# THE JIHADIST THREAT

**Some of Paul Moorcraft's other books on military topics**


*A Short Thousand Years: The End of Rhodesia's Rebellion* (1979)

*Contact 2: The Struggle for Peace* (1981)

*Africa's Superpower* (1982)

*African Nemesis: War and Revolution in Southern Africa, 1945-2010* (1994)

*Axis of Evil: The War on Terror* (with Gwyn Winfield and John Chisholm) (2005)

*The New Wars of the West* (with Gwyn Winfield and John Chisholm) (2006)

*Inside the Danger Zones: Travels to Arresting Places* (2010)

*Shooting the Messenger: The Politics of War Reporting* (with Phil Taylor) (2011)

*The Rhodesian War: A Military History* (with Peter McLaughlin) (2011)

*Mugabe's War Machine* (2011)

*Total Destruction of the Tamil Tigers: The Rare Victory of Sri Lanka's Long War* (2012)

*Omar al-Bashir and Africa's Longest War* (2015)

# THE JIHADIST THREAT

*The Re-conquest of the West?*

PAUL MOORCRAFT

Pen & Sword
**MILITARY**

First published in Great Britain in 2015 by
PEN & SWORD MILITARY
an imprint of
Pen & Sword Books Ltd
47 Church Street
Barnsley
South Yorkshire
S70 2AS

ISBN 978 1 47385 679 0

The rig... **LANCASHIRE COUNTY** ...to be identified... s the
author ...f this work has been asserted by him in accordance
wi...h the Copyright, Designs and Patents Act 198...
**LIBRARY**

All rights rese...ed. No part of this book may be reproduced or transmitted
in any for... (or by any means, el...tronic or mechanical, including
photocopyi...ording or by any information storage and retrieval
syste... without permission from the Publisher in writing.

Typeset in Times New Roman
by CHIC GRAPHICS

Printed and bound in England
by CPI Group (UK) Ltd, Croydon, CR0 4YY

*Pen & Sword Books Ltd incorporates the imprints of*
Pen & Sword Archaeology, Atlas, Aviation, Battleground, Discovery, Family
History, History, Maritime, Military, Naval, Politics, Railways, Select, Social
History, Transport, True Crime, Claymore Press, Frontline Books, Leo Cooper,
Praetorian Press, Remember When, Seaforth Publishing and Wharncliffe.

*For a complete list of Pen & Sword titles please contact*
PEN & SWORD BOOKS LIMITED
47 Church Street, Barnsley, South Yorkshire, S70 2AS, England
E-mail: enquiries@pen-and-sword.co.uk
Website: www.pen-and-sword.co.uk

# Contents

# About the Author

**Professor Paul Moorcraft** is an internationally respected expert on crisis communications, especially relating to security issues. He worked for *Time* magazine, the BBC and most of the Western TV networks as a freelance producer/correspondent. He completed his studies at six British, Middle Eastern and African universities, thereafter lecturing full-time (consecutively) at ten universities in the UK, US, Africa, Australia and New Zealand in journalism, politics and international relations. He was most recently a visiting professor at Cardiff University's School of Journalism, Media and Cultural Studies. He has worked in thirty war zones in Africa, the Middle East, Asia and the Balkans, often with irregular, and sometimes jihadist, forces. Most recently he has been operating in Afghanistan, Iraq, Palestine/Israel, Nepal, Sudan, Zimbabwe, Syria, Turkey, Sri Lanka and, for a pleasant change, the Maldives.

Dr Moorcraft spent five years as a senior instructor at the Royal Military Academy, Sandhurst, and later at the UK Joint Services Command and Staff College. He also worked in Corporate Communications in the Ministry of Defence in Whitehall and in defence procurement in Bristol. The MoD recalled him for service during the Iraq war in 2003.

Dr Moorcraft is a regular broadcaster (BBC TV and radio, as well as Sky, Al Jazeera, etc.) and op-ed writer for international newspapers (including the *Guardian, New Statesman, Washington Times, Canberra Times, Business Day,* etc.). He is the author of a wide range of books on military history, politics and crime. One of his recent books is the co-authored *Axis of Evil: The War on Terror* (Pen and Sword, 2005). An updated version, *The New Wars of the West*, was published by Casemate in the US in 2006. His *Shooting the Messenger: The Politics of War Reporting* (Potomac, Washington, 2008) was co-authored with Professor Phil Taylor. An updated version was released in 2011 (Biteback, London). The first of many editions of *The Rhodesian War: A Military History* (with Dr Peter McLaughlin) was published by Pen and Sword books in 2008. *Mugabe's War Machine* (Pen and Sword) came out in 2011. *Total Destruction of the Tamil Tigers:The Rare Victory of Sri Lanka's Long War* was released by Pen and Sword in 2012. Three volumes of memoirs have been published, the most recent being

*Inside the Danger Zones: Travels to Arresting Places* (Biteback, London, 2010). He is an award-winning novelist as well as the author of a publication related to his charity work (*It Just Doesn't Add Up: Explaining Dyscalculia and Overcoming Number Problems for Children and Adult*s (Filament, Croydon, 2014).

Paul Moorcraft is the director of the Centre for Foreign Policy Analysis, London, founded in 2004 and dedicated to conflict resolution. He was Head of Mission, for example, of fifty independent British observers at the Sudan election of 2010. He lives in a riverside cottage in the Surrey Hills, near Guildford.

# The Jihadist Timeline

**300-600 AD**
The superpowers of their day, the eastern Roman Empire and the Persian Sassanians, exhaust themselves in constant fighting over the Middle East. The Arabs in the Arabian peninsula are considered insignificant barbarians.

**570**
Birth of Muhammad.

**624**
Battle of Badr. Muhammad leads or commands over twenty-seven military campaigns and raids in ten years.

**627**
The date when Islamists believe the worldwide war between Jews and Muslims began.

**628**
Considered by some Islamist historians as the beginning of the war against Christians when an Arab Christian outpost of the Byzantine Empire was attacked.

**632**
Death of Muhammad.

**633**
Muslim Arabs start to conquer Syria.

**634**
Beginning of conquest of Iraq.

**637**
Arab defeat of the Persian Sassanians and the sack of their capital, Ctesiphon.

**638**
Conquest of Jerusalem.

**642**
Islamic armies complete conquest of Persia/Iran and Iraq and move into India and Afghanistan. Control of Egypt and penetration of Sudan.

**674**
First Arab siege of Constantinople.

**642-705**
Conquest of North Africa.

**650**
Islam starts to expand into Asia via trading posts in Sumatra, Indonesia, India and Pakistan. Also moves into China and east African coast.

**711-713**
Conquest of Spain and, briefly, south-western France.

**732**
Charles Martel defeats the 'Saracens' at Battle of Tours, and pushes Muslim armies out of much of France.

**750**
The 'Call of Islam' penetrates central Asia and southern Caucasus.

**900**
Arabs control most of northwest India

**922**
Parts of Bulgaria converted to Islam.

**950**
Arabs consolidate position in Aceh, Indonesia

**1050**
Muslim ships begin to raid the Philippines. Mombasa established as a key Islamic trading post for ivory and slaves. Islamic conquests in Nigeria.

**1071**

Byzantines pushed out of fertile areas of Turkey.

**1164**

Saladin starts his campaign against the Crusaders.

**1174**

Saladin conquers Damascus.

**1200s**

Muslim armies reach Bengal and mass conversion of Hindus. Sultanate based in Mogadishu in Somalia.

**1250**

Sultanate established in Aceh. Beginning of small sultanates in the Philippines.

**1229**

Oz Beg, Khan of the Golden Horde, converts to Islam, which spreads to Kazakhstan, Uzbekistan, Turkmenistan, Tajikistan, Kirghizia and Siberia.

**1389**

Turks defeat the Hungarians at Kosovo and start occupation of Balkans and eastern Europe.

**1396**

Key trading centres in Ukraine are captured.

**1400**

The King of Malacca converts to Islam and takes the Malay peninsula with him.

**1453**

The Ottoman Turks capture Constantinople, heralding the end of the Byzantine Christian Empire.

**1457**

Some Thai provinces convert.

**1463**
Turks conquer Bosnia.

**1518**
Barbarossa becomes admiral of the seaborne Jihad as commander of the Mediterranean fleet. Muslim fleets start to raid as far as Cornwall, Ireland and the French coasts. Hundreds of thousands of European Christians are taken as slaves.

**1526**
Battle of Panipat creates the base for the Muslim Moghul Empire in India. Pest in Hungary falls to the Turks.

**1530s**
The Muslims in Somalia start to penetrate Christian Abyssinia.

**1538**
The Ottoman navy defeats the combined Christian fleets, led by Venice.

**1571**
The Battle of Lepanto. Combined Christian fleets destroy the Muslim Mediterranean fleet and liberate 10,000 Christian galley slaves. The Turks soon rebuild their fleet. Mass slave raids by Muslim corsairs continue throughout the seventeenth century.

**1650**
The Sultan of Oman expels the Portuguese.

**1677**
Modern-day Senegal, Gambia, Guinea-Bissau are captured and forcibly converted.

**1683**
The Battle of Vienna. Combined Christian forces finally halt the Ottoman advance outside the gates of Vienna. But the Turks drive the Austrians out of Belgrade, Bulgaria and Transylvania.

**1729**
Muslims retrieve Mombasa from the Portuguese.

**1738**
The Iranian Shah invades Afghanistan and India.

**1804**
A new Jihad establishes a caliphate in northern Nigeria.

**1832**
A slave revolt led by a Muslim calls for a Jihad in Jamaica.

**1840s**
The Sultan of Zanzibar controls many of the ports of East Africa.

**1860s**
New sultanate forged in Guinea and Senegal.

**1870**
Russian forces expel Islamic leaders from Dagestan, Georgia and Armenia.

**1871**
The British threaten a naval blockade to force the Sultan of Zanzibar to close his slave market.

**1874**
Sultan of Somalia invades part of Abyssinia, expels Christians and destroys churches.

**1881**
Mahdist uprising in Anglo-Egyptian Sudan.

**1885**
Siege of Khartoum and killing of General George Gordon.

**1914**
Ottomans join war alongside Central Powers.

**1916**
Jihad in Darfur crushed by Anglo-French forces.

**1916**
Beginning of Arab revolt against the Turks. Sykes-Picot agreement to divide Arab lands between Britain and France.

**1917**
Balfour declaration.

**1918-1922**
Defeat in First World War collapses Ottoman Empire, end of caliphate. Britain and France take over Arab lands. British govern mandate in Palestine.

**1939-1945**
The Second World War divides Arab nationalists (and Islamists) – some support the Axis, others the Western Allies.

**1947**
Pakistan is one of the first Muslim-majority countries to achieve independence.

**1948**
Israel declares independence.

**1952**
Egyptian independence.

**1956**
Suez Crisis.

**1957**
Start of Algerian War.

**1960s**
Muslims in the Philippines begin their insurgency. Funded by Saudi Arabia, and later armed by Iran and Libya, they start fighting for independence, via the Moro National Liberation Front.
   Overwhelming victory for Israel in June war.

**1973**
Yom Kippur War leads to OPEC oil power.

**1976**
Pakistan declares it will build an 'Islamic' bomb.

**1979**
Russia invades Afghanistan. Islamic Revolution in Iran.

**1983**
Islamic Jihad attacks US embassy in Beirut and sixty-three killed; same year attacks US and French bases; 299 killed.

**1989**
Soviets retreat from Afghanistan. First Sunni Islamist revolution, in Sudan. War against the largely non-Muslim south declared a Jihad.

**1991**
US leads a coalition to liberate Kuwait from Saddam Hussein's forces.

**1991-1995**
Jihadists flock to Bosnia.

**1993**
26 February, first attack on World Trade Center in New York.

**1995**
Bombings on Metro in Paris.

**1998**
Islamist attacks on US embassies in Dar es Salaam and Nairobi. Pakistan's first test of nuclear device, 7 August.

**1999**
Start of Islamist campaigns in Chechnya.

**2000**
12 October, attack on USS *Cole*.

**2001**
11 September, attack on Twin Towers and Pentagon. Start of 'war on terror'. US intervention in Afghanistan. May, renewed Islamist insurgency in Indonesia.

**2002**
23 October, Moscow Theatre hostage crisis.

**2003**
Iraq war begins, to finally remove Saddam Hussein.

**2004**
11 March, Madrid train bombings.

**2005**
7 July, attack on London transport system.

**2008**
Massacre in Mumbai.

**2011**
Arab Spring begins in Tunisia and spreads through north Africa. Change of government in Egypt and Libya. NATO intervenes in Libya to oust Gaddafi. Massacre in Hotan, China, 18 July. Unrest spreads to Syria. 2 May, Osama bin Laden killed in Pakistan by US special forces. US begins drawdown from Afghanistan and complete withdrawal from Iraq.

**2013**
15 April, Boston Marathon attack.

**2014**
June, Islamic State forces conduct successful blitzkrieg and capture Mosul. 29 June, Islamic State declared. September, US leads coalition against IS.

**2015**
Saudi Arabia leads Sunni coalition to intervene in Yemen civil war and entrenches Sunni versus Shia schism. July, US leads great-power nuclear deal with Iran. Turkey enters war on IS.

# List of Maps

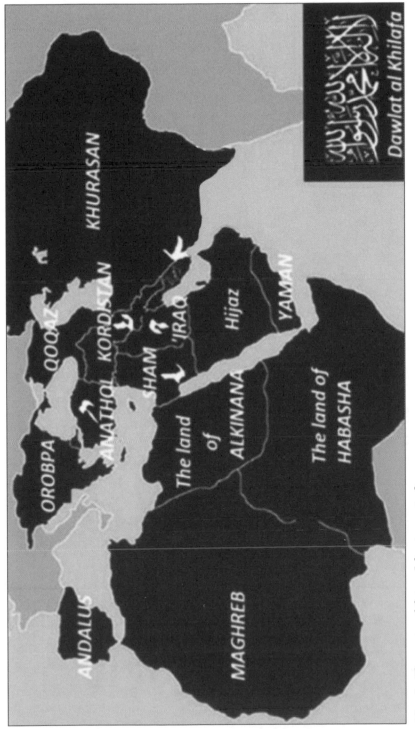

Map 1.  *The past and future Islamic empire?*

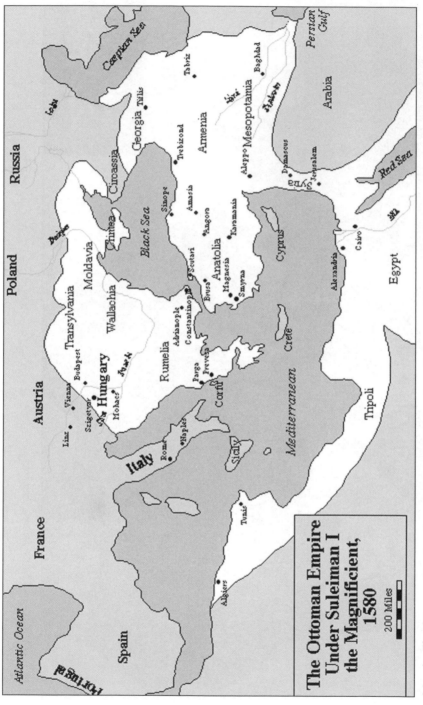

*Map 2. The Ottoman Empire almost conquered Vienna three times.*

*Map 3. Afghanistan.*

*Map 4. Iraq.*

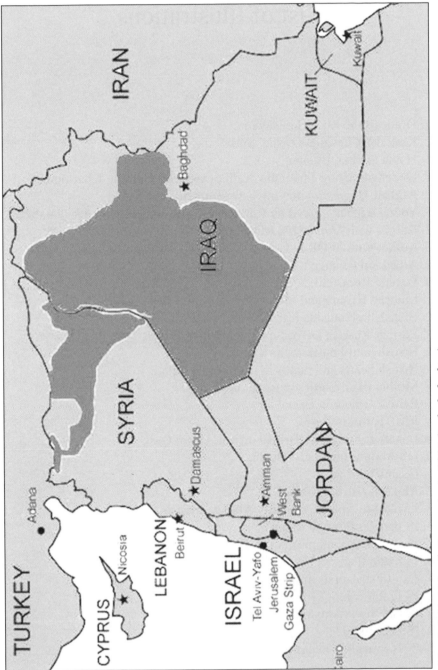

*Map 5. Initial Islamic State gains in 2014 (in dark shading).*

# List of Illustrations

1. Dome of the Rock, Jerusalem.
2. Krak des Chevaliers castle, Syria.
3. Hagia Sophia, Istanbul.
4. Underestimating Jihad: the death of General Gordon, Khartoum.
5. Afghan *Mujahedin* praying before attack, near Kabul.
6. Young Afghan injured by Russian anti-personnel mine, near Jalalabad.
7. Author with *Mujahedin*, tribal area.
8. Author with SFOR in Bosnia.
9. Attack on Pentagon, 9/11.
10. Donald Rumsfeld.
11. Lindsey Hilsum and Marie Colvin, Jenin, West Bank.
12. British base outside Kabul.
13. Former Russian OP occupied by British forces.
14. British patrol outskirts of Kabul.
15. British hearts and minds in a school in Kabul.
16. Mother of all Battles mosque, Baghdad.
17. British armour in Basra.
18. RMP patrol in Basra.
19. Locals arguing with British officer, Umm Qasr.
20. US Abrams tank in Baghdad.
21. Osama bin Laden.
22. Abu Bakr al-Baghdadi.
23. IS likes to emulate the early Arab conquests.
24. IS parades through Raqqah.
25. IS captured numerous tanks and Humvees in Mosul.
26. IS battle flag.
27. Can IS sustain its armoured fleet?
28. IS in Raqqah.
29. IS convoy in Anbar province.
30. IS beheading.
31. IS is spreading its influence to north Africa.

# Introduction

*What is the threat?*

This book is about the worldwide Jihadist threat, although I focus primarily on Britain, the country of my birth. The research, however, is based on forty years of travel, including working alongside Jihadists in daily combat in war zones such as Afghanistan. I have also spent much time more recently with devoted Islamists and ardent Jihadists in countries such as Sudan. I also draw on my own direct experiences of living and working in countries with Muslim communities as diverse as those in Bosnia, Kosovo, Iraq, Syria, Palestine/Israel, the Maldives, Morocco, Ethiopia, Turkey and Sri Lanka. Some of the information comes from my time in government service, in the British Ministry of Defence, sometimes liaising with American security organisations. So this book is based on decades of thinking about and working with the grain of the Jihadist danger and is not an opportunist knee-jerk reaction to recent atrocities in Europe and the expansion of the so-called Islamic State in Iraq and Syria.

I will seek to join the dots about how international Jihad operates not just in the developing countries, especially in the Middle East and Africa, but also in advanced economies in Europe and America. My main thesis is that the failure to integrate many if not most Muslims into British and European society is making the security dangers far worse. It is not politically correct to say this, but it is nonetheless true: Europe is facing an existential challenge from Islamic society, not just from those perceived as the violent extremist minority. What is most troubling is how many support acts of extremist violence even if they would never do them themselves. I accept that only a minority has been sufficiently 'radicalised' to want to plant bombs in European capitals or augment the ranks of the 'soldiers of God' fighting in the Middle East.

By concentrating on the small minority of violent extremists – and doing a poor job of de-radicalising them – the security authorities are missing the point. A large number of British Muslims support *Sharia* law in the UK and want criticism of the Prophet Muhammad, infamously via cartoons, to be punishable by law, in some cases saying they want capital punishment. Many Muslims, second- and third-generation Britons, feel alienated from the mainstream, based on a mix of what they perceive as social, cultural, racial or employment discrimination. MI5 calls this 'blocked mobility'.

The Jihadists want to drive a wedge between the UK government and British Muslims. The greater the divide the easier it is to radicalise Muslims and convert them to the Jihadist cause. Logically, then, fully integrating Muslims into British society, inculcating British values, should be the goal of the anti-Jihadist strategy. Multi-culturalism failed a long time ago. Allied with mass migration, the result has been physical and cultural ghettoes.

Of course not all Muslims are Jihadists, though all Jihadists must by definition be Muslim. Nor can all Muslims easily be classified, except in their commitments, to a lesser or greater degree, to the basic tenets of the faith. Besides the ancient Sunni-Shia schism, Muslims adopt all sorts of local and international variants of both Sunni and Shia precepts. Muslims are divided by language, geography, nationality and politics as well as culture. That is why no one effective body exists to represent the majority of Muslims in Britain. That is why motor-mouths representing a few, or just themselves, grab so much airtime.

Almost all Muslims believe in the concept of the *Umma*, the universal ideal of a worldwide Islamic community that perhaps one day will dominate the planet. Some believe it fervently, others nod vaguely in its direction, just as Christians are supposed to believe in heaven and sometimes even hell, although the latter has gone out of fashion. Since Christ was crucified, Christianity has changed with the times; Islam has altered very little since Muhammad died. Just as Catholics come in many varieties of sinner, so do Muslims. Interestingly, the bacon-munching, beer-swilling, skirt-chasing, hip-hopping types often repent; many of the 'Jihadi-cool' young warriors who came from Europe to join the Islamic State have a wild past and a police record to prove it. Hell hath no fury like a sinner saved.

*The international perspective*
The worldwide Muslim greeting is *As-Salamu Alaykum* – peace be upon you. Yet Muslims divide the world into the land of Islam (*Dar al-Islam*) and the land of war (*Dar al-Harb*). Like the Hebrew scriptures/the Old Testament, Islam is not primarily a religion of peace, although the Koran boasts some peaceful admonitions. I will trace briefly the violent and dramatic expansion of Islam from its beginnings in the Arabian peninsula. Then I will examine the growth of the Ottoman Caliphate, which the West managed to work with eventually — after its military expansion had been halted. *If* the majority of today's Sunnis want a renewed caliphate I will

argue later that it might be better to think about negotiating with the Islamic State rather than trying to eradicate it, a policy that will radicalise even more Muslims. That does not necessarily mean appeasing domestic or international Jihadists. I agree with the Prophet, peace be upon Him – and also Sun Tzu RIP – sometimes it is better to parley than fight.

I use the phrase 'join the dots', as a reference of course to the dot-joining failures of US intelligence in the lead-up to the 9/11 attacks. I will explain how modern Jihadism began and how the recent surges in violence in the Middle East and Africa relate to each other. It may be a cliché to say the West is responding with 'whack-a-mole' tactics, though whack a mole is what it is. Treating Islamism from northern Iraq to northern Nigeria to the London Underground individually is a mistake. It is an understandable one given the local nuances and the West's reluctance to react robustly to the burgeoning dangers. Just as the threats have to be joined up to understand them, so too the response must be holistic. For example, leaving Boko Haram to Nigeria's rag-tag army is a recipe for Jihadist victory in the region.

I will explain how the Jihadists co-operate and how their franchises are armed and funded. It is no secret that many long-time Western allies, in Saudi Arabia and the Gulf, are financing, or have until recently financed, their religious brothers-in-arms. I will also show how Jihadist warriors are seducing thousands of Muslims, men and women in Western countries, to join their cause.

*The domestic factors*
Very few, even in the British intelligence services, joined up the *domestic* dots. The French intelligence agencies nagged the British for decades to contain the Jihadist centres in London, or 'Londonistan' as they dubbed it. I remember a leading Sudanese official in Khartoum saying to me at the beginning of the 'war on terror': 'If the Americans want to hit Jihadist centres or terror training camps, they should bomb London or Riyadh not Khartoum.' The Sudanese Islamist had a point. Osama bin Laden had an office in London for most of the time he was also living in Sudan. Belatedly, British counter-terrorism officers woke up to the internal threat, but it is only since the 'Trojan Horse' scandals in British schools and the flood of young British volunteers to Syria that the domestic ramifications of the Islamist threat have been more fully understood. It was just not politically correct to talk about the growing radicalisation in British schools. Some headmasters who did complain were gagged or sacked. Why should the taxpayer fund secular or faith schools that in effect undermine British

values? Indeed a case can be made for withdrawing state funding from *all* faith schools, though it could also be argued that Methodist fundamentalists, ardent Church of England bell-ringers or Jewish ideologues are not shredding the UK security budget. Likewise, British police forces were initially afraid to clamp down on Muslim gangs – almost entirely of Pakistani descent – who were sexually abusing and exploiting thousands of young 'white' girls in places such as Rotherham.

*The complete picture*
For decades Special Branch and MI5 had been unable to act because of small budgets and the ignorance and pusillanimity of politicians. It is surely time to look at the whole picture, domestically and internationally, without pulling any punches or succumbing to group-think. Defining the Jihadist threat correctly is the first step. How to fight and then contain and maybe even defeat that security threat is a massive challenge; simultaneously trying to fix social cohesion at home is even harder. And to do all this without creating a garrison state that undermines the liberal values that the Jihadists are hell-bent on destroying is a very tall order indeed. But I will try.

*Chapter 1*

# The Origins of Jihadism

*Early days*

Muhammad's words on war and peace have been endlessly debated. According to an often-quoted saying of the Prophet:

> Do not look for a fight with the enemy. Beg God for peace and security. But if you do end up facing the enemy, then show endurance, and remember that the gates of Paradise lie in the shadow of the sword.

Muslim scholars have continuously dissected Islam's central concept of Jihad or Holy War. They have debated fundamental questions such as whether Jihad needs to be violent external conflict or an internal spiritual struggle; or, if defined as a physical battle, whether Jihad should be deployed only defensively or legitimately used to expand the frontiers of Islam. And is it a stern obligation or rather a voluntary activity for observant Muslims?

The Koran and sayings (*Hadith*) of the Prophet have been re-interpreted and re-translated as often as the Bible. Contemporary records of Muhammad are even scarcer than those of Jesus Christ. Indeed, they are practically non-existent. Arabs are not a people famed for their rhetorical reticence, especially after conquering most of the known world, so it is very strange that there is no single Muslim record from the age of the Prophet, except for two tiny fragments of papyrus and vellum. At the same time in the wilds of northern Britain the savage Northumbrians were capable of preserving *inter alia* the writings of the Venerable Bede. As historian Tom Holland wrote of the Prophet: 'Why not a single Arab account of his life, nor of his followers' conquests, nor of the progress of his religion from the whole of the near two centuries that followed his death?'[1] The variants on the Koran, the numerous collections of *Hadith* and biographies of the Prophet all were dated over two centuries and usually much later than two centuries after Muhammad died.

Muhammad, who is said to have lived from AD 570-632, was apparently a man of many parts. To Muslims he was primarily God's last prophet, after Abraham, Moses and Jesus. He is said to have perfected the monotheism of the Jews and Christianity into a final revelation from God – many Christians and Jews lived around his hometown of Mecca. He preached that all humanity should and would submit to the one God, Allah — Islam literally means submission to God. The Prophet took on many roles besides prophecy: he was also a merchant, commander, diplomat and a social reformer. Muhammad displayed different aspects of his personality and mission depending on the local political exigencies of his time, especially during the hostility between the tribal groupings in Mecca and Medina. In short, sometimes he taught peace and at other times war, depending on the prevailing balance of power. In battle sometimes Muhammad was merciful and yet on other occasions hostages were beheaded. Frankly, modern-day Islamists can deploy the Prophet's words to justify almost anything, just as Christian clerics blessed guns in numerous recent conflicts sanctified in the name of 'just war', quoting chapter and verse from the scriptures or theologians. Religion has been a source of war throughout history. A few pacifist creeds emerged, but were usually overwhelmed by the martial majorities.

Muhammad was not a peacemaker. He inspired the most dramatic military expansion in the history of the world. Perhaps, in the short term, the Mongol hordes were more bloodthirstily successful, yet the Islamic conquest of Arabia and then the amazing expansion of the empire from the Pyrenees to China must then have seemed evidence of God's blessings on the all-conquering Muslim warriors. And where are the Mongols today? whereas, in most of the Arab conquests, Islam is still the dominant culture and religion and the language is Arabic. The sword was not always the main instrument of domination. Many converted through conviction. Sometimes commerce was the hidden persuader. Also, the Arabs' sense of racial superiority discouraged absorption or often it made more sense to tax unbelievers, by making them pay *Jizyah*. This was a poll tax, roughly double the *Zakat* tax on Muslims; if unpaid, it usually led to expulsion, enslavement or even death. Like early communists, most Muslims believed in the inevitable triumph of their creed throughout the known world. Often Muslim leaders practised tolerance towards other religions, especially towards 'people of the book', Christians and Jews, whose prophets had been revered by Muhammad. At other times Christians and Jews were expelled, killed, enslaved or forcibly converted. The ethics of Islamic conquest were as chequered as the ravages of the Crusades, when Christendom tried to reverse the Muslim hold on the Holy Land.

The initial territorial expansion was hailed as proof that a strict adhesion to the teachings of the Prophet brought success then and would do so again. This is the essence of the current appeal of Jihad today – a return to the early fundamentals of Islam, as practised by the Prophet and his companions; in military ambition, dress, strict obedience to the *Sharia* laws and so on will inevitably bring a return of God's favour. Many Jihadists also believe that they are imminently facing 'the end of days', a belief not uncommon among many Christians in the southern states of the USA.

Islam spread from Mecca in the time of the Prophet to conquer much of the known world, overwhelming the remnants of the two ancient empires, the Byzantine and Persian. Soon Allah's warriors would penetrate the heart of western Europe. This was not a single coherent expansion – Islamic empires such as those of the Abbassids, the Mughals in India or finally the Ottomans were often concerned with more regional matters, yet they all believed in the inevitably universal success of their faith.

*The conquest of Arabia*
Arabs in the deserts of the northern Arabian peninsula could not eat faith so the initial expansion had many practical imperatives, not least access to water and fertile soil or at least goods from the more temperate neighbouring lands. Muhammad was said to have been born in Mecca in AD 570. Very little concrete historical evidence exists about Mecca (or Muhammad) at this time; the 'city' was probably involved in trade between the Mediterranean and the Indian Ocean. It was near the border of the Byzantine Empire which centuries before had established Christianity as its sole official religion. In Mecca, Jews and Christians lived in separate quarters; paganism was also rife.

The story goes that in around 610 Muhammad, who was probably illiterate, started receiving messages from God via the Angel Gabriel, at least according to the Koran. He claimed that he was a prophet in the line of succession from Moses and Jesus. Initially, Muhammad was tolerant of other monotheistic religions, especially Christianity and Judaism. After all, their traditions infuse the Koran. But Muhammad attacked the idol worship of the pantheists, who comprised the majority in Mecca. At first, the pagan Arab leaders tried to compromise with Muhammad and his growing band of followers. When this failed, Muslims – as they came to be known – were persecuted. Some followers of Muhammad sought exile in the Christian kingdom of Axum in Ethiopia. In 622 Muhammad and many of his supporters fled to nearby Medina. This flight or *Hegira* marks Year 1 of the Muslim calendar.

At first the Muslims co-existed amicably with the local Jewish tribes, who lived in their own fortresses outside the town. The Jews were largely traders, but many of the new Muslim inhabitants lacked skills or capital, so they resorted to raiding Meccan caravans. Soon the raids turned into pitched battles. Muhammad's opponents in Mecca tried to protect a major caravan heading back from Syria; the Meccans were defeated at the Battle of Badr, however. Muhammad tightened his grip on the people of Medina, first expelling some of the Jews who resisted conversion. After a reversal in another battle against the Meccans, Mohammad turned once more on the remaining Jews, and expelled them after seizing their possessions. Some of the expelled Jews allied with the Meccans and Medina was besieged. Muhammad managed to deploy diplomacy to spread dissent against the coalition facing him. The Prophet then turned on the remaining Jews, beheading hundreds of the males and enslaving the women and children. Previously his Jewish opponents had been expelled, but they had allied with his enemies. This time, modern Muslims would argue, Muhammad could not afford to be merciful. These expulsions and beheadings around AD 627 are considered by some Islamist historians as the beginning of the worldwide battle between Islam and the Jews.

In 628 Muhammad led his war bands against Christian as well as Jewish towns and villages, and this year is sometimes portrayed by Islamist historians as the beginning of the war on Christians. Some were killed and many forcibly converted. Others were allowed to keep their lands and pay a heavy tax. Muhammad accumulated vast wealth as well as many wives (though only four at a time) and concubines. One of his wives, Aisha, was just six years old when he married her, though the marriage was not consummated until she was nine.

Soon, in 630, Muhammad achieved his main goal – to capture his home town of Mecca. He had assembled 10,000 troops and the city fell without fighting. The inhabitants agreed to convert to Islam. Only seven Meccans were executed, including two female singers who had sung satirical songs about the Prophet. Right from the start of the religion, artistic criticism could be met with harsh retaliation. It is often said that Muhammad's behaviour, especially beheadings and enslavement, has to be judged by the morality of the times. This is of course true – the Romans and their Byzantine successors were equally brutal. The problem is that nowadays fundamentalist Muslims believe that the Koran and *Sharia* (which means 'path') apply to *all* peoples in *all* times. Historical relativity is absent. The world view of modern Jihadists is deliberately the same as the Prophet's, who sanctified killing and plunder – against non-Muslims – as religious duties. Muhammad is estimated to have led in twenty-seven raids and battles himself, thus acquiring much treasure. These events were memorialised centuries later in the Koran and *Hadith*, though Muhammad admitted that some of the original prophecies were contradictory 'Satanic verses' (whispered by the Devil not the Angel Gabriel) and most Islamic scholars judged many of the *Hadiths* to have been bogus. Despite offering a prescription for the planet, the Koran is deeply ambiguous and its provenance very dubious – just like the Bible.

Muhammad celebrated the triumph over paganism and Mecca's holy *Kabba*, once a site for idols, was turned into a mosque. Muhammad's forces spread out from Mecca to destroy pagan temples and peoples. Some pagan tribes resisted and selected their own prophets to counter the power of Islam. When Muhammad died in 632 a number of the tribes renounced Islam, refused to pay tax and sometimes supported the rival prophets. Muhammad's father in law, Abu Bakr, led the 'faithful' armies in what was called the 'wars of apostasy'. Within a few years of the Prophet's death, Christians and Jews were expelled from the whole of the Arabian peninsula. Islam had triumphed. The next step was to conquer the two neighbouring superpowers, the Byzantine and Persian empires. This was approximately the view of al-Qaeda in the late 1980s. Russia was defeated in Afghanistan – the next superpower to be targeted was the USA. We are jumping ahead by 1,400 years, however.

*The initial Arab conquest*
The Arabs' dramatic territorial expansion, based upon the sword and plunder, was little different, in effect if not religious motivation, from the barbarian invasions of the collapsing Roman Empire, the Viking depredations in northern Europe, the Norman conquest of England or the later ravages of the Mongol hordes. A hundred years after the death of the Prophet, Muslim armies were rampaging through central France as well as through the old domains of the Persian Empire in the east. Just over a century after Muhammad, Rome was ransacked. Such a rapid subjugation was bound to leave many Byzantines, Persians, Christians and Jews, especially outside the towns, living as they had been under previous empires, not least for practical reasons. Arabs were – and arguably are still – not

generally talented state administrators, though they proved highly effective warriors. Provided the vanquished peoples submitted and paid taxes, many of the old ways of life did not change, especially agriculture, to feed Muslim armies which lived off the land. Many Muslim military leaders were hostile to conversion, willing or forced, simply because it both reduced income from the tax base and slavery as well as the status advantages of the Arab conquistadors. In the century or so after Muhammad until 750, called the Umayyad period, less than 10 per cent of the lands conquered outside the Arabian peninsula were inhabited by followers of Islam.

First the Arab armies pushed into regions controlled by the bankrupt Byzantine Empire in Constantinople. From 633 to 634 the Islamic warriors moved into Syria and then Iraq. In 637 Muslim armies seized Ctesiphon, the Persian Sassanian capital. In the next year the Christian and Jewish icon of Jerusalem was taken. By 642 Arab forces controlled nearly all of the old Persian Empire and had begun to penetrate Afghanistan and India in the east, and Egypt and Nubia (Sudan) in Africa. In 674 the Arabs besieged Constantinople for the first time, although its mighty walls resisted the attacks. Also, the Western Christian powers had the advantage – for a while – of more advanced sea power.

The astounding military advances and impressive generalship in the campaigns masked divisions in centralised command and control. The Koran had stipulated no clear rules for successors to the Prophet. The descendants of Muhammad and his close companions fought over the right to rule. Those who emerged as rulers were called *Khalifa* in Arabic – or, in English, Caliphs: the successors to the Prophet. The murder of caliphs, beginning with Omer and later Ali, the Prophet's cousin, caused continuous rifts. In particular, the confrontation between Ali and Muawiya led to Ali's assassination. This spawned an eternal division between the followers of Muayiwa, later called Sunnis, and Ali's followers, Shias. While these schisms, often termed *fitnas*, were based initially on tribal or family divisions, they soon became ideological chasms that are still today the cause of savage civil wars. As I write these words in the summer of 2015, Yemen, Syria and Iraq are being torn apart by rival Sunni and Shi'ite armies and militias, while similar antagonisms fester throughout the Arab lands.

Despite the infighting, the initial Arab conquests were remarkable feats, achieved with no obvious military advantage, especially in technology. And the armies were surprisingly small. The later chronicles of the conquests are notoriously contradictory in detail, especially on numbers, but a good guess is that the Arab army that conquered Syria was never more than 30,000 men

– and they were rarely combined in one force. The army that conquered Iraq was probably no more than 12,000 warriors, less than the contemporary Jihadists who conquered most of Sunni Iraq in 2013. The initial Muslim army that marched into Egypt was probably no larger than 4,000 men.[2]

In just over a century the Arabs had seized territory stretching far wider than the Roman Empire. Setting aside the argument that God was on their side, how did they do it? They were lucky in the timing – a generation or so earlier Muhammad's men would have been seen off by the then more sophisticated, better organised and bigger armies of the Byzantine and Persian empires. The climactic battles between the new Romans and the old Persians had destroyed an imperial system based on sound bureaucracy, standing armies and efficient taxation in much of their domains. Plague and largescale depopulation followed. Infighting in the surviving elites in the military and competing churches added to the implosion of imperial rule in the Near East. The strength of the empires had been partly based on the centralised standing armies. The imperial Arab levies – some Christian – had defended the respective borders of the two empires, but the long-standing *cordon sanitaire* of Arab militias was disbanded, partly to save money and partly because the unruly Arab nomadic raiders from the desert were not then considered a major threat.

The internal weakness of the declining superpowers of their day was not sufficient explanation for the sudden eruption of power from the Arabian deserts. The strength of faith, especially the lure of paradise via martyrdom, was a galvanising factor. To this was augmented the traditional warrior ethos of the desert tribes and their kinship cohesion. The loyalty was extended from their own commanders often chosen on merit, not birth, to faithful obeisance to the central direction of the caliphs. The armies did not have the numbers or the technology, though they did have rapid mobility. Their ground coverage was astounding. It was more than 4,000 miles from Morocco to the far reaches of the Muslim world in Asia – the Roman Empire extended for less than this, around 3,000 miles from Hadrian's Wall to the Euphrates. The Arab armies lived off the land. Used to travelling in the dark in the desert, they excelled at night fighting. The quality of their operational leadership was almost consistently high. Byzantine forces were often disrupted by mutinies; this was very rare in Arab armies.

Unlike the Mongol hordes, the Arabs generally imposed comparatively easy terms on the conquered peoples, who rarely rose in revolt once they were overrun. In the absence of the former imperial structures, it was usually better to surrender to the invaders, agree on terms and pay taxes, rather than to fight to the death. Yes, sometimes harsh penalties were imposed in the initial conquest, but thereafter the Arab rulers, tiny in number, were prepared to live and let live – provided they were obeyed. Sometimes the occupied peoples considered their taxes to be lighter than before and, in the early period, Christianity and Judaism were largely respected. The locals probably thought that the Arabs were temporary invaders; when they stayed they usually lived in their own areas of existing towns and cities or occasionally founded new ones. This avoided the inevitable frictions of an invading army living cheek-by-jowl with indigenous and perhaps disgruntled inhabitants. Also, the social mobility of the new Islamic order appealed to many of the conquered peoples. The lower orders had been excluded from the hierarchical class system of the Byzantine and Persian empires. In theory a Muslim convert could rise to the highest ranks. Of course not all was harmony between old and new Muslims and Arab and non-Arab, yet that did not entirely undermine the universal theocratic message that Islam was open to all. All could believe in Allah if they so chose (although they could not then change their minds). Another unifying factor was Arabic. God had spoken to Muhammad in Arabic which became the language of administration and culture, although in the short term accounts were often kept, for example, in Greek. Full absorption took centuries. It was likely that by the year 1000 the majority of the conquered population trod the path of Islam. There was much in Islam that could be understood by conquered Christians and to a lesser extent by Jews; after all, Islam was fundamentally about perfecting, not destroying, its monotheistic predecessors. Nevertheless, the armies' initial military success was the obvious precondition of the gradual Arabization and Islamization that ensued over centuries.

In Hugh Kennedy's sweeping account of the great Arab conquests, he concluded:

> In the final analysis, the success of the Muslim conquest was a result of the unstable and impoverished natures of the whole post-Roman world into which they came, the hardiness and self-reliance of the Bedouin warriors and the inspiration and open quality of the new religion of Islam.[3]

*The conquests of the later caliphs*
The Umayyad caliphs were displaced in 750 by the Abbasids, who took their name from Muhammad's uncle, Abbas. This second dynasty ruled until

1258. The Abbasid caliphs shifted their capital from Damascus to Baghdad and a new wave of conquests ensued. Islam came to dominate Spain for 781 years and pushed into France. The expansion into northern Europe, however, was halted in October 732, at the Battle of Tours/Poitiers. Contemporary sources are scant and contradictory, though the Christian army, with perhaps 20-30,000 men, was probably outnumbered. The centrepiece of continuous historical debate, this clash of arms has often been portrayed as the definitive battle to halt the encroachment of Islam in Europe: the decisive fight between Cross and Crescent. Charles Martel, the leader of the Franks, did crush the Saracens' able commander, Abdul Rahman al-Ghafiqi, the Emir of Córdoba. The Emir hailed from the same area as another better-known emir, Osama bin Laden, and both seriously endangered western Europe. Islamic historians have downplayed this defeat, which they call the Battle of the Palace of the Martyrs, and not just because it was a failure. They argue that it was a mere raid in force, not a determined effort to conquer northern Europe. And it has to be seen in the context of concurrent Islamic defeats at the hands of the Byzantines as well as a major revolt of the Berbers in north Africa, plus schisms within the caliphate that all contributed to its collapse in 750.

Contemporary Western historians have sometimes agreed with this version, although the classical interpretation is that without Charles Martel – his cognomen means 'The Hammer' – Islam would have taken over the rest of Europe. Muslims were fighting in central France, over 1,000 miles from their main base in Gibraltar; without Martel they could have moved another 1,000 miles into the Scottish Highlands and their warships could have sailed into the mouth of the Thames. Martel certainly changed Europe in that he combined great military acumen with superb skills as an administrator. He created the first standing professional army since the fall of Rome. He also adapted quickly to the Arabs' military tactics. Previously the Christian armies had been caught in the open and sliced up by Saracen heavy cavalry. Martel, however, deployed in a wooded area on a high point to draw in the Muslim forces; by maintaining strict military discipline he kept his men in a tight phalanx formation which, with the tree cover, prevented the Muslims from using their advantage in heavy cavalry. Before Tours, the Arab armies had regarded the enemy as unruly bands of ill-organised barbarians. Martel, however, was well prepared and well-organised. He sent scouts to harass the Muslim camp and this led to parts of their army retreating to ensure the safety of their booty, especially slaves in the ill-guarded encampment. This version of the battle confirms the opinion that the Arabs were intent on plundering the very wealthy monastery of St Martin of Tours. With the death in battle of their emir, the Islamic armies soon retreated to Spain. Martel recovered many of the Arab saddles and started to develop the use of stirrups to create within five years Christian heavy cavalry, the precursors of the traditional heavily armoured knights on horseback.

The lessons of 732 are clear. Martel won because he adapted and turned the advancing Muslims' strategic advantage, heavy cavalry, against them. This is essentially the challenge facing western European governments today. They have to adapt and turn Islamic State's strategic advantage, its skilful use of the Internet and social media blitzkrieg, against its creator. Otherwise, the conquest of Europe by a virtual caliphate is possible.

Tours was a very important battle for Christendom. Whether it was *the* decisive battle of the West is open to debate, as even more dangerous incursions from Spain soon followed. The Emir of Córdoba's son wanted revenge for his father's death and used naval power to expand Muslim conquests along the coast of southern France. Martel returned to the fight though some Arab forces remained in France. Martel's son, Pippin the Short, took up the fight against the Crescent and his son, Charlemagne, built the first western empire from the ashes of the Roman imperium. Western Europe became better organised, centralised and more militarised. The Arab conquest of France was halted and soon the *reconquista* of al-Andalus/Iberia would gather momentum.

The development of Arab maritime power had played a significant role in the second invasion of France. Islamic warships soon helped to overwhelm Corsica, Sardinia, Crete and Malta and, finally, Sicily in 902. In 922 parts of Bulgaria converted to Islam. The conquests in Asia gave a breathing space to the patchwork of European Christian kingdoms, however. By 900 Arab armies had consolidated their position in north-western India. Muslim trade and influence spread to Indonesia and the Philippines. By 1050 Mombasa in east Africa had become a Muslim trading base for ivory and slaves. In the west, northern Nigeria came under the sway of Islamic militias.

The main bulwark to Muslim advance against the Christian West had long been the armies of the Byzantine Empire, but they were pushed out of the fertile areas of Anatolia (in modern-day Turkey) by 1071. The salvation of the Orthodox Christians in Constantinople was then deemed to be in the hands of diverse Catholic military powers in Europe and the naval strength of the Italian states, plus the key support of the Papacy. The West, however, was involved in a similar schism to the Sunni versus Shia hostility. Muslims had already conquered many smaller squabbling sects of Christianity, but the Catholic versus Greek Orthodox enmity was to enfeeble Western Christian defence. The Papacy's meddling in the Byzantine Empire by sponsoring the Crusades initially buttressed the defence against Islam, yet in the end it helped to topple the Roman remnants in Constantinople. In 1095 the first of a series of seven ill-co-ordinated though often savage invasions of the Holy Land began, establishing various Christian Crusader kingdoms in the Levant. Over the course of 200 years the undiscriminating Crusaders preyed on Byzantine Greeks as often as Jews, Arab Christians or Muslims. Some Christian states allied with Saracens in battles between the small, often precarious, Christian kingdoms. The great Muslim warrior Saladin started his campaign against the Crusaders in 1164 and conquered Damascus in 1174 and Jerusalem in 1187. By 1291 the last Christian fortress at Acre had fallen.

The Crusader states had been summoned into existence in 1095 when Pope Urban II called for a Christian rescue of the Christians allegedly being abused by the Saracens, especially when they were on pilgrimage. Many of the accusations were pure propaganda. Four main crusades followed during the 200-year adventure; other smaller failed ones should be included as well as the numerous crusades *within* Europe, for example against the Albigensian 'heretics', the pagans in the north-east of Europe and the re-conquest of Iberia. Despite the papal influence, no central command structure emerged for the crusades in the Levant. Christians travelled across Europe, living off the land, to reach Jerusalem for a host of reasons – penance, salvation, adventure, booty, military experience or because of feudal obligation. The fighting men were usually raised and led by lords and sometimes kings, so the Crusaders were deeply localised and feudal in their loyalty; hence the lack of unified command that ultimately created the conditions for their defeat by a much bigger, perhaps better-motivated and, certainly more important, *local* enemy whose logistics chain did not ultimately depend on the poor connections with faraway Europe.

Islamic growth was still not just at the point of a sword. The fourth Abbasid caliph, Harun al-Rashid (763-809), was a renowned patron of learning in the often ignored Muslim tradition of the 'scholar's ink is holier than the martyr's blood'. Caliph Harun is probably best known in the West because of his connection to the stories in the *Arabian Nights* or *One Thousand and One Nights*. It became popular in the Western world in the nineteenth century, but has generally been disdained in Arab literature and culture. Most scholars trace the beginning of this so-called Islamic Golden

Age to Harun and describe its end as the sack of Baghdad by the Mongols in 1258, while other historians extend this period of artistic and scientific achievement a few hundred years later. Far from just focusing on the narrow confines of the Koran, Islamic scholars reached out to the ancient texts of classic antiquity of Greece and Rome as well as Persia and Judaism which were translated into Arabic and preserved. Without this Arab scholarship, Western Europe would have had no Renaissance and perhaps remained stuck in the Dark Ages. The first universities were founded. The University of Al Karaouine in Morocco was set up in 859 and is often considered the first degree-granting institution. Baghdad, Cairo and Córdoba became intellectual centres in medicine, science, education, philosophy and mathematics as well as trade hubs. The literature and cultural artefacts of the Greek, Roman, Chinese, Persian and Phoenician civilisations were collected, copied and synthesised. For the libraries the use of paper spread from China to Al-Andalus on the Iberian peninsula. Above all, Islamic culture exulted in its command of architecture. Witness the majesty today of the Alhambra in Granada, the Dome of the Rock in Jerusalem or India's Taj Mahal.

In some places Christians were still persecuted – forced to wear distinctive clothing and forbidden to build new churches, for example. In other places, such as Egypt, run by the Shia Fatimid dynasty from the tenth century, religious tolerance and promotion in government service on merit, not religion or tribe, were common.  Education and hospitals flourished. This caliphate was conquered, however, by Saladin in 1171 and absorbed into the Abbasid Empire.

Islamic scholars often try to comprehend why Muslim culture was so dominant in warfare, arts and sciences as well as commerce in the Golden Age. In the millennium since this age of reason, the total number of books translated into Arabic is less than those translated into Spanish in just one recent year. The question of why Islamic states are so backward in governance and indigenous scientific and cultural development has hinged on the unresolved debate about modernisation versus faith.

The decline in Islamic cultural glory was not sudden, although the 1258 sacking of Baghdad by the Mongols was a clear-cut watershed. External and internal rivalries played a role. From the 950s the Seljuk Turks from today's Uzbekistan started to embrace Islam. They were to become both allies and opponents of the Arab-inspired empire. The Turks, or Ottomans, started to encroach on Byzantine lands in Anatolia. As we saw, the Byzantines allied with Frankish armies to lead a counter-offensive against Islamic power in the Levant. Later, Christian armies were to launch another series of Crusades in Spain, eventually re-conquering the entire peninsula by 1492. The biggest challenge to the Islamic territories came in the east, however. In 1215 Genghis Khan captured Beijing. His brother, Hulaga Khan, overwhelmed Persia and wiped out the Abbasid Empire. He then swallowed Aleppo and Damascus. The hordes pushed into Russia and central Europe, taking a break to swim in the Adriatic Sea off the Dalmatian coast. The surviving Islamic realms in Egypt and North Africa were saved by the Mamluks. These mercenaries, descended from slaves originally from the Black Sea region, defeated both the Mongol hordes and, earlier, the Crusaders. The Mongols destroyed nearly all they could not transport back to the steppes. Libraries, mosques and centuries of accumulated knowledge were torched. Although some of the Mongol armies converted to Islam, the zenith of Islamic culture had been destroyed. The Islamic world never fully recovered from the Mongol devastation, though the ideal of Jihad did.

### The Ottoman empire

The word 'Ottoman' derives from the anglicisation of Osman I, the founder of the Ottoman dynasty. Nomadic horsemen from Turkmenistan, displaced by Mongol invasions, rode into Anatolia to aid the Seljuks of Rum in their conflict with the Byzantines. Osman I (1258-1326) extended what became known as 'Turkish' settlement and thus created an Islamic empire which endured for 600 years. Like the Arab nomadic armies, the Turks relied on conquest, plunder and slavery – sometimes in the name of Jihad – to control North Africa, the Middle East and much of south-eastern Europe. Warfare with the Christian West was sporadic; sometimes, for example, the French allied with the Turks to defeat their European rivals, especially the Habsburgs. The Ottomans defeated Serbian forces in Kosovo in 1389, which led to the rapid penetration of Muslim-led armies into Europe. In what is sometimes described as the last Crusader counter-offensive, at the Battle of Nicopolis on the Danube in September 1396, an alliance of Christian armies was thrashed, partly because of poor preparation, drunkenness and arrogance, especially among the French knights. The nobles who survived were ransomed (although it took twenty-seven years to finalise all the ransoms via Venetian intermediaries). Christian commoners, who were judged to be aged over 20, were beheaded or dismembered (in retaliation for a Christian massacre of Muslim prisoners). Various smaller 'crusades' were attempted. After the humiliating defeat of Nicopolis, however, Europe appeared to be largely defenceless against the Ottoman onslaught.

The apex of Western humiliation was the tumultuous fall of

Constantinople in 1453. It had been besieged many times, though usually naval power from the Italian republics or the intercession of Christian armies from the Balkans had saved the empire, which by then had been reduced almost to the size of a city-state, surrounded by hostile forces. The last Byzantine emperor, Constantine XI, fought hard on sea, land and in underground tunnels against armies, led by Sultan Mehmed II, that outnumbered the defenders by ten to one. It had been the dream of Muslim rulers for centuries to conquer the new Rome. Constantinople became Istanbul and the heart of the Ottoman Caliphate. The exquisite patriarchal basilica of Hagia Sophia was transformed into a mosque. The Muslim empire now controlled the major overland routes between Europe and Asia. The armies and navies were modernised under a series of warrior sultans and their rule expanded in the fifteenth and sixteenth centuries. Persia and Egypt were taken back under the caliph's rule.

Suleiman the Magnificent had assumed the reins of power in Istanbul in 1520 at a critical and especially quarrelsome time in European history. A young Medici pope, Leo X, ruled in Rome. A Habsburg, Charles V, had just been crowned the Holy Roman Emperor and, as all schoolboys used to know, it was neither holy nor Roman nor much of an empire. In England, Henry VIII had just married Charles's aunt, Catherine of Aragon. More crucially for Christendom's divisive tendencies, in Germany Martin Luther was challenging the roles of popes and Catholic kings in the mighty movement that was to split the West and which became known as the Reformation. Religious wars were to ensue – the perfect opportunity for an ambitiously militaristic sultan in Istanbul and moreover a sultan who was determined to avenge the recent loss of Islamic lands in Iberia. Saying farewell to the grandeur of Granada and the glories of the Alhambra and to a Muslim civilisation of over 700 years was hard for such a proud ruler to bear. In 1521 Suleiman led his armies out of Istanbul to march north to the heart of Europe.

Suleiman captured Belgrade and absorbed most of the Kingdom of Hungary. In the high tide of expansion into Europe, he besieged Vienna in 1529, but was pushed back, only to return in 1532. If Vienna had fallen, the heart of Europe would have been exposed. The Ottomans were repelled, although in the east the Turks seized control of Baghdad in 1535 as well as naval access to the Persian Gulf.

With a Christendom sundered by religious schism, the sultan could play off one European power against the other. France in particular was not keen on European alliances against the Muslims, and sometimes did backhanded deals with Istanbul against its own Christian neighbours. Venice, Spain and the Habsburgs also made opportunistic deals with the advancing Ottomans. The Turks' conquests in Cyprus, accompanied by massacres, finally united the Christian states that were formed by the Pope into an uneasy alliance called the Holy League. Islamic land grabs as well as threats to naval commerce were as much inducements as defence of Christ. In October 1571 the Holy League finally assembled a fleet in Greece's Bay of Patmas near Lepanto. The sultan had more ships and more men, though far fewer cannon. Spanish sailors managed to capture the commander, Ali Pasha, on his flagship, the *Sultana*, and displayed his head on a pike. Demoralised, the surviving Ottoman ships withdrew. Over 12,000 Christian slaves were freed from their oars. The Christian forces lost fifty galleys and suffered 13,000 casualties. One of the wounded on board a Genoese ship was Miguel de Cervantes, who wrote *Don Quixote*, perhaps the first modern European novel. When he previously served in the Spanish navy, he had been captured by Algerian corsairs and had spent five years in captivity before his parents managed to raise the ransom money.

The Ottomans soon rebuilt their navy and augmented their army. They also faced down challenges in the eastern parts of their empire. Eventually they once again marched north into Central Europe. At the last moment, on 11 September 1683, the King of Poland with 60,000 troops joined with German and Austrian armies outside the Gate of Vienna to defeat the 250,000 troops of the Grand Vizier. This was the last time that Muslim troops threatened to conquer the West. It was a decisive moment in the alleged clash of civilizations. It is also sometimes said to be the reason al-Qaeda chose 9/11 to attack the symbolic Twin Towers in New York.

The American connection with the Muslim world long preceded 2001. As President Obama noted in 2009, 'The first nation to recognise my country was Morocco'. As far back as 1627 Algerian Muslim pirates claimed to have raided Iceland and carried off 400 slaves. North African corsairs had been raiding European coasts and seizing tens of thousands of slaves from France, Ireland and southern Britain. In the biggest single slave raid on Britain, in June 1631, Barbary pirates captured the entire village of Baltimore in West Cork. Most were to spend the rest of their lives as galley slaves, secluded in harems, or as slave labourers on building sites. Less than a handful managed to get back to Ireland. The tyrannical Moroccan sultan, Moulay Ismail, had 500 wives and concubines, most European slaves, as well as 30,000 white male slaves who built his palace at Meknes and the city walls. One of the slaves, an Englishman by the name of Thomas Pellow, became an officer in the sultan's guard. During his twenty-seven years as a slave, he kept a record of the mercurial behaviour of the sultan, who would personally flog his slaves and, in the days before unions, occasionally saw offending slaves in half while wearing his favourite red riding boots. Thomas Jefferson, before he became US president, was actively involved with slave redemption after two American ships were captured and held for ransom by the Barbary pirates. At one stage it was estimated that such ransoms were taking up to 20 per cent of the US federal budget. When Jefferson became president he sent in the US Marines who later captured Tripoli and put a temporary halt to the corsairs. The first Barbary War (1801-05), America's first war since the Revolution, and the Second Barbary War (1815), were immortalised in the US Marine anthem: *From the halls of Montezuma to the shores of Tripoli.* In the 1805 Battle of Derna, fifty-four US Marines – after marching through hundreds of miles of desert – led a group of mercenaries to overwhelm a much larger Ottoman force in Tripolitania. Ironically, Derna became a centre of Jihadism in modern-day Libya. Perhaps even more ironically, the US Marine Corps officers' dress weapon is still a scimitar-shaped Mameluke sword because of America's first overseas campaign in Derna.

America was generally, however, not involved in the European wars against the Ottomans. The caliphate's failure to take Vienna, on the second try in 1683, marked the high tide of militant Islamic expansion. After this, the Ottoman Empire slowly began to decline. In the beginning of the Ottoman period nearly all the sultans were capable. After Suleiman the Magnificent, well, they were not so magnificent; they were often lackadaisical or plain incompetent, more interested in their palaces and harems rather than their armies and navies. Their military standards diminished while the technology of Western forces advanced rapidly. Corruption at the imperial centre grew apace and the provinces, increasingly ill-governed, started to go their own way. Once Istanbul dominated the trade network between Europe and Asia; the discovery of new maritime routes had suborned the Ottoman monopoly. Portugal and Spain and later England, Holland and France forged new maritime empires. The Russians expanded into the Volga and Caspian regions and also helped their Slav Christian allies in the Balkans. The Serbs rose up against their Turkish overlords, although the most famous rebellion in the West was the Greek fight for freedom in the 1820s, immortalised by the poetry and subsequent martyrdom of Lord Byron. By the mid-nineteenth century the crumbling Ottoman Empire was dubbed 'the sick man of Europe'. The French and the British had to prop up the Turks in their life-and-death struggle with the Russians during the Crimean War of the 1850s. Britain and France later exacted a price as largely Christian territories in the Balkans were granted their nominal independence, starting with Serbia.

Determined to hold on, Istanbul resorted to outright coercion. In 1876 the *Bashi-Bazouks* (literally crazy heads) – ill-disciplined irregulars – killed over 100,000 Bulgarians in their doomed bid for independence. This and other atrocities catapulted the so-called Eastern Question into regular discourse in the parliaments and newspapers of the West. In Westminster, William Ewart Gladstone, four times prime minister, fulminated about the abominable Turks killing Christians. The Russo-Turkish war of 1877-78 culminated in a decisive victory for the Russian Tsar: Bulgaria gained virtual independence as did Serbia and a smaller Montenegro. Austria-Hungary also annexed Bosnia-Herzegovina. In Europe, the Ottoman Empire was being nibbled to death. At the Congress of Berlin in 1878, Britain took over Cyprus and, after 1882, displaced French influence in Egypt, nominally under Ottoman rule.

Shrinking in size, the sultanate turned in on itself, killing perceived enemies, most notoriously the Christian Armenians who were alleged to sympathise with the Russians. In turn, many Balkan Muslims migrated to the heartlands of Anatolia. In 1908 the Young Turk revolution tried to reform the politics and military and introduce a more democratic state. Nevertheless, Istanbul lost Libya to Italy and then nearly all its remaining European territories in the Balkan wars of 1912-13. By the eve of The First World War in 1914 the once great Muslim empire consisted of around 15 million people in modern Turkey and approximately 4 million Arab subjects in Syria, Lebanon, Palestine and Jordan, with over 2 million in Iraq. Another 5 million Arabs were under nominal Ottoman suzerainty in the Arabian peninsula, where the whole Islamic expansion had begun.

The Ottoman Empire entered the world war on the side of the Central Powers (Germany and Austria-Hungary). Since the shrunken imperium now contained a large majority of Muslims, a global Jihad was declared. Whether they opted primarily for God or empire, Turkish troops were hardy and fought well. French and British forces were beaten in the Gallipoli campaign, a result of Winston Churchill's hare-brained advocacy of the scheme to capture Constantinople and outflank the stalemate on the Western Front. The Turks also did well against the British in Iraq when their forces were besieged in 1916 at Kut near Baghdad; German officers had initially done the staff work. Anglo-Indian troops under Major General Charles

Townsend were compelled to surrender in one of the most humiliating defeats of British military history. The dashing Arabist, T. E. Lawrence, had tried to bribe the Ottoman commander to buy the freedom of Townsend's men; the offer was rejected. Many of the British and Indian troops who surrendered died of disease or ill-treatment in captivity. Russian troops made much better headway against Ottoman forces in their Caucasus campaign. As the Russian Caucasus army advanced into eastern Anatolia, Istanbul began deporting and ethnic cleansing its Armenian population, portrayed as pro-Russian. Perhaps as many as 1.5 million Armenians died. Armenian soldiers in the Ottoman army were disarmed and killed. Many civilian Armenian leaders followed them to their graves. The wives and children of those killed were often forced to convert from Christianity and assimilate with families of Arabs and Turks. The less fortunate were either killed or just driven into the deserts to die. The Ottoman government hid the scale of crimes and argued that it was a reasonable response to the rebellious behaviour of a traitorous minority. This was arguably the first genocide of the twentieth century. Greek and Assyrian minorities were also persecuted.

The genocidal response to the Armenians had been partly prompted by the epic defeat of Ottoman arms at the battle of Sarikamis in the winter of 1914. Of the 100,000 Turkish troops sent into battle, scarcely 18,000 survived the harsh winter conditions and the Russian onslaught. On the Middle Eastern front the Turks made better progress in the first two years of the Great War. Then Anglo-French diversionary tactics colluded with the Arab revolt of 1916. The prime purpose for the British was to tie up Ottoman forces and to prevent their advance on British positions in Egypt, especially the Suez Canal. Much romantic nonsense has been written on the Arab revolt against their co-religionists in Istanbul. Lawrence of Arabia played a smaller role than is depicted by Hollywood. Arguably, a British Arabist, Gertrude Bell, did more to win over Arab leaders, especially in Iraq. And other British officers played significant roles in persuading some of the Arab tribal leaders that they should pursue independence from the Turks and set up a unified Arab state. Often portrayed by historians as a secular nationalist revolt, it was also depicted in religious terms by both Muslim sides that did the fighting.

German propaganda worked equally hard to stir up support for the caliph's call for Jihad throughout the British Empire. In a little known attempt at Western pro-Jihadist mobilisation, Kaiser Wilhelm II supported the *Halbmondlager* (Half Moon Camp) in Zossen, near Berlin. This spectacularly unsuccessful pet project of the Kaiser to fire up Muslim sentiment on behalf of Germany was inspired by an aristocratic crank and Orientalist called Max von Oppenheim. The aim was to create a Muslim rebellion throughout the French and British empires. At any one time, up to 5,000 Muslim prisoners of war were detained, in relative luxury. Initially the captives came from colonial French forces raised in Morocco, Algeria and Tunisia. Besides good food and access to a new mosque, the inmates were subjected to lectures and even on occasion asked to appear as extras in films made in Berlin. Despite extensive attempts to indoctrinate their prisoners, the Germans never quite worked out how the Jihadists were to distinguish hatred towards *some* unbelievers (the French, say) from the Austrian unbelievers. Around 3,000 of the Muslim volunteers were eventually sent to fight on pro-Ottoman fronts in Iraq and Persia; they appear to have proved ineffective, not least in fighting for Islam. The Germans tried to develop this campaign at the Half Moon camp and other prisons, by trying to seduce Sikhs captured from the Indian Army. The new inmates enjoyed the good conditions, but they were very rarely induced to betray their British overlords. The Germans then tried to work on Irish prisoners. Predictably, their unruly behaviour made prison authorities despair of turning them into anti-British troops. Nevertheless, the Germans were soon to take pro-Jihadist and especially anti-Jewish propaganda much more seriously in the next world war. German and Ottoman intrigues were not a complete failure. One of the most significant responses to the summons to holy war was in Darfur, which abutted the Anglo-Egyptian territory of Sudan. The Darfurians heeded the caliph's call, though the rebellion was soon quashed by British and French officers leading Arab levies. British military intelligence in Cairo may have played a role in producing fake documents to entrap the Sultan of Darfur, Ali Dinar, to fight for his nominal Muslim overlord, the caliph in Istanbul, with the intention of annexing the independent sultanate.

Another more long-lasting effect of the caliph's call to Jihad came in the North-West Frontier area of the Raj. In the 1880s the Deobandi movement had been formed to purify Islam and end the corruption of Western influence, most specifically the British. The movement wanted to make up for the losses inflicted by the failed revolt against the Raj during the Indian 'mutiny'. The Deobandis had cross-fertilised with the Wahhabi movement set up by Muhammad Ibn Wahhab (1703-1792) in Najd in the heart of the Arabian peninsula. This ultra-conservative form of Islam was taken on board by the local ruler, Muhammad Ibn Saud. This fusion of political power and religious fervour became central to the later emergence of the Kingdom of Saudi Arabia and its subsequent influence on worldwide Jihadism. While some Arabs in central Arabia were to join the British in the Great War, the Deobandi Muslims in the Raj started to fight *against* the British. Militant Deobandi elements sought refuge in the lawless Afghan-Raj border region to fight alongside rebel Pathans. The Indian Army suppressed a series of minor revolts which had more to do with traditional Pathan resistance than Jihadist-inspired preaching by the Deobandi. The border troubles were to contribute to the short Third British-Afghan war in 1919. Nevertheless, the seeds of the Saudi-Deobandi alliance were – much later – to grow into the Taliban and al-Qaeda in the twenty-first century. Today around half of British mosques are Deobandi-oriented.

If the Caliph's call to Jihad had little short-term influence in British India, it had even less effect in the old Islamic heart of Arabia. Just as the Raj sent tens of thousands of Indian troops, of all faiths, to fight in the Middle East and on the Western Front, Arabs – in much smaller numbers – fought alongside the Union flag. Many of the Bedouin who fought in the main Arab revolt against Istanbul did so for gold coin – paid in advance. The money helped them distinguish their old antipathy to Turkish bureaucrats and tax-collectors from their residual loyalty to the religious leadership of the caliph. The motivations for the revolt were a mixture of religion, nationalism, tribal loyalty, adventure and avarice. A small number of irregulars and a few regular forces, mainly Arab Bedouin and British officers, including Lawrence of Arabia, and a small French detachment, tied down a very large number of Turkish troops (and their frequently loyal Arab conscripts) in largely defensive positions, especially in Istanbul's attempts to defend the vital Hejaz railway. The tide was turning against the Ottomans by 1917. The British regrouped in Mesopotamia under the capable General Sir Frederick Stanley Maude, who captured Baghdad in March. He died from cholera and was buried in the city he had just conquered. But conquered only for a while; after the war the Iraqis rose up in a revolt that was savagely suppressed by British-led imperial forces. 'In recent days there has been bloodshed and the destruction of populous towns and the violation of the sanctity of places of worship to make humanity weep.'[4] This was written by an Arab journalist based in Najaf in October 1920; the same words could have applied to the American occupation in 2006 or the Islamic State in 2014.

In Palestine the Egyptian Expeditionary Force under General Sir Edmund Allenby broke out of Sinai. The Ottomans scored a temporary victory at Gaza, but it was not enough to stop the advance into Palestine proper. The withdrawal of Russian forces on the northern front as a result of the October Revolution could not help the Ottomans to concentrate their troops in the south. British regular forces defeated Turkish and German forces to capture Jerusalem just before Christmas 1917. British Prime Minister David Lloyd George described it as a 'Christmas present to the British people'. To show respect, Allenby entered the Old City on 11 December, humbly on foot, rather than riding in on horseback through the Jaffa Gate as the German Kaiser had done twenty years before. Allenby was the first Christian ruler of the City in many centuries. Both the British general and Lawrence of Arabia considered the possession of Jerusalem as the supreme moment of the Great War. Eventually, British forces and Arab allies rolled up Palestine; Allenby's troops alongside the Arab nationalist Northern Army decisively defeated the Ottoman Seventh Army at the battle of Megiddo in September 1918. Arab and Allied troops also occupied Damascus.

The Turks signed an armistice in October 1918 which ended the fighting in the Middle East theatre. Bent on a draconian peace settlement, the Allies occupied Constantinople, much to the relief of surviving Armenians. 'While Istanbul's Christians celebrated, the Muslim majority watched the Allied soldiers take possession of their city in silence from behind their shuttered windows, overwhelmed by humiliation and despair.'[5] The Allies did not stay long; they had walked into an internal civil war which resulted in the Turkish nationalist leader Mustafa Kemal (Atatürk) setting up a republic in 1923. The caliphate was officially abolished on 3 March 1924, although the last ruling sultan, Mehmed IV, had left the country on 17 November 1922 on board a British warship for Malta and a final exile on the Italian Riviera. The thirty-sixth and last sultan had been condemned by Turkish nationalists for reluctantly conceding to the Allies' dismemberment of the empire. The House of Osman had fallen as had the physical manifestation of Islamic centralised rule. The caliph's call for Jihad had not worked. In fact, the Western allies, terrified of a pan-Islamic revolt throughout their imperial domains, had taken the call to Jihad much more seriously than Muslims themselves had. (The same might be said about the overreaction of the West in the war on terror.) The British and French had hoped that by picking off the apparently weakest of their enemies, they would shorten the war. Instead the Turks' resistance meant that hundreds of thousands of troops were diverted from the Western Front, thus prolonging the war. The Hashemite princes had responded to T. E. Lawrence's call to fight for a pan-Arab state, but they got relatively small pickings in Trans-Jordan and Iraq, while Ibn Saud took possession of Saudi Arabia. Many Arabs would continue to dream of forging a pan-Arab Muslim state rising from the ashes of the Ottoman edifice. They would be frustrated by the emergence instead of French and British dominance in the Middle East and North Africa.

## The collapse of the Arab dream

T. E. Lawrence had promised his Arab friends freedom, but the Sykes-Picot agreement of 1916 planned to carve up the Arab lands once the Sublime Porte in Istanbul was prostrate. The Russians had been involved too, looking for bits of the Ottoman pie to slice up. Once the Bolsheviks took over in October 1917 they published the details of the secret deal, severely embarrassing the Anglo-French conspirators, infuriating the Arabs and delighting the Turks. The old colonial powers resorted to another version of the Scramble for Africa, this time under legal veneers of protectorates and mandates, sometimes under the aegis of the League of Nations. After the Versailles Peace Conference punished Germany, at the succeeding conferences for other defeated states the haughty imperial cartographers literally redrew the Middle East into spheres of influence. The Holy Land became proverbially the 'thrice-promised land'. Under the pressure of war, London made extensive promises to Arabs and influential Jewish lobbyists while intending to take over the territories themselves. Palestine was 90 per cent inhabited by Arabs; to make it a Jewish homeland was bound to spark and then fuel anger for many decades. The French took control in Syria and Lebanon, and the British set up puppet kingdoms and satrapies in the region including Trans-Jordan and Iraq. Palestine was ruled by a traditional colonial apparatus. Aden, taken over in 1839, remained a formal British protectorate, while the emirates in the Gulf clung to Britain for their security against their bigger neighbours.

Lawrence was consumed by guilt at the failure of the British to honour all their wartime promises, although the Hashemites had received some pay-off. He wrote at length about his angst, although perhaps one of the most concise summaries of the Arabists' post-war sense of betrayal was by Walter Smart of the Egyptian Service:

> The Anglo-French bargaining about other people's property, the deliberate bribing of international Jewry at the expense of the Arabs who were already our allies in the field, the immature political juggleries of amateur Oriental experts, the stultification of Arab independence and unity … all the immorality and incompetence inevitable in the stress of a great war.[6]

In the inter-war period some Arabists in Whitehall proselytised for the Arab cause, but mostly London was concerned with strategic and commercial interests, especially oil, at minimum costs to the British Exchequer. Even more than in India, it was empire on the cheap, albeit an empire in its menopause. The long affair with the Hashemites, who provided the kings of Jordan and, briefly, Iraq, was based often on a genuine belief that by bolstering the conservative forces of Islam and the ruling families from the ancient Bedouin tribes, the British could maintain Arab stability not least against the radical forces of secular nationalism, tinged with the Bolshevism spreading from Russia.

*The Second World War*
Over 55 million people were killed in this war, most of them civilians. According to the iconoclastic British historian Norman Stone, 'It would be cruel, but not inaccurate, to say that the British war effort consisted of taking American dollars to pay for Russians to kill Germans, while the British just dropped bombs on civilians.'[7] Despite Anglo-American propaganda during and after the war it is inescapably true that the 1939-45 war was won and lost on the Russian steppes, where the Red Army destroyed 607 divisions of the German and Axis forces. To the British and Russians especially it was seen as a great patriotic war, but how did Muslims, especially Arabs, view the conflict?

Some Arab soldiers fought alongside the Allies in Syria and Lebanon to contain determined pro-Vichy French forces. They also soldiered alongside British forces in Iraq. The small but well-trained Sudanese defence force fought by the side of the British in defeating the Italians in Ethiopia and Somaliland.[8] In Iran, Russian and British forces ejected the pro-Nazi shah and replaced him with his son. Over 30,000 Jews from Palestine joined the British army.

On the other hand, many Arabs sided with Axis forces as the best way of booting out their colonial masters as well as curbing Zionism. The best-known pro-German Arab leader, the Grand Mufti of Jerusalem, sought exile in Nazi-occupied Europe from where on 25 November 1941 he declared a Jihad against the Allies. According to Albert Speer's reasonably reliable memoirs, Adolf Hitler expressed sympathy with the Arab cause on a number of occasions, and sometimes discussed the martial success of the first Islamic invasion of Europe. The mutual hostility to Jews was another inducement to the Führer. Technically, Nazi doctrine would denigrate Arabs as members of an inferior Semitic race, but convenience dictated that pro-

Nazi allies should be made honorary Aryans. The obvious example again was the Grand Mufti, Haj Amin al-Husseini, but there were others, especially Iraqi nationalists. The Germans supported the Arab revolt in Palestine (1936-39) as well as backing a pro-Axis government in Iraq in May 1941, when a Führer Directive stated: 'The Arab Freedom Movement in the Middle East is our natural ally against England.'

There never was and never will be a single Arab opinion – in the Second World War, or any time. Arabs espoused many conflicting viewpoints, from Marxism through to Western liberalism, and on to Islamic fundamentalism. Despite the German (and Italian) propaganda campaigns to win over Muslim opinion, relatively few Arabs joined the half-hearted clones of the European Fascist parties. The Syrian national party, and for a while the Young Egypt Party did flirt with fascism, as did some of the founders of the Ba'athist movement. The Catholic Maronites in Lebanon also set up the avowedly fascist Phalange party in 1936, with brown shirts and Nazi salutes. Eminent generals such as Erwin Rommel were feted in Arab society, and Hitler praised. In Damascus after the fall of France in 1940, some Arabs chanted (in Arabic):

> No more Monsieur
> No more Mister
> Allah's in Heaven
> And Hitler's on earth.

Pro-Nazi Arab exiled leaders, ejected from Palestine and Iraq by the British, helped to form a Muslim Waffen SS division that wore distinctive scimitars as well as swastikas. Many were Bosnian Muslims, who fought in anti-partisan operations. They also issued propaganda, not least on the Voice of Free Arabia radio station. One of the most influenced by Nazi propaganda was a young Anwar Sadat, later to be president of Egypt. Some pro-Nazi Arabs in North Africa were involved in extensive sabotage and intelligence operations.

Five million citizens of the British Empire joined the armed forces in the Second World War. Of these almost two million were from South Asia, probably the largest volunteer army in history. In many of the most crucial battles – El Alamein, Monte Cassino and especially Kohima – a significant proportion of the 'British' troops were Indian. Many of these were Muslims. Britain declared war on behalf of India without any discussion with the leading Indian politicians. Many nationalists objected to the diktat and so opposed the war effort that they might have supported if they had been consulted. Secular leaders such as Jawaharal Nehru were imprisoned. His rival, Mohammad Ali Jinnah, who became the founder of independent Muslim Pakistan, supported the imperial war.

Likewise, despite their own dislike of colonialism, the majority of Arab leaders tended to sympathise with the Allies. Despite the size of the pro-Vichy forces, the number of Arabs who volunteered to fight for the Axis was small compared with those who enlisted with the British and Free French. Fascism was a minority taste among the intelligentsia. The extreme anti-Semitism of leaders such as the Grand Mufti was contrasted by many Arab families who sheltered Jews during the Axis occupation of Tunisia. In Morocco, for example, King Mohammed V refused to make the 200,000 Moroccan Jews wear yellow stars (although this discrimination was practised in France). After the fall of the Reich, some elements of fascism survived in Ba'athism in Iraq; in the Egyptian national movements, an early admirer of Hitler, besides Anwar Sadat, was Abdel Gamal Nasser.

Islamism was manipulated by all sides in the propaganda campaigns of the Second World War. Some of it was mere window dressing. Where it was believed passionately was in a movement formed in 1928 which was to have a very influential and permanent role in the Middle East – the Muslim Brotherhood. The immediate years of the Cold War witnessed an age of dictators and Arab nationalism marked by secularism rather than Islamism. Despite the eclipse in 1945 of the fascist dictators (except in Iberia), decolonisation in the Middle East fashioned a new vogue for the man on horseback, nationalist leaders who were each courted by the rival superpowers in Washington and Moscow.

*The Age of Dictators*
Britain had stood alone in 1940 and had fought the Axis powers from start to finish. Without Winston Churchill, London would probably have done a deal with Hitler, not least to preserve the empire. Despite Washington's financial power and Moscow's military manpower, in late 1945 Great Britain could still pose as one of the Big Three (or Four if France is included) as the Iron Curtain began to fall. Britain may have won the war, but it had lost its wealth, and more importantly its will. As the chronicler of empire, James Morris, observed: 'The Royal Navy had failed, the British armies had been outclassed; white men had been seen in states of panic and humility; the legend had collapsed in pathos.'[9] The imperium was to totter on for a few more years, yet in the heartland of the Arab world, Egypt, it

was about to be dealt a fatal blow by the most charismatic Arab dictator, Gamal Abdel Nasser.

Military coups were fashionable in the Islamic world. Pakistan, Iraq and Sudan all despaired of Western-style civilian democracy – bequeathed by the departing British – and instead turned to the military. Arguably, a relatively efficient British-trained military, honed in combat in the Second World War, was the most powerful legacy of the imperial recessional, not parliaments, judiciaries and universities. The new dictators toyed with a variety of *isms* from Arab socialism and Islamism to communism, though usually a form of muscular nationalism triumphed. And anti-imperialism was the dominant *leitmotif*.

President Nasser waited until British troops left the Canal Zone in 1954 and then nationalised the (French) company that managed the canal. Even though the lease ran for another decade there was no reason why Egyptians should not administer the major asset that flowed through their own country. Besides, with the independence of the Raj in 1947, it was no longer the 'jugular of Empire'. To the old men in power in London, and their propagandists, Nasser was another Hitler, however. Appeasement would not be repeated. In a secret, dirty deal with the Israelis, Britain and France invaded the Canal Zone under the pretext of separating Israeli and Egyptian forces and supposedly safeguarding it on behalf of the UN. In a last roar of the British lion, London wanted to display its sham virility to oust Nasser. It was regime change before the term became fashionable. Washington threatened a run on the pound, and Moscow, busy invading Hungary, offered to rain down rockets on the Anglo-French imperialists. Britain and France had to withdraw immediately and Nasser was hailed as a hero throughout the third world.

Suez was a humiliation of the first order for London, which thereafter did little in foreign fields without the express permission of the USA. France was more of a slow learner. Humiliated by the rapid Nazi conquest in 1940 and then the loss of its colonies in South East Asia, the French government internalised the myth that Algeria was as French as Paris. It wasn't – it was an Arab state in a nationalist ferment, and armed by an over-confident Nasser.

Writer Albert Camus captured the mood of the savage Algerian war (1954-62). 'In this admirable country in which a spring without equal covers it with flowers and its light, men are suffering hunger and demanding justice.' The French authorities condemned the Algerian nationalists as communists and waged one of the most inhumane of all colonial wars. The war ended the careers of six French prime ministers – and promoted the rise and nearly the fall of Charles de Gaulle who survived thirty-eight assassination attempts – and twice led France to the edge of civil war at home. After endless atrocities on both sides, a million Algerians had been killed and a similar number of French settlers had fled. France was defeated, and the pan-Arab media underscored another Arab triumph.

Britain and France were thoroughly humbled in the Arab world, although Britain hung on briefly in Aden, for a while perhaps the busiest port in the world, and longer as a protector of the Gulf statelets. When, in the 1970s, Britain was forced to withdraw from its position 'East of Suez', a synonym for retirement from empire, its power projection was largely spent. True, many of the Arab potentates in Oman and the emirates in the Gulf still sent their sons to the Royal Military Academy, Sandhurst, and bought British weapons to protect their oil assets. Nevertheless, Britain and France had been replaced by America and Russia as the new regional colossi.

The Arab states became thoroughly authoritarian. They were nominally Muslim of course, though any hints of Islamism, especially any sort of the more radical political Islam, were usually erased or pumped underground. Syria's dictators cosied up to Russia. Egypt flirted with Moscow, but eventually ended up a close ally of Washington, as did Saudi Arabia. During the height of the Cold War the dictators, especially the House of Saud, used their oil and influence to dominate the Sunni world. In Shia Iran, the shah was backed to the hilt by Washington. During the Cold War most Arab dictators played the dating game with the superpowers to ensure they stayed in power. Many of the Arab leaders forgot their socialist mantras and became corrupt oligarchies, buttressed by their secret police. The *Mukhabarat,* the secret service, was often the most, and sometimes only, efficient state organ. Washington rarely protested on the simple principle: 'He may be a bastard, but he's *our* bastard.'

In the wider Islamic world, Indonesia underwent years of internal strife. Pakistan was racked by war with India. Turkey was buffeted by regular army coups. In the Arab states oil wealth brought rapid economic development unmatched by progress in democratic freedoms. Stability was what mattered both to the internal oligarchs and their foreign allies. The West turned a blind eye to regular beheadings in Saudi Arabia, even of princesses. Iraq descended into a terror state under Saddam Hussein, though it was tolerated by Washington as a brake on revolutionary Iran. Much of the debate in the Arab world was not so much about internal social improvements. Rather, most ills were displaced onto the perpetual Arab-Israeli dispute. Israel was

28 *The Jihadist Threat*

often portrayed as *the* central problem of Arab politics. On the contrary, it was the only thing that the Arab League could usually agree on. Arabia, arguably, would have been more fractious without the existence of Israel.

Despite the never-ending disputes between Sunni and Shia in Lebanon and elsewhere in the Fertile Crescent, all impelled by the rise of Iran, the spiritual spark of a Sunni revival of the true beliefs of Islam was never extinguished. Scholars, idealists, dreamers, poets and imams talked of a return to the essential beliefs of the Prophet, although they could not of course agree on what precisely the true path was.

### The Muslim Brotherhood

Almost since the death of Muhammad, thinkers have talked and written about the correct interpretation of Islam. For centuries revivalists have tried to restore either the spiritual or temporal power of the Islamic community, the *Umma*. In modern times the Sufi movements, which concentrated on the inner mystical elements of the faith, have played an inspirational role. Sometimes the more spiritual reforms have morphed into direct political action. A classic example is the rise of the Mahdi, Muhammad Ahmad ibn Abdullah, who led a messianic movement that drove the British out of Sudan and inflicted one of the Victorian empire's biggest defeats when General 'Chinese' Gordon was killed in the siege of Khartoum in 1885. The imperial retribution soon followed in the re-conquest of the country. Nevertheless, London fretted that the Mahdi's message of Jihad would spread to the regional imperial heartland in Egypt and also to Muslims throughout the empire.

Earlier, in the eighteenth century in central Arabia, the Wahhabi religious movement had taken a political grip that was to result in a long-lasting deal with the House of Saud. With its mega-riches from oil, Saudi Arabia was able to pump billions of dollars into setting up tens of thousands of Wahhabi-leaning madrassahs, especially in Pakistan with its old allies, the Deobandi. Most Islamists don't like the term Wahhabi, so it might be polite to call it the ultra-conservative Saudi branch of Salafism. This branch of Salafism became super-rich, hyperactive and very political.

Spiritual renaissance and political adventurism were often related – that is why most of the more secular Arab leaders since 1945 have been wary of Islamists. One of the most significant spiritual revivals in recent times has been centred in the Muslim Brotherhood or the Society of Muslim Brothers to give its full title in English. Founded by a schoolteacher and Islamic thinker, Hassan al-Banna, in 1928, it has grown to influence the entire

*Umma*. In 1989 Muslim Brothers in Sudan helped to introduce the first modern Islamist revolution in the Sunni world. (The first in the Shia sphere was Iran in 1979.) The more radical Islamists in Sudan were eased out by the military and Field Marshal Omar al-Bashir still rules the country after ending the official Jihad in the largely Christian and animist south. In Egypt, despite constant persecution, in 2012 the Muslim Brotherhood created the first democratically elected ruling party in the country's long history. At the time of writing it is a banned terrorist organisation and the former president, Mohammed Morsi, has just been condemned to death.

The Brotherhood's reputation for piety, non-corruption and above all charitable works has inspired a big following throughout the Arab world. It believes that the *Sunnah*, the Islamic way of life based upon the Koran and reputable *Hadiths*, will create the perfect society on earth, with Allah's blessing. The Brothers allocate a portion of their income to the movement, although the Saudis also financed various branches of the Brotherhood for decades. The Saudis' austere branch of Islam, based upon Wahhabism, shared some of the ideals of the Brotherhood; later the Saudis removed their support, especially after the Arab Spring of 2011. Egypt cracked down on the Brotherhood on many occasions. In 1948, 1954 and 1965 many Brothers were jailed and some executed. The most famous Islamist 'martyr' was Sayyid Qutb, a prolific writer and scholar, who was executed in Egypt in 1966. His magnum opus was *In the Shade of the Koran*, a thirty-volume commentary on the holy book. He hated the USA for its materialism and sexual indulgence and loathed Jewish influence. Above all he was determined that his scholarship should encourage political action. He is often seen as the leading light of modern Jihadism. Qutb's brother Muhammad moved to Saudi Arabia and is said to have influenced Osama bin Laden. Certainly, the current leader of al-Qaeda, Dr Ayman al-Zawahiri, has extolled Sayyid Qutb's influence on his and his movement's philosophy.

Some Brotherhood leaders have distanced themselves from al-Qaeda. The movement is still legal in the United Kingdom, although in many lengthy discussions with its leaders in London, they expressed their fears to me that the government would ban them. They went to great lengths to present their democratic and peaceful intentions. The Brothers have been banned and persecuted in various Arab states, most notably Saudi Arabia, Syria and Egypt. Yet the Brotherhood is probably the most cohesive and effective of all Arab political organisations with very strict and tight hierarchical structures that bear a passing resemblance to the Freemasons. Their discipline and self-reliance have enabled them to survive decades of persecution. Particularly in the West, the Brothers tend to espouse political activism though they eschew violence on the model of al-Qaeda and the Islamic State. When pressed on the violence of Hamas, for example, they insist that defensive action is justified, including firing unguided missiles into the Jewish state. The Muslim Brotherhood's ability to survive, metamorphose and multiply means that its many off-shoots are likely to continue to be significant political players. The Brothers may be temporarily down, but they are not out. Not even in Egypt.

*Chapter 2*

# The Renaissance of Militant Jihad

Islamists disagree as to what precisely triggered the revival of modern military Jihad. Western historians are hardly in accord on the matter either. After the Cold War it was conjectured by some that there was an 'end of history' – that Western liberal democracy and modern capitalism would inevitably accompany globalisation. The notions of a clash of civilizations and the re-emergence of faith-based politics were hotly contested well into the twenty-first century. How did the existential threat of Jihadism emerge from a world divided first by the rival secular ideologies of the superpowers to the collapse of the Berlin Wall and then to the recent establishment of the warrior Islamic State? That old charlatan Nostradamus is said to have predicted the Islamic State, but few others did and certainly no-one in the multi-billion dollars' worth of Western intelligence agencies. Its sudden explosion in Iraq and Syria, and its numerous franchises, have shaken the tectonic plates of the Middle East and now Europe.

Some Muslim historians tend to focus on the sins of Israel, notably its winning 'the war of independence' in 1948-49. Arabs and particularly the Palestinians refer to this as the *Nakba* – the day of catastrophe. They also point to the utter Arab humiliation in the Six-Day War of 1967. The constant failures of Arab armies in 1948, 1956 and 1967 required a scapegoat – especially US succour inspired by Jewish lobbies. The humiliation of Egyptian armies in Yemen added to the collapse in the belief in secular Arab socialism as the way forward. Perhaps God should be given a chance. Or so a growing minority began to think.

Some confidence was restored with the very partial success of the 1973 Yom Kippur/Ramadan War and the new muscle-flexing of the Organisation of Petroleum Exporting Countries (OPEC). In 1979, much to the surprise of the Americans (and the CIA), the Islamic revolution in Iran deposed the pro-Western shah. In the same year the Soviets invaded Afghanistan – that would lead to the influx of holy warriors, *Mujahedin*, from the entire Muslim world. This was clearly a watershed moment in the rise of the modern Jihad.

The exodus of Russian soldiers in 1989 was celebrated by Islamists worldwide as a vindication of Allah's blessing.

Fighting, rather than armchair, Jihadists also stress the importance of Bosnia. They say that the influx of *Mujahedin* to protect the most endangered of Muslim communities, on the frontier of the *Umma,* was the Rubicon of modern Islamist warfare. At the same time the Chechens fought two wars against their Russian overlords. These wars were initially fired up by nationalist sentiment; then the anger was recharged within the international Jihadist network. Thereafter hardened and usually very competent Chechen *Mujahedin* were to be found on nearly all the Jihadist battlefields. The wars against Saddam Hussein and the alleged presence of uniformed American soldiers near the holy places in Saudi Arabia were also volatile accelerants. Meanwhile, Islamist insurgency began to spread in Asia, in the Philippines and in Indonesia. In Africa the implosion of Somalia left the ungoverned spaces ripe for the Jihadists to exploit.

Obviously 9/11, the cataclysm of the attack on the Twin Towers, was portrayed in Jihadist circles as a major counter-blow to the American-led Christian crusade. Many Arab states were privately tolerant of the American reprisal in toppling the Taliban in Afghanistan in late 2001. The removal of Saddam Hussein in 2003, if not entirely condoned in the Islamic world, was tolerated because Saddam was not a popular figure, even in the Arab League. The occupation fiasco in Iraq immediately raised hackles, however. Atrocities in Europe, such as the 7/7 bombings of the London transport system in 2005, were seen by Jihadists as an inevitable progress of the expanding consequences of Western attacks on the *Umma.* This was dramatised by Hamas's defence against the Israelis and the perceived double standards of the West towards the Jewish state.

The Arab Spring was welcomed in the West as a means of undercutting the radical message of al-Qaeda and its expanding number of franchises that were blossoming in North Africa and Yemen. It was hoped in Western capitals that the toppling of the tyrants, even if pro-Western, would finally introduce a new dawn of liberal democracies. The fall of Saddam, remember, was supposed to be the key to unlock democracy in the area. Instead, along with the overthrow of Colonel Gaddafi in Libya, it became a classic example of dictatorship giving way to mayhem. The political vacuum was soon filled by Islamist extremists, not liberal democrats. In Libya, the North Atlantic Treaty Organisation had simply and inadvertently acted as the air wing of al-Qaeda, soon to be displaced by the more radical Islamic State. Libya was awash with weapons that were dispersed to fanatics in Algeria, Mali and

Nigeria and elsewhere in the arid Sahara and Sahel. Soon, from A-Z – Algeria to Zanzibar – Jihadist groups, most notoriously Boko Haram in Nigeria, rushed to swear allegiance to the new caliphate.

State boundaries were collapsing throughout the Arab world. The straight-line mania of European cartographers had created artificial 'nations' in Africa after the Congress of Berlin in 1878. Nearly a century later, the shibboleth imposed by the Organisation of African Unity and its successor, the African Union, tried to prevent any border revisions. Yet the last colonialist fiat was bound to crumble. Eritrea's secession from Ethiopia, at first amicable, was to spawn one of the most bitter and pointless wars in African history. South Sudan became independent in 2011 after Africa's longest struggle (dubbed a Jihad by Khartoum), which soon toppled into tribal anarchy. It was no coincidence that the peripheries of Ottoman imperium should start to disintegrate when the successors to caliphate rule – Britain and Sudan in the case of South Sudan and Darfur – eased their grip. Kurdistan was another heritage of the botched settlement after the Great War. In fact, it is amazing the Sykes-Picot deal had endured so long – nearly a century. Most of the artificial states and borders conjured up by the French and British bureaucrats made little sense in 1916, let alone today. The whole edifice of the Middle East is collapsing, so it is no surprise that a new wave of Jihadism should reject not just the cack-handed imperialists in London and Paris of a century ago, but also the whole Arab firmament, and indeed anything not ordained by Allah.

*The steps to the new caliphate*

Three major Western interventions helped to prompt the Islamic State crisis of 2014-15: Afghanistan, Iraq and Libya. The West stumbled in other places, but events in these three countries were paramount. That is not to say that Western military action in these three states was solely responsible, the only recruiting sergeants for the Jihadist advance – just as Israel is not the sole factor, despite its use as a whipping boy by Arabs for all their woes. Or just as African states still resort to blaming colonialism for their problems instead of examining their own poor governance. The American-led interventions in Afghanistan and Iraq and more reluctant involvement in Libya did create, however, numerous unintended adverse consequences. The destruction of the Ba'athist regime in Baghdad was directly responsible for the then unchecked rise of Iran, one of Washington's great *bêtes noires*. Worse, the growth of Jihadist forces in Afghanistan, Iraq and Libya caused numerous 'blowbacks' in the West, not least the training of young Jihadists keen to extend the campaigns to the Western heartlands in retaliation for what they think are grievances in the war zones in the *Umma.*

Russians in Afghanistan

The war that began, or rather intensified, in 1979 had a profound effect on the whole Islamic world. When the Soviets invaded, hatred of the USSR was grafted on to raw nationalism, local Afghan tribalism and religious fervour. A Jihad was declared *before* Russian tanks rolled in on Christmas Day 1979 to support the Marxist regime in Kabul. The tribal warriors disliked *any* government, let alone an atheist communist one backed by foreign infidels. Previous attempts at land reform and improvements in women's rights had incensed rural conservatives, both landlords and peasants. The Soviets soon discovered what the British had learned in the nineteenth century: defeating and controlling the Afghans were two entirely different feats. In the first years the Soviets' war did not resemble the American debacle in Vietnam. The Russians were fighting on their own doorstep. Despite the mounting casualties, Soviet press and public opinion were successfully muzzled. And although Afghanistan was generally ideal guerrilla terrain, the tribal fighters were not natural soldiers. Convinced of their innate martial qualities, they were reluctant to train and spent as much time praying as working out tactics or maintaining their weapons.

As an aside, there is nothing worse for trained Western soldiers than to be involved daily in close combat alongside the disorganised rabble which many of the *Mujahedin* were. In summer 1984 I accompanied well-trained ex-soldiers, some special forces, while we filmed the insurgency near Kabul.[10] A minority of the 'Muj', as they were called by Western observers, were very good indeed, especially the insurgents in the north led by Ahmed Shah Massud. By sheer doggedness, however, even the ill-disciplined insurgents managed to keep the Red Army at bay. The Soviets controlled the cities and especially the air. The Muj, comprising some forty major groups, controlled perhaps 80 per cent of the country.

The Americans helped the Muj, although the CIA connection with Osama bin Laden has been overstated. But they certainly encouraged, armed and – via Pakistan – helped to train the Jihadists. Short term, their aim was to force Russia to suffer its own Vietnam; long term the conflicts produced a cadre of well-trained and ultimately triumphalist Jihadists. China also helped with weapons and Saudi Arabia donated much of the funding. On the ground the foreign backers failed to produce a cohesive strategy. The insurgents fought sometimes on local tribal issues based on clan or personal feuds, more than a sense of national or international Jihad. From personal experience, the insurgents spent as much time ambushing and stealing from fellow *Mujahedin* as attacking the invaders. Their rigid individualism was both their main strength and weakness. No Tito or de Gaulle emerged to seize overall leadership. The persistent divisions were partly a legacy of traditional social structures in which elders reached the decisions by lengthy consensus and fighters were hesitant to venture outside their own immediate areas. As the inveterate traveller and photographer Nick Danziger observed, 'The civil war was more about tribal and sexual apartheid than about the defeat of a foreign invader.' The fractiousness was sometimes exacerbated by the influx of foreign fighters. Usually the Arab volunteers were kept in separate bases to avoid clashes with the local Afghan insurgents. The holy warriors had to work out a fundamental dilemma: to fight a modern war they had to give up their instinctive individualism and tribal ways, which is what they were fighting communism to defend.

Many of the part-time *Mujahedin*, numbering around 150,000 men, regarded military operations as a highly individual ritual performed on a whim or to save face according to their eccentric, if often ferocious, code of honour. The intensity and tide of the war varied immensely. The conflict in the Tajik-inhabited highlands of the north often bore little resemblance to the fighting in the Pushtun desert regions of the south. A heavy Soviet offensive, tribal feud or the death of a popular commander could quickly and dramatically alter local conditions, although the news could take weeks to trickle back to the guerrilla headquarters in Pakistani cities such as Peshawar or Quetta.

The weaknesses of the insurgency were obvious to me on my first trip and initially I thought the Russians would contain the revolt. The same weaknesses must have been more obvious to bin Laden, whose base I passed – but my Afghan companions forced me to make a short detour around it to avoid 'troubles with the Arabs'. As bin Laden pondered on the nature of Jihad, the ideal prerequisites – unity, central direction, clearer ideological messages and, above all, charismatic leadership – would have been obvious.

After the Soviets did finally quit with their tails between their legs in 1989, Afghanistan fell off the map in terms of news coverage. This blindness applied fatally to the Western intelligence agencies. Just a handful of Westerners chronicled the rise of the Taliban and its umbilical links with Pakistan's very powerful Inter-Services Intelligence Agency (ISI). Even fewer tracked the rise of the one-eyed mullah, Muhammed Omar, as the Taliban's presiding genius, 'the saint on the satellite phone', though the title mullah had as much connection with spiritual integrity as the term comrade has with workers' solidarity.

If Omar was to focus on co-ordinating the Taliban in Afghanistan alone, bin Laden worked on re-organising an internationalist solution to the deficiencies in Islamist military responses to Western encroachment on the *Umma*. The Taliban were soon to rise to power in nearly all of Afghanistan, while the Saudi warlord developed al-Qaeda as an organisation to strike at the heart of the infidels in America. But 9/11 and the 'war on terror' did not follow on immediately from the sense of Jihadist triumph – after defeating one superpower, Russia, the next to fall would be what Iran called the 'Great Satan', the USA.

Iran

Professor Edward Said's critique of the Western media's role in the Islamic world was amply vindicated in the case of the 1979 fall of the Shah of Iran, Mohammed Reza Pahlevi.[11] Only one of the 300 journalists who flocked to Iran could speak Persian. Western intelligence agencies were also caught off-guard. The Cold War was still in full swing and the opponents of the shah were dubbed, interestingly, Islamic Marxists. The shah had been considered in the West as a moderniser and was supposed to be popular among his people, except for a handful of fanatics, be-turbaned, black-robed and self-flagellating Shi'ites. Most correspondents, though, neglected to ask why the shah needed a large and vicious secret police if he were really so popular. In Afghanistan the same turbaned extremists were battling in the holy war against communism. Afghan fundamentalists were freedom fighters, Muslim militiamen – at worst, noble savages, and, at best, plucky anti-Soviet heroes. Osama bin Laden, organising those same Afghan fighters, was then a pin-up poster boy for the CIA.

The Islamic leaders who brought down the shah were usually portrayed in the Western media as history's slow learners, anti-modern fanatics, and their militancy as a form of madness without roots. The reportage of Iran was largely related to US interests in the region. In the West, the Iranian revolution was crudely depicted as ultra-religious conservatives' reactions against a shah determined to drag his stubborn backward people into the present century rather than a mass movement, led by clergy, to rectify deep-seated economic and social inequalities. The Western media portrayed the shah's regime as liberalising when it was in fact notorious for stifling criticism, torturing dissenters, censoring the media and outlawing opposition parties.

Sometimes Americans compared the loss of Iran with the loss of China in the 1940s; certainly the US government and CIA had completely misread the situation. When revolutionary students stormed the US embassy in Tehran on 4 November 1979 and held 400 hostages the US military attempted a rescue mission, Operation EAGLE CLAW. It was a disaster, partly caused by a C-130 aircraft colliding with a helicopter in the Iranian desert. The world learned of the fiasco when pictures were sent from Iran of grinning mullahs picking through the wreckage. The TV pictures were a huge blow to US President Jimmy Carter and to the prestige of the American military. So Washington soon recruited proxies to do its work. When secret US ally Saddam Hussein, a thoroughly secular Arab leader, invaded Iran in 1980, Baghdad and Washington expected a quick victory, the rapid seizure of disputed territory and the collapse of the mullahs. Instead it became a long conventional war with more than one million casualties. Unfortunately for Baghdad and Washington the invasion consolidated the Islamic revolution. The Iranian counter-invasion of 1982 had the parallel unintended consequence of strengthening the rival Ba'athist regime in Baghdad. Washington had wanted to weaken both but achieved the opposite. Iran was to become the main Islamist thorn in the side of the American superpower, then bestriding a unipolar world – briefly. Baghdad also recruited support from key Sunni allies such as Saudi Arabia and helped to stoke the Sunni-Shia enmity that later was to tear apart the Middle East. The US concept was called 'dual deterrence'. The Americans armed both sides, but Washington was found out. The Irangate scandal was revealed in 1986: in addition to militarily backing Iraq, the US had been selling arms to Iran, officially branded a terrorist state, ostensibly in exchange for the release of American hostages in Lebanon.

Lebanon was the site of another hammer blow to the American military. On 27 October 1983 Islamic Jihad, acting under orders from Tehran, deployed suicide truck-bombs to hit the US Marine barracks in Beirut as well as a French base at the same time. Within minutes 299 troops, including 241 American military personnel, mainly Marines, were killed. Both forces had been part of a multinational peacekeeping contingent. For the Marines it was the biggest loss of life in a single day since Iwo Jimo during the Pacific War. And it was the largest loss to the French since the Algerian war. The Western multinational force soon left Lebanon. Naturally Iran denied any involvement; in 2004, however, the Iranian government erected a monument in Tehran to the 'martyrs' who had driven the truck bombs.

If Tehran had intended the Beirut bombs to discourage US support for Saddam Hussein, it didn't work. The Iran-Iraq war dragged on for eight years and ended in a military draw. Iran initially concentrated on building its revolution in one country, a replay of the Bolshevik experience of the 1920s. Iraq was militarised even more and was soon to threaten US interests in the region, most notably by invading Kuwait. Iran was to return to an internationalist role by arming Shia regimes or terrorists throughout the Middle East, notably in Syria and Lebanon and later Yemen. Tehran even backed radical Sunni Islamists such as Hamas, when it suited them. Saudi Arabia, not to be outdone, intrigued throughout the region to arm Sunni groups, many of them Islamists. The Saudi-based Wahhabi creed was the backbone of the most radical, especially al-Qaeda. The stage was being set for the massive realignments of borders and allies, most as proxies for the religious and power rivalry between Riyadh and Tehran. This was to become a war between two contending approaches to Islamist extremism.

*Islamist insurgency before 9/11*
Although tensions in the Middle East and West Asia were the most critical in the genesis of the new Jihadism, Europe should not be ignored. Libya, for example, supplied arms to the Provisional Irish Republican Army during Europe's longest insurgency. In 1972 the politics of the Middle East intruded at the Munich Olympics when eleven Israeli athletes were murdered. Criminal gangs also became embroiled in European politics as people and arms smuggling, as well as drugs, financed a large black economy. Afghan heroin, Russian weapons and other illegal goods provided by Albanian smugglers created an underworld in which the embryonic Jihadist movement could operate clandestinely. The Balkan wars and Chechnya were also significant factors.

Bosnia
Although most Yugoslavs were Catholic or Orthodox Christians, the federation also contained Europe's largest concentration of Muslims. It was no accident that the Soviet and Yugoslav federations began to unravel at the same time. First Slovenia broke away and then Croatia. The Serb centralists did not care so much about tiny Slovenia, but Croatia contained many Serbs. Bitter conflict was likely, though not inevitable. Next-door NATO did nothing until tens of thousands were killed. Many of the tensions were

recent, whipped up by local politicians and bigoted domestic media. 'Ancient tribal rivalries', however, became the handy, if incorrect, international media shorthand for the opposing Balkan factions. Great pictures abounded; sound analysis was rare. Journalists could not usually master the complex languages and Tolkienesque names where, as P. J. O'Rourke famously quipped, 'the unpronounceables were killing the unspellables'. There were few white hats in the Balkans. Memories still persisted of the atrocious behaviour of the pro-Nazi Croats in the 1939-45 conflict. Yet the foreign hacks chose – with some justification – to blame largely the Serbs. They did commit the most, and worst, atrocities. Serbia was dubbed the land of Mordor by the more literate journalists, in honour of writer J. R. Tolkien's dark vision of the fallen kingdom.

By the spring of 1992 the civil war had spread to the breakaway state of Bosnia (Bosnia-Herzegovina). The newest state in Europe looked as though it would be the most short-lived. Sarajevo, the Bosnian capital, came within a whisker of falling to the Serbs; its largely Bosnian Muslim inhabitants – and also brave Serb and Croat Sarajevans – fought on for three years however. It was certainly the heaviest fighting in a European capital since 1945. The close urban fighting I witnessed reminded me of what I had read about in the siege of Leningrad. Just outside Sarajevo on Mount Igman, for example, I was in a bus, full of women and children, during a supposed truce, when a Serb anti-aircraft gun with a depressed trajectory, ripped through the bus, and then the Serbs followed up the attack with ground forces with spotlights. With my Australian translator we helped two people escape, and then tried to join a group of Muslim volunteers who were trying to break into the city. I also witnessed concentration camps where Auschwitz-looking locals were held in Serb camps. The ill-equipped and poorly mandated United Nations Protection Force could record, but not protect.

Sarajevo had been an integrated city where Muslims and Christians freely intermarried. The drumbeat of hate-filled media, especially from the Serbs, and the intensity of the siege, made Muslims – largely secular before – identify themselves as distinctly and primarily Muslims; the influx of Islamists from outside intensified this shift. Some of the tensions *did* relate to the distant past when the division of the eastern and western Roman Empire became the fault line between the Christian West and the Ottoman domains. Most Western journalists heard variations of a Bosnian Muslim combatant raving about a Serb crime in the medieval period. In utter exasperation the journalist would say, 'But that happened in the fourteenth century!' 'Yes,' the Muslim soldier would reply, 'but I heard about it only last week.' The three sides in the Bosnian civil war were obsessed with maps – nearly every debate would guarantee literal cartographic versions, often for hours.

Most of the anger was caused by very recent atrocities, however: the mortar and artillery attacks on the civilian markets, the deliberate destruction of ancient buildings and always the constant sniping. Civilians and frequently journalists were chosen Serb targets. The normal way to cross a main intersection was by walking across to one side of an armoured personnel carrier, taking cover from the incoming fire. The inhabitants lived indoors or underground much of the time, though sometimes people met in cafés shielded by tall buildings, to avoid the tireless sniping, and talked late through the night because of the curfews.

Many of the Muslim officers I spoke to were very bitter: 'Do you think NATO would stand by for years and watch if we were a Christian army besieged by Muslims?' Another officer said to me, 'If we had oil, the West would invade to protect us.' Many commented that the aid that trickled in was 'just a means of fattening us up to make it easier for the snipers'. Not many Sarajevans were fat – most lost a great deal of weight because of food shortages. When I asked someone why he was collecting grass, he insisted it was a form of lettuce.

Despite the UN declaring certain towns in Bosnia as safe havens, they were neither safe nor havens. In July 1995 the Bosnian Serb army overran Srebrenica, with tragic and momentous consequences. Scornful of the UN, its 400 inadequate Dutch peacekeepers and the foreign media, the Serbs massacred 8,000 male Muslims – the largest mass murder in Europe since the Second World War. Finally, with Washington's permission, NATO intervened. Western air power rolled up Serb forces and Bosnians and Croats were able to fight back. NATO had fired its first shot in anger, though only after tens of thousands of killings in Croatia and Bosnia.

The British Conservative governments of the period had been reluctant to enter the Balkan wars, despite Mrs Thatcher's military adventure in the Falklands more than a decade before. In 1997 Tony Blair became Labour prime minister and wars of intervention, usually shoulder to shoulder with the US, became fashionable. And the first of the Blair wars was Kosovo.

## Kosovo

The nominally Muslim majority in Kosovo, another region of the former Yugoslavia, often saw the NATO intervention as an atonement for

Srebrenica. Serb atrocities in the Kosovo province – considerable but exaggerated by the Western media and NATO – encouraged the Alliance to bomb Slobodan Milošević, the Serb president, into submission. NATO thought that a short sharp air war, perhaps less than seventy-two hours, would dismantle the Serb strongman's regime. 'Air power,' as Eliot Cohen observed at the time in *Foreign Affairs,* 'is an unusually seductive form of military strength because, like modern courtship, it appears to offer gratification without commitment.' (As late as 2015 the Western allies still overestimated air power, this time against the Islamic State.)

After a lengthy bombing campaign and preparation for a ground offensive, the Serbs capitulated in June 1999, without NATO suffering a single casualty, although stray bombs had killed lots of the Kosovars, the very people whom the West was supposed to protect. The Allies had to pay millions of dollars to repair bomb damage in Serbia. During 40,000 bombing sorties, NATO destroyed, besides civilians and infrastructure, just thirteen elderly Serbian tanks. It would have made economic sense to have offered Milošević $10 million for each one and thus save a lot of lives.

Serb forces began to withdraw from the capital of Kosovo, Pristina. The Russians sent in a flying column and they were treated as heroes by the local Serbs. Advancing British forces were ordered to fly in helicopters to take Pristina airport where the Russians had holed up. The tough British commander, General Mike Jackson, did not play poodle to the American overall commander, Wesley Clark. 'General, I'm not going to start World War Three for you,' the British officer famously declared. Clark was forced by Washington to back down. When British forces arrived at the airport they had to feed the Russians. I spoke with some of them and asked to look inside the armoured personnel carriers; they seemed like relics from the 1960s if not the Second World War. The race to Pristina was seen then as the last 'battle' of the Cold War, or at least Cold War Mark 1.

Unlike Bosnia, Kosovo was a short sharp successful war for NATO that did not significantly radicalise the nominally Muslim majority. Nor did it radicalise opinion in the West. Given the zeitgeist and the acceptance of humanitarianism via casualty-free virtual war throughout Western Europe, NATO governments and their electorates largely backed this war. Nor was there hostility from the Islamic world. The victory was celebrated by a visit to Pristina of pop-singer Yusuf Islam, formerly known as Cat Stevens. The most popular person in immediate post-war Pristina, and perhaps the only place where he is still lionised, was Tony Blair. Many cafés and children were named after him. Still, the region was an odd place: the 1950s slapstick comedian Norman Wisdom was the biggest star in next-door Albania.

Intercession in Kosovo helped the Muslim inhabitants, and did not incite anger or Jihadism in the Islamic world. It was perhaps unique. The rest of Blair's compulsive interventionism caused catastrophes for many Muslims. And Kosovo was deployed by the Kremlin as a template for its own interventionism later in Georgia, for example, and most dangerously in Ukraine.

Chechnya

In 1858, after decades of robust resistance, Chechnya was conquered by Russia. This followed the defeat of Imam Shamil, whose fighters had vowed to establish an Islamic state. During the chaos of the Russian revolution, the Chechens briefly secured independence; then Germany's invasion brought renewed hope of freedom from the Soviet yoke. When the Second World War ended, Josef Stalin exacted vengeance by wholesale deportation of the Chechens, mainly to Siberia. Many were allowed to return after Stalin's death. If any Muslim community in Europe should have been Islamised because of infidel persecution, Chechnya was the prime candidate.

When the USSR collapsed in 1991, the Chechens again declared independence. In 1994, the Russians bungled a poorly planned bid to regain control. They attacked at Christmastime, as they had in Afghanistan fifteen years before, perhaps assuming the West would be distracted by the festivities. About a tenth of the population was killed in the onslaught, especially in the capital, Grozny. David Loyn of the BBC observed, 'For the first time since the Second World War, thousands of shells were fired into a city in a single day. The snipers of Sarajevo seemed almost gentlemanly by comparison.'[12] The main resistance leader, General Aslan Maskhadov, fought well and hard. The founder of Frontline TV News, Vaughan Smith, commented on the widespread support that the Chechens gave Maskhadov: 'If you were a fighter, you didn't get a shag from the missus that night unless you killed a Russian.' Amid growing public concern at heavy losses of their own troops, Moscow withdrew its forces. Chechnya achieved substantial autonomy, though not full independence.

It did not achieve stability either, as warlordism and organised crime proliferated. In August 1999 Chechen fighters crossed into the neighbouring Russian republic of Dagestan, as part of a planned Islamist insurrection in the whole region. The following year the Russians blamed the Chechens for a series of explosions in Moscow apartment blocks. Suspicions abounded that the Russian security services had bombed them to create a pretext for war and the re-election of Vladimir Putin in 2000. The assertive ex-KGB officer turned president then launched a second Chechen war. A few Western journalists had managed to cover the first war; now Putin imposed a total ban on reporting. The Russian army captured and obliterated much of Grozny, with little quarter given. Soon, Putin – after the September 2001 attacks on the Twin Towers – projected his Chechen adventure as part of the wider war on global Jihadist terror, not least to mute criticism from Washington and Europe. At the height of the Cold War, the West would probably have armed the Chechens as they had the Afghans. Instead, Putin's response to George W. Bush's call for solidarity ('You are either for us or against us') worked. Now the West and Russia – and later China suffering from its own Islamist protests among the Uyghur people – were lining up against al-Qaeda. Putin's strategy worked, the West gave Putin almost *carte blanche* in Chechnya and his crackdowns throughout the Caucasus.

Chechen rebels seized a Moscow theatre in October 2002 and held 800 people hostage; 120 of the hostages were killed when Russian special forces stormed the building. Then Moscow blamed the Chechens for organising the siege at North Ossetia's Beslan school, which ended in a bloodbath. In 2007 Putin declared the war to be over, yet the fighting by dissident Islamist fighters continued against the pro-Moscow Chechen leader, Ramzan Kadyrov. The pro-Russian forces condemned the malevolent influence of foreign Jihadists. They were relatively few in number partly because of the inaccessibility of Chechnya – unlike Turkey in 2015, an almost open door for wannabe Jihadists flooding into Syria and Iraq.

Jerusalem – the eternal city of discord
Jerusalem has been at the centre of East-West conflicts for centuries. American writer P. J. O'Rourke once quipped, 'The press stands accused of holding the Israelis to higher moral standards than it holds the other peoples of the Middle East. That's not our fault. Moses started that.' Muslims consistently accuse Western media of bias. This charge is analysed in Palestinian-American literary theorist Edward Said's influential work, *Covering Islam*, which was published in 1981. In this work Said argued that Western reporting of Islam has been superficial and cliché-ridden, tainted by cultural bias and at times dangerously xenophobic. Said also said that the Western media were conditioned by strategic and economic interests, namely the threats to the production, distribution and pricing of oil. Obviously, Western interests are more complex than oil, or the protection

of Israel, or even the current obsession with defeating the Islamic State. It is also simplistic to argue for a fundamental clash of civilisations, as Professor Samuel Huntington had done.

Yet there is undoubtedly a problem with media coverage of the Islamic world, not least the inescapable event-based stories rather than the far more complex issue-based context. As in Africa, the news in the Middle East has generally been negative. Al-Jazeera changed this somewhat; this was the first time that real news was broadcast from East to West instead of vice-versa. Nevertheless, wars, coups, terrorism and underdevelopment have tended to dominate Western coverage. While Israel was not the cause of Arab underdevelopment, it became a symbol of the Arab world's failures to address its many deficiencies.

After the Holocaust, Israel's underdog status guaranteed it sympathetic media coverage in the West. Many Western correspondents believed that Israel deserved to succeed, though why the Muslim (and Christian) Palestinians should pay for the Christian West's guilt about Jews' treatment during the Second World War was never fully explained. The Palestinian-Israeli dispute has been a head-on collision between Western and Middle Eastern values, a dispute over borders and historical rights compounded by highly distorted images of the adversary, sophisticated propaganda and a chronic regional arms race initially tied to superpower intrigue. It may have been a sociologist's paradise, but it has been a diplomat's hell.

The surprising victories of 1948-49, 1956 and 1967 against combined Arab armies began to undermine Israel's underdog image, especially as major foreign powers, notably France and later the USA, nurtured the infant state. Military success led to conquest of territory and a hubris, which led in turn to a reluctance to trade land for peace. And then came permanent occupation of most of the West bank. Israel's occupation was often harsh, though it has to be said that if one has to suffer occupation by a foreign army, I personally would prefer the Israeli forces, especially compared with the Germans, for example – and Israelis are often compared with Nazis by Islamists. I was arrested regularly, shot at and often treated arrogantly by Israelis in the West Bank, so I hold no particular affection for the occupation.

One of Israel's most distinguished political scientists, Yehoshafat Harkabi, said: 'Israel's problem is that with the best will in the world it cannot meet the Arabs' demand, because it is unlimited and cannot be satisfied as long as Israel exists.' At least organisations such as Hamas agree on this. Ceasefire not agreement is the best on offer. Nevertheless, statesmen have spent forty years trying to establish a two-state solution, perhaps possible once, but highly unlikely now that the whole region is in ferment.

In 2015 the Islamic State adheres to an end-times philosophy. This apocalyptic idea is reflected in the West too. The Jewish lobby's influence in the US to protect the region's sole democracy is often noted; less so is American evangelicals' fascination with the Holy Land now united under Israeli rule (apparently prophesied in the Bible and, who knows, Nostradamus and his ilk as well). Such fortune-telling has played into a powerful Armageddon complex among the American Christian right. This 'doomsday chic' ascribes Israeli victories to the timing of Christ's return.

The biblical interpretation of military success suffered some bruising when Israel almost lost the 1973 war, when Egypt and Syria caught the Jewish state off guard on its holiest day. Prime Minister Golda Meir gave the order to assemble Israel's nuclear weapons at Dimona in the Negev desert. This order soon leaked to Washington, probably intentionally, and the USA provided the biggest airlift of weapons the world had yet seen. Israel counter-attacked effectively and the USSR had to intervene to prevent another total Arab defeat. Yet again, to Islamists, the secularists in power in Cairo and Damascus might not have needed Russian help if the Arab leaders had followed the true path and thus secured Allah's blessing.

Israel, too, was divided by its own version of secularists versus religious fundamentalists, especially the large number of ultra-Orthodox Jews, who were not obliged to do active military service – although the Orthodox settlers in the West Bank are well armed. Nevertheless, Israel buttressed its military image in the West, after the shocks of the 1973 war, by its daring and successful rescue mission of the hostages held at Entebbe, Uganda, in July 1976. Books and movies ensued. For an American military traumatised by the recent Vietnam disaster, and haunted by the searing pictures of Americans escaping in helicopters from the US embassy in Saigon, the Israeli Defence Force raid on Entebbe exemplified the successful use of force. According to an American cultural historian, 'After Entebbe and after Saigon, Israel became a prosthetic for Americans. The "long arm" of Israeli vengeance extended the body of an American nation no longer sure of its own reach.'

## Gulf War 1
Technically the first Gulf War was the Iran versus Iraq conflict, but popular usage describes the First Gulf War as the Arab-Western liberation of Kuwait

after Saddam Hussein's invasion in 1990. This conflict brought Western infidel troops, including female soldiers, to the holy land of Mecca and Medina and prompted fears of a new era of crusades in the minds of some devoted Muslims who were prepared to turn to extremism. On the other hand, many Arab states joined the remarkable thirty-five-nation coalition to take on the Iraqi army, mandated by UN resolutions and under US command. This was Operation DESERT STORM, or GRANBY to the British. Crucially, Israel was persuaded to stay out of the fight, despite the provocations of Iraqi Scuds landing on the Jewish state (though causing relatively little damage).

The media coverage was alike in form and content despite the new age of real-time reporting pioneered by CNN. As one commentator quipped, 'Never in the field of recent conflict has so little been disclosed to so many by so few.' It emerged after the war that only 8 per cent of the ordnance used to bomb Iraq was electronically guided – or 'smart'; this meant that 92 per cent was indiscriminate or 'dumb'. From the onset, the real war was largely absent from the media war. Iraqis, however, were killed in their thousands by the dumb bombs, although many were also terminated by laser-guided weapons. For example, over 400 people, mainly women, children and elderly, were incinerated when two smart bombs smashed through the roof of the Al Firdos installation in Baghdad's Amiriyah suburb. As a result of outdated intelligence this air raid shelter was targeted as a command and control centre.

The war consisted of a five-week aerial bombing campaign followed by a rapid ground assault into Kuwait and southern Iraq that was over in a hundred hours. Journalists were allowed to see little of the carnage and often copied the military's disingenuous phrase 'collateral damage' using it to draw a veil over the death and injury to civilians. Media analyst Norman Soloman described it as 'linguicide'. Live reporting of the rocket attacks on Israel and Saudi Arabia were dubbed 'Scudavision'. This was allied to the publicising of cameras in smart weapons hitting their targets (though never missing them). A collective fantasy developed in which conflict had become entertainment, a video game in which the horrors of real war – the death and brutality – were absent.

Regime change then was not official policy, despite the constant questioning as to why the Allies did not push on to Baghdad and dethrone Saddam. Had the coalition pursued the defeated Iraqi army farther into Iraq the Arab members undoubtedly would have split away causing more diplomatic problems than the war had allegedly solved militarily.

Nevertheless, the CIA organised a series of black ops to ignite the Kurdish rising in the north and Shia rebellion in the south. When they did rise up, the Americans failed to support them and they were crushed by a vengeful Saddam. When the Americans did finally return over a decade later, many sceptical Shi'ites remembered the 1991 'betrayal' and reached for guns not rose petals to greet their supposed liberators.

If many Iraqis felt betrayed in 1991, many other Arabs (except the Kuwaitis) were aghast at the ease with which the mainly Western forces cut through even the supposedly elite Republican Guards of supposed strongman Saddam. The Iraqi forces had developed a reputation, even among the Israelis, for being the toughest of Arab troops. Once more the Arabs were humiliated; once more the West had come in to sort out Arab quarrels.

Intifadas

The Gulf War resonated throughout the myriad conflicts in the region, not least in Lebanon. In June 1982 Israeli armour had reached Beirut in a mere six days, though a prolonged siege ensued. Constant pictures of Israeli artillery pounding Palestinian camps aroused world-wide opprobrium, especially on the Arab street. Here was yet another humiliation and destruction of (mainly) Muslim communities. The Israelis gave the Lebanese Christian militias control over the Palestinian camps, which resulted in mass murder at Sabra and Shatila. The Israelis withdrew, though they maintained a security belt in the south, and an international peacekeeping force drawn from the USA, Italy, France and Britain entered Beirut. They did not stay long. Hezbollah, a radical Shi'ite group, suicide-bombed the US embassy killing sixty-three people in April 1983. It was the worst ever attack on a US diplomatic mission. Then in October came the major assault on the American and French bases murdering 299 people. Although the French were attacked at the same time, it was photographs of the American disaster that seized international attention, and excited Islamic extremists' desire to emulate the mass-casualty tactic.

Lebanon's multiple conflicts almost defied classification, and still do. Internal religious rivalries, such as Muslim versus Christian and Shia versus Sunni, allied with ideological and class hostilities interlaced with tribal feuds have been constantly manipulated by outside powers. For years a sign hung in the office of Timur Göksel, the official who dealt with the press in the UN-controlled southern zone. It read: 'If you think you understand Lebanon, you've not been properly briefed.'

The Israeli invasion displaced from the country the Palestine Liberation Organisation (PLO) leaders, notably Yasser Arafat; and in 1991 the Palestinian cause was further damaged in the West by the PLO's support for Saddam. This was a poor PR move by Arafat who – as the Israelis loved to repeat – 'never missed an opportunity to miss an opportunity'. As radical Islamist groups began to win over more and more adherents, the relationship between the Palestinian people and the PLO began to sour.

A series of uprisings collectively known as the intifada, which means literally 'a shaking off', accelerated the discord between the PLO and the Palestinian people it was supposed to represent. The first Palestinian uprising began in 1987 and lasted six years. Both the first and the more aggressive second intifada, which began in 2000, were born out of deep-seated and bitter frustration with both the Israeli occupation and ineffectual Arab leadership.

The Gulf War had improved Israel's conventional military position. Its enemy Syria had lost its Russian patron (for a while) and Iraq had been humbled. The Arabs, cowed by American weapon wizardry in the Gulf, had lost interest in fighting Israel. In one sense, though, Saddam had won an accidental victory: he had placed the Palestinian uprising back at the centre of the world stage. The defence of the Palestinians had been a major plank of his propaganda campaign in the lead-up to the 1991 war in order to win over Arab opinion. By 1993, after a series of peace deals, the Palestinian Authority was established in jigsaw parts of the occupied territories. Arafat seemed unable or unwilling to control the endemic corruption or the rise of Islamic fundamentalist groups such as Hamas. The Israelis withdrew from southern Lebanon, but found no peace. The Israeli Defence Forces (IDF) reacted with reprisal raids as the Islamic zealots sent suicide bombers into the Jewish state, mainly from the West Bank.

Hamas was allegedly assisted in its early days by Israeli intelligence as a counterbalance to the Al-Fatah domination of the PLO. Funded in part later by Saudi Arabia and Kuwait, Hamas garnered enough money to provide a basic welfare system for the Palestinian poor. Hamas leaders enjoyed a reputation for austere lifestyles, while Arafat's Palestinian Authority, awash with EU funds, wallowed in corruption and nepotism. Contrary to most Western opinion, the Palestinians, especially in Gaza, came to support Hamas not because of its violence or Islamism, but because of its provision of schools and clinics.

The dramatic pictures of the rebellion in the West Bank created a sense of immediacy in the Arab world. Israel could no longer claim to be using reasonable force to contain the Palestinians when Al-Jazeera showed otherwise, daily and hourly. The propaganda war over the intifadas became a real TV war in a way that the Gulf War was not. Media-savvy Palestinians and Al-Jazeera had outflanked the Israelis who had previously won the media battles hands-down. This Arab success was a foretaste of the clever propaganda campaigns later waged by al-Qaeda and the Islamic State with its command of social media.

The advantage lay with the Palestinians only briefly because almost inevitably they fought among themselves. Hamas conquered Gaza, while Fatah, a main component of the PLO, held on to the battered Palestinian Authority in the West Bank. Israel stood back as its enemy collapsed in on itself. The media now proclaimed a 'two-state solution': Gaza ruled by Islamists who refused to recognise Israel, and in the West Bank the more secular Fatah was prepared to talk to the Jewish state.

Hundreds of news bureaux staff members and also freelance journalists were based in Jerusalem and continued to sift the ancient, overworked soil for new scoops. About 900 articles on events in Israel, the West Bank and Gaza are published each day in the English language alone, seventy-five times more than any other area of comparable population. Israelis bemoan this constant attention, but the Old City is the home of three great world religions. It is also a fulcrum of the long-running Middle East crisis and perhaps even the edge of a tectonic plate if Huntington's thesis of a clash of civilisations is correct. Compared with the vast desert terrain of the Gulf War, Israel's small area was conducive to rapid and comprehensive reporting. And most Israeli leaders spoke excellent English. Like Saigon, Jerusalem boasted comfortable hotels with well-stocked bars. Nor was any understanding of military technology required as in the Gulf War. US military briefers used to joke that most journalists couldn't 'tell a tank from a turd'. Correspondents could cover the intifadas, however, without ever having attended a single class in 'Army 101'.

Travel anywhere in the Middle East and a TV or two will be blaring in every café. During crises the twenty-four-hour Arabic language channel of Al-Jazeera was a crucial ingredient in shifting the political balance of power in favour of the Palestinians. The Qatar-based TV station's English-language channel was also influential, though to a far lesser degree in the West. AJ – as it was called – spawned numerous international copycats, including in Arabic and Persian, and forced the dreary national Arab stations to up their game. Better TV coverage heightened the already simmering sense of Arab grievance at the perceived injustices – imposed by Zionists or Americans and their own governments. Yes, there were increasing numbers of Islamic channels, but Al-Jazeera was a crucial ingredient in churning up Arab anger. Pictures of the fighters in Afghanistan, Bosnia, Chechnya and the West Bank had stirred the hearts of many young Sunnis, just as Hezbollah appealed to would-be Shia warriors in the war to punish and exterminate Israel and its ally, the Great Satan. One of the main effects of this televised rebellion and resistance was the rise of Jihad as a solution to these many perceived wrongs. Al-Qaeda became the symbol if not always the driving force of this Islamist ferment. And it was planning something for the cameras that would shake the pillars of the earth.

*Chapter 3*

# The War on Terror

'Buildings collapsed. Democracy stands' ran the leader of the *Los Angeles Times* a few hours after the 9/11 attack. Despite this bravado, al-Qaeda's onslaught was a brilliant masterstroke in asymmetric warfare. With the exception of Pearl Harbor, the War of Independence and the self-inflicted wounds of the Civil War, 9/11 was the first time Americans had suffered major military harm on their own soil.

The 9/11 abominations changed the world dramatically, as did the events which flowed from them – the war on terror, the invasions of Afghanistan and Iraq, the Bush doctrine of pre-emptive war and new legislation in Western democracies that threatened traditional civil liberties, all in the name of security. Some analysts claimed that 9/11 had radically changed the DNA of Western democracy. In fact, 9/11 crystallised long-existing trends in world politics. The optimism of the post-Cold War order had already faded as had the supposed peace dividends. Jihadism had long been a real threat as evidenced, for example, by a previous attack on the World Trade Center in 1993.

The 2001 onslaughts were a serious intelligence failure in the same way that Pearl Harbor was. In both cases the writing was already on the wall. The attacks provided an opportunity for the George W. Bush administration to implement pre-existing plans, such as the removal of Saddam Hussein, to transform the regimes of the oil-rich Middle East into a system – in theory a democratic one – favourable to Western interests. Instead, the use of military might, especially in Iraq, alienated even some Western allies and certainly potential ones in the Muslim world. In the Cold War, the West eventually won the battles of ideas and ideologies. In the long war that followed 9/11, the West increasingly lost not only the media war, but also the struggle to claim the moral high ground, at home, in the developing world and more crucially in the Middle East. Washington declared war on al-Qaeda (just as al-Qaeda promoted war against America and the Jews). Yet on the battlefields of Afghanistan and Iraq the West's military superiority was often outflanked by the insurgents' propaganda. It was by no means clear who was going to triumph in the self-fulfilling clash of civilisations.

## Al-Qaeda

Osama bin Laden was born of Yemeni stock in Riyadh, Saudi Arabia, in 1957. He was the seventeenth of fifty-two children of a Yemeni immigrant contractor, Muhammad. The father subsequently divorced Osama's mother, a Syrian who was a follower of the Alawite sect, considered heretical by the pervasive Wahhabi culture in Saudi Arabia. The lanky youth grew up as a devout Muslim in a very wealthy family in a large family mansion in Jedda. He scorned music on religious grounds, though he was said to be keen on football. After university in Saudi Arabia he was attracted to the struggle in Afghanistan against the Russians. Although he had an interest in engineering and construction – on which the family fortune had been built – he became fascinated by Jihad, especially after studying the writings of Sayyid Qutb, the Egyptian scholar, who is generally regarded as the Lenin of the Islamist movement. Although a somewhat shy and reserved young man, Osama took as his inspiration the declaration of the Prophet that 'a few moments spent in Jihad in the path of Allah is worth more  than seventy years spent praying at home.'

Bin Laden used his personal fortune to fund an Arab legion in the war on the Soviets. He also took part in a small number of battles and skirmishes himself. In 1984 he helped to form the *Maktab al-Khidamat* to channel foreign fighters, mainly Arabs, into the Afghan war. The offices of the organisation were set in a leafy middle-class suburb of Peshawar to the north-west of the bustling, almost medieval, old town. Perhaps as many as 25,000 young Jihadists passed through these offices, from the most militant groups in the Middle East. The locals tended to keep their distance from the 'Arabs', as they were called, though many honoured their courage and sacrifice. Pakistan's all-powerful intelligence organisation, the Inter-Services Intelligence organisation (ISI), kept a close eye on the comings and goings through bin Laden's office and also set up a parallel bureau to funnel young Mujahedin into the Afghan battles.

The Americans helped to fund the war, though much of the money came from Saudi Arabia, and the arms and training were strictly controlled by the ISI. The CIA and bin Laden had connections, but relations were very limited by Pakistani generals, eager to pull the strings themselves, and to cream off some of the funding. The training camps for the foreign Islamists were often in the 'tribal' border areas of Pakistan, a region only loosely controlled by the central government. The camps for mainly Afghans I visited in 1984 had basic facilities and the main instructors were Afghan army officers who had defected to the insurgents, as well as Pakistani officers. In 1988 bin Laden split from the *Maktab* to concentrate on leading his own organisation for Arab fighters, as he had grown disillusioned with the ever-fractious Afghan *Mujahedin*. It was around this time that he established what later became known as al-Qaeda, meaning the 'base' or 'foundation'.

After the withdrawal of the Soviets, bin Laden returned to Saudi Arabia as something of a hero. Although the lionised warlord practised the same austere Wahhabi creed as the ruling royal family, bin Laden did not share his government's enthusiasm for their dalliance with the United States. When Iraq's invasion of Kuwait endangered his homeland, bin Laden offered his loyal Arab legion to defend Saudi Arabia, rather than allow US soldiers in the land of the holy cities of Mecca and Medina. The Saudi government took the superpower option. That caused a serious rift with the messianic bin Laden who eventually took refuge in Sudan in 1991. From Khartoum, he lambasted his own government for the conduct of the war against Iraq in alliance with Washington. Unsurprisingly, the Saudis retaliated by withdrawing his citizenship, cut off his family funding and discussed his assassination.

Sudan had launched the first successful Sunni Islamist revolution in 1989; the spiritual mentor was Dr Hassan al-Turabi. A man equally at ease in turban or tie, and in Arabic, French or English, the madcap imam later was dubbed the 'Islamic pope'. Bin Laden moved in close to al-Turabi in a plush suburb of Khartoum; he was a frequent house guest and took al-Turabi's niece as his fourth wife. (I was al-Turabi's house guest as well, but unfortunately I failed to share the same dinner table as bin Laden.) Despite his private jet and other symbols of wealth, bin Laden enforced a strict survivalist code on his family: although living in a mansion, he would not allow the use of refrigerators or air-conditioning to temper the scorching heat in Khartoum. And he took his sons out for desert trips to toughen them up. I have written extensively elsewhere on his five-year stay in Sudan and explained how bin Laden was treated as a VIP because of his Afghan exploits.[13] Khartoum's official line was that he was not engaged in training Jihadists. Rather, he was busy once more in construction work, especially much-needed road building. He bought vast tracts of land especially in the east of the country, primarily to employ some of his Jihadist followers.

The Americans and Saudis exerted great pressure on Khartoum to kick him out. A very angry bin Laden told a senior Khartoum government minister: 'The Saudis and the US didn't even pay you – you are throwing me out for nothing.' The warlord's parting shot was to call the Sudanese administration 'a mix of religion and organised crime'. Khartoum never refunded the $50 million bin Laden left behind him in Sudan.

On 18 May 1996 a chartered plane took the Saudi chieftain, his wives, children and over 100 of his followers to Jalalabad in eastern Afghanistan. En route the plane refuelled at the Gulf state of Qatar – which had close ties with Washington – but was allowed to proceed unhindered.

The Sudanese *Mukhabarat* (intelligence service) claimed that it had tipped off the CIA about the flight. Later, as Sudan came under more economic sanctions and US military pressure, the Khartoum line was that they had even offered to hand over their guest to the Americans in exchange for the removal of sanctions and the deletion of Sudan's name on the list of states supporting terrorism. Sudanese officials cited the recent example of their donation to the French of Carlos the Jackal, who had taken refuge in Khartoum. The offer to hand over bin Laden on a platter, once he had left, was almost certainly a PR gimmick. It would have been unIslamic, *haram*, to hand over a Muslim guest to *kuffars* (unbelievers), it was later admitted, albeit in more diplomatic prose. Washington regarded the ejection of the 'Emir', as his followers called him, as a victory. The Americans just wanted him out and said he could go anywhere – except Somalia, where they had recently suffered a political and military embarrassment during the US military intervention alongside UN forces in 1993, graphically depicted in the Hollywood version, *Black Hawk Down*.

The expulsion of bin Laden to Afghanistan changed world history. Not long after the Emir left, I interviewed General Gutbi al-Mahdi, who had just retired as head of the Sudanese *Mukhabarat*, one of the most effective intelligence agencies in Africa. He denied that the Saudi had been busily developing al-Qaeda while he was in Sudan. The spymaster told me:

> When he was here, he was under close surveillance. We were watching him. He was busy. He was preoccupied by his business … . Kicking him out was a big mistake … . In Afghanistan no one could watch him, not even the Americans.

The Sudanese version was that bin Laden would have concentrated on engineering and not gone back into the Jihad business, and thus saved the planet a lot of angst. That argument is not entirely convincing as bin Laden had already trod the Jihadist path in the previous decade. Moreover, the spiritual leader of the Sudanese revolution, al-Turabi, was obsessed with international Jihad, even though the president of Sudan, Field Marshal Omar al-Bashir, was focused on the *national* Jihad, the conflict in the south against the animist and Christian majority. This was the longest war in Africa; it ran on and off from 1955 until al-Bashir signed a peace deal in 2005.

Over the years I spoke to many people in Sudan who knew bin Laden well. In elite government and business circles they all described him as gentle, intense and courteous. He always asked people about their children and enjoyed talking in fine detail about construction equipment. Apparently he was happiest talking about JCBs, not Jihad. His Khartoum travel agent fondly reminisced about the warlord giving him lots of business and paying with his American Express gold card. I asked a senior local journalist in Khartoum if keeping bin Laden would have made a real difference.

'At least the road to Port Sudan would be in better shape,' I ventured. 'The roads bin Laden built soon fell apart,' was the curt reply.

That was not entirely accurate as recently I journeyed on these roads, for example to reach the marvellously unvisited pyramids three hours' drive north from Khartoum.

In 2014 I interviewed the powerful Sudanese vice president who had just retired. Ali Othman Taha said:

> I tried to persuade the Americans to talk to him, not to kick him out. He hadn't dropped the Jihadist issues, but his main concentration was on engineering …. I told visiting US diplomats to engage him. [As they had done when they were effective allies over the Russian occupation of Afghanistan.] But they always fobbed me off with an excuse about it not being part of their mission in Sudan. Then Osama bin Laden's concentration was genuinely with commerce. Those Americans made the mistake of their lives.

Whether bin Laden would have stayed as a one-man NGO in Sudan is one of history's imponderables. He arrived back in Afghanistan determined to cultivate the international Jihad. Certain that the Taliban-ruled state was the only pure Islamic country in the world, he started working out how to remedy the mistakes of the anti-Russian struggle and thus expand the Taliban emirate into a universal caliphate. He wanted first to impose full-scale *Sharia* law in the Maghreb and the Arabian peninsula. The states would be radicalised by Jihadist insurgency. At the same time, just as the Russians had been ground down by the Cold War and then the Jihad in

Afghanistan, so too constant onslaughts on Western interests would bleed
the USA dry, especially if it could be provoked into attacking Islamic
countries. This would overstretch the US military and economy, as well as
radicalising the *Umma*. The strategic plan included an Islamic 'awakening'
and 'opening their eyes' and then a 'standing up' – to translate loosely from
the Arabic. He prophesied that a core caliphate would be established by 2016
and perhaps a definitive victory over the US-led unbelievers by 2020. His
main enemies were what he called 'apostate' Muslims – particularly in the
secular Arab states (the 'near enemy'). Describing them as 'apostates' thus
allowed al-Qaeda to circumvent the Koranic edict about not killing fellow
Muslims. To a Sunni absolutist such as bin Laden, the Shia were not
considered even Muslims. In his various later manifestoes and *fatwas*,
increasingly broadcast on channels such as al-Jazeera, he proclaimed how
he would destroy his enemies, especially the Americans (the 'far enemy')
and Jews. If he had actually been Mr Nice Guy in Sudan, he had now
completely changed his tune.

Mullah Mohammed Omar was a close ally and hospitable host in the
Afghan emirate. Bin Laden ruled his growing mini-empire with a *Shura* or
council of between twenty to thirty loyal commanders. Other allies – for
example from the Egyptian Islamic Jihad – would soon swell his numbers.
The running costs were about $30 million a year, though soon his many
individual admirers in the Gulf and Saudi Arabia would boost his funds.
Here bin Laden would help train the Jihadists for the worldwide mission.
The first major al-Qaeda attack was the World Trade Center bombing in
1993: a truck bomb that killed six and injured hundreds. Once bin Laden
was free of the scrutiny of the Sudanese *Mukhabarat* (and a special CIA unit
in Khartoum), the stakes grew much bigger. The main precursor to 9/11 was
the mass-casualty 1998 bombings of the US embassies in Kenya and
Tanzania. Then came the four planes hijacked and flown into the Twin
Towers and the Pentagon while the fourth, out of control, crash-landed in
open terrain; the last plane was probably supposed to hit the White House.
Sixteen of the suicide hijackers were Saudi nationals, from supposedly
Washington's closest Muslim ally. The murder of nearly 3,000 innocent
people was a dagger thrust at the heart of America and precisely designed
both to weaken US resolve and reputation in the Muslim world. It was also
intended to provoke a military intervention and thus crank up the action-
reaction cycle that would result in the establishment of the new caliphate.
Initially, bin Laden chose to deny involvement in the attack, though he later
publicly and proudly accepted responsibility. Nevertheless, walk around any

bazaar in the Middle East and ask who was responsible for 9/11 and a large majority will tell you immediately it was the work of the CIA and/or Mossad. It was a Western conspiracy, most Arabs still believe.

*The Empire strikes back*
The president of the US, George W. Bush, declared 'a war on terror', although he also initially and thoughtlessly used the word 'crusade'. At the time I co-wrote a book on what the so-called war on terror was supposed to mean.[14] What was the Clausewitzian end state – to use the military jargon – of such a campaign? What was the precise purpose in attacking Afghanistan and especially Iraq? Regime change alone could not justify a long war against al-Qaeda, a stateless enemy fighting an asymmetric war. What was the definition of victory before Western troops could be withdrawn? Unless that was clear they may soon have to return empty-handed, I wrote at the time. Terrorism was a means, a method, not an ideology as in the Cold War. Terrorism, like Islam, goes back many centuries. Was this to be a cultural or religious war, as some Islamists predicted? How could a struggle be won via hearts and minds as well as military power, if the counter-terrorism was seen as a form of xenophobia or, worse, Islamophobia? All successful counter-terrorism and counter-insurgency have usually been based upon long-term social engineering – political, economic and social change. (There have been a few exceptions, for example the military defeat of the highly effective Tamil Tigers in Sri Lanka.)[15] In this context should Islamic hostility to the West be seen as crisis of modernisation, not faith? Fourteen years on, and many wars and lives lost, the same basic questions are still pertinent.

Initially the answer seemed plain – to destroy al-Qaeda bases in Afghanistan. The short war was waged successfully by US air power and special forces allied with the Northern Alliance, hostile to the Taliban, who held over 10 per cent of Afghanistan's rugged territory. Many in the ruling elites in the Arab world displayed some sympathy or at least tolerance for American action, though in retrospect many Muslims thought perhaps the sincerity of the Taliban's offer to try Osama bin Laden under *Sharia* law should have been tested. With what the military call 'economy of effort', with heavy airpower support – that old warhorse, the B-52, as well as the American navy's Tomahawk cruise missiles – the Northern Alliance rolled into Kabul. Despite pockets of tough resistance the Taliban sought refuge in their villages in the south or once again over the border in Pakistan. It looked as though the war had ended.

Although President Bush had vowed to kill or capture bin Laden, ultimately he failed. The Saudi commander escaped from Afghanistan into Pakistan, despite major US and SAS engagements at Tora Bora in December 2001 and in Operation ANACONDA in March 2002. Both engagements were staged in the forbidding Afghan highlands, where guerrillas had traditionally fared better than conventional armies. The explanation offered at the time by the Americans was that bin Laden had bribed key local warlords to help him escape. Yet with a $25 million bounty on his head, later doubled, a more plausible explanation – besides US military and intelligence failures – was the shared affinity of religious and political sympathies, allied to a visceral hatred of the infidel Americans. Apart from the significant failure to grab bin Laden, the initial war in Afghanistan was an outright American victory, especially over the media. The coalition relied on air power, which is almost impossible for the media to cover, and special forces' operations, which are always off-limits to journalists.

Both the Taliban and their allies in al-Qaeda regrouped in Pakistan. Quetta replaced Kabul as the Taliban capital. Pakistan's president, General Pervez Musharraf, responded to George W. Bush's challenge – you are with us or against us – by accepting military and economic inducements to side publicly with Washington. Secretly America threatened to bomb Pakistan 'into the Stone Age' if they didn't play ball. The Muslim president, secular at least in his taste for good whiskey, could not alienate his own Islamic parties and the hard-line Islamists in his intelligence services by abandoning the Taliban completely, particularly since Pakistan's great rival India had supported the Northern Alliance. Moreover, fiercely independent tribal areas – a long strip along the eastern Afghan border – had always ignored Islamabad's writ.[16] Thus Bush's Manichean imperative was never going to be followed in full in the Islamic world, even by moderate apparently pro-Western governments.

*The invasion of Iraq*
Many Islamic rulers viewed the American build-up to war with grave suspicion, despite the personal dislike most felt for Saddam Hussein. Nearly all regarded the Anglo-American policy with even more suspicion: they felt that its pre-emptive strategies based on dubious dossiers and poor intelligence about alleged weapons of mass destruction (WMD) were part of a crusade against Islam in general, not alleged Jihadist terrorists in particular. Many sensed that the American administration agreed with the old Washington jest: 'What is all *our* oil doing under *their* sand?' US officials deliberately duped public opinion into war by manipulating the UN

weapons inspections process as well as strong-arming Saddam into war by launching an escalation of operations over the southern no-fly zone, which was effectively the beginning of the war in May 2002. Tony Blair was also secretly committed to war as early as April 2002, a war his government sought to justify with the notorious 'dodgy dossier' claiming intelligence backing for allegations of Iraqi WMD.

In addition, it was the one-sided backing of Israel, with Washington's blind eye to UN resolutions critical of the Jewish state, that continued to rankle in the Arab world. The security barrier – a great big Berlin-style wall – that Israel was building to keep out suicide bombers appeared as de facto borders in the West Bank. The Israeli Defence Force occupied several towns in the occupied territories in April-May 2002, most notoriously Jenin. For eight days Israeli troops, deploying Merkava tanks, armoured personnel carriers and Cobra helicopters, waged war on Hamas and Islamic Jihad insurgents in the town. Giant armoured bulldozers the size of double-decker buses were brought in to flatten the centres of resistance. About 25 per cent of the cinder-block houses were destroyed. I witnessed Palestinians tearing at lumps of rubble with their bare hands to reach the bodies of the dead and perhaps the living, while an old man rescued a TV from the wreckage. I saw insurgents running from house to house with light machine guns, as I weaved my way carefully around the numerous booby traps which claimed the lives of many Israeli troops. A few residents, on realising that I was British, harangued me, blaming Foreign Secretary Arthur Balfour for his pro-Zionist declaration in 1917. Like the Irish, the Palestinians have long memories. One young boy, aged about eleven, told me his mother and brother had been killed by Israeli soldiers. 'When I grow up I want to be a suicide bomber too,' he said firmly.

Over fifty-two Palestinians were killed. Al-Jazeera's reporting of the siege of Jenin galvanised Arab opinion throughout the Middle East, though its coverage of the casualties was fair (I counted the bodies and visited the hospitals) and contradicted the Palestinians' exaggerated claims of deliberate whole-scale massacres. I was arrested twice by the Israelis and narrowly avoided deportation for illegally sneaking into Jenin with three other journalists, after being guided in by the PLO. Despite the media flak over the Israeli actions in the West Bank, Britain's Tony Blair continued to side with George Bush's stance on the Arab-Israeli conflict, though in private the British prime minister urged his American counterpart to accelerate a two-state settlement.

Though the neo-conservatives in the US Congress needed little persuasion to go to war against Iraq, the House of Commons did. The case depended on a series of propositions regarding the nature of the Saddam regime: its secret obsession with weapons of mass destruction; its co-operation with Jihadists and other terrorists and its willingness to hand over WMD to them; its ability to deceive UN weapons inspectors; the fragility of Saddam's domestic popularity; and the possible consequences of his removal for the whole region. The propositions drew on intelligence information that would not be refuted until it faced the audit of war and the invasion of Iraq was over. Although pre-emptive war strategies have to be founded on good intelligence, the British and American intelligence services were largely misled or misguided on the above propositions. Intelligence agencies corrupt their purpose if they fall into line with political demands and fail to voice doubts about their evidence, especially if used publicly as a *casus belli*. Bush and Blair stand accused of hoodwinking both national and international opinion, unwittingly or otherwise. Senior generals in the US and the UK advocated extreme caution about invading Iraq, but they were ignored in the drumbeat of war. In a chain of Chinese whispers the Anglo-American media regurgitated much of the bogus intelligence and political hype. Constant repetition and embellishment acquired its own sense of truth and reality.

The truth was the decidedly secular and relatively religiously tolerant regime of Saddam had no connection at all with al-Qaeda or any Jihadists. He had no weapons of mass destruction, though he had used chemical weapons against the Kurds, most notoriously at Halabja in March 1988. The Western intelligence agencies got nearly everything wrong (and those who called it right within the services were silenced, especially in Britain). Soon Washington and London were about to face the reality in what Winston Churchill once called 'the thankless deserts of Mesopotamia'. Or as Jon Stewart of America's tongue-in-cheek programme the *Daily Show* would dub it, 'Mess-o-potamia'.

Saddam was tolerant of other religions. His No. 2 in the regime was a Christian, for example, and Sunni and Shia Muslims had freely intermarried. But Saddam would brook no political opposition, hence his persecution of the Kurds and Islamists. Just before the war I asked to speak to the Archbishop of Canterbury, Rowan Williams, about his views on the impending invasion, even though he was in interview *purdah* for three months. His PA flippantly said he was giving interviews only in his native tongue. I took up the offer, although I had no idea what the correct Welsh translation was for WMD. In our long conversation he warned that an invasion would threaten Christians in Iraq and possibly the whole Middle East. How right he was.

I found myself in Baghdad on the eve of the war. One of the advantages of working in a dictatorship such as Saddam's was that if you slipped your minders you could get around the back of the bazaars, not only in safety, but also get people to talk, discreetly. Imagine a lone unarmed Westerner walking around Baghdad at night today, or around the magnificent old souk in Damascus, one of my favourite places. It was much better then in so many ways. Admittedly, the mood in Baghdad was nervous – most knew the war was coming. But the leaders I spoke to, such as Tariq Aziz, the Christian deputy prime minister, seemed to be oblivious of the extent of the American blitzkrieg that was about to descend on them. The Americans would come to call it 'shock and awe'.

For the Americans the attack on Iraq in 2003 was part of 'the global war on terror'. The coalition of the willing, however, that was assembled to actually fight, consisted of only four nations – the United States, Britain, Australia and Poland. As veteran British journalist Martin Bell said, 'To call them a coalition was a supine use of language.' Significantly, although US bases in Arab states were used, there were no formal Arab military contributions, unlike in 1991, and with absolutely no clear-cut UN resolutions authorising the invasion. For Britain, Operation TELIC, the UK designation of what the US labelled Operation IRAQI FREEDOM, was perhaps the most controversial foreign military intervention since the 1956 Suez debacle. The controversy became more intense when the post-war truths began to emerge, not least about WMD. Fear of WMD was not a bluff, though. When the British army crossed from Kuwait, they were fully expecting a chemical attack. I had returned to government service and my Bergen was two-thirds full of the bulky protective suits as I lugged the damn things around southern Iraq. When I went on patrol in Basra with the Royal Military Police, the locals were not actively hostile – in the beginning. Such was the misguided confidence then about a benign occupation that berets not helmets were worn. And the Brits refused to copy the Americans in the full Star Wars body armour and, of course, sunglasses. The Brits believed they knew a lot more about peace enforcement than their American allies. They were wrong. The British army, still one of the best forces in the world, was later humiliated in Basra and forced out, partly because of poor military and political leadership, but mainly because it was totally under-resourced.

Baghdad fell quickly, despite the Western generals once more assuming that Saddam had drawn a red line around his capital and would use tactical

WMD. The Iraqi leader himself remained at large until December 2003 when his capture became a global media event. Iraqi insurgents – both Sunni and Shia – had killed more American troops by this point in Iraq's post-invasion liberation than during the entire combat phase of operations. This was the shape of things to come as large parts of Iraq seemed to be embroiled in a full-scale insurrection. The vaunted liberators had become oppressive occupiers to many if not most Iraqis even if the majority of the Shia and Kurds were glad to see the back of the Sunni tyrant. After the liberation, opposition would soon rapidly outgrow a narrow pro-Saddam fringe.

Right at the start Western politicians did not know what was happening on the ground in Iraq. The southern Iraqi town of Umm Qasr was reported by the media to have been taken on nine separate occasions before it actually fell. The UK Ministry of Defence, which should have known more than the media, announced that the town was secured three times on three separate days, before it actually fell. Geoff Hoon, the UK secretary of state for defence, blamed imprecise language: the coalition had not clearly differentiated the port and the town itself, which shared the same name. 'Umm Qasr is a town similar to Southampton,' he explained to the House of Commons, meaning that the port and town were in separate places. 'He's either never been to Southampton or he's never been to Umm Qasr,' quipped one British soldier on patrol in Umm Qasr. 'There's no beer, no prostitutes and people are shooting at us. It's more like Portsmouth.'

It was a short one-sided campaign: one reporter argued that one of Saddam's statues put up more of a fight than Saddam had himself. Despite the short war, there was still time for atrocities. President Bush commented on the images of two British soldiers slain execution-style that were aired on al-Jazeera. Both the British and the Americans played up the propaganda about the cruelty of Saddam before and during the war. Both sides tried to show that the enemy was attacking civilians. On 9 April 2003 the Americans stage managed the toppling of the huge Saddam statue in Baghdad's Firdos Square to give the media a sense of closure. That scene, enacted in front of the Palestine Hotel where the international press corps was quartered, was supposed to symbolise the American exit strategy. Three weeks later President Bush, wearing a macho bomber jacket, rammed the point home with his speech on board the USS *Abraham Lincoln*; above him stood a massive banner emblazoned with 'Mission Accomplished'. It was, however, the beginning of real fighting. And yet for the Islamic world the most powerful images were not taken by Western media, but by American soldiers: the appalling pictures of the Iraqi prisoners at Abu Ghraib incensed the Arab street and undermined Washington claims to higher moral purpose. This was reinforced by the detention of al-Qaeda suspects and other Islamists from all over the world in the notorious Guantánamo prison in Cuba. Some had been 'rendered for extradition' in very shady circumstances; others were tortured in sordid jails belonging to Washington's Muslim allies and, even in the cleaner cells run by Americans, suspects were forced to undergo illegal treatment including the notorious 'water boarding'. This was not a good look for promoting democratic modern values to counterbalance the lure of Jihadism.

*The Occupation of Iraq*
The intelligence thinking in Whitehall was that Saddam would be ousted by his generals when the Anglo-Americans started to invade. Thus the new Iraqi top brass would be sensible enough to concede to *force majeure* and do a deal. The Americans would run the show briefly, fly in one of their tame Iraqi exiles and the Iraqi army, minus a few of the most loyal and cruellest Saddamites, would stay on to do the policing in an 'occupation lite'. The British Foreign Office and US State Department wanted the Iraqi army to stay largely intact, but the Pentagon called all the shots – and nearly always missed. The US Defense Department was dominated by the adamantine personality of Donald Rumsfeld. The military largely ran the show in Iraq, but the State Department had its own man in the form of Paul Bremner who headed the occupation authority. No American since General Douglas MacArthur's administration of Japan had assumed such a powerful foreign post. Bremner had studied at Harvard, Yale and the *Institut d'Etudes Politiques de Paris*, and had also been a close associate of Henry Kissinger. He was not simply Rumsfeld's representative on earth. He ran his own show, very badly. Former Speaker of the House Newt Gingrich called him 'the largest single disaster in American foreign policy in modern times'.

The first nine months were certainly marked by disaster, from the security vacuum that led to a locust-storm of looting, to the US army's insane de-Ba'athification, which sent tens of thousands of armed, angry, unemployed young men and their well-trained officers onto the streets. The initial military impetus and latent Iraqi attitude of gratitude (especially among the Shia) for the downfall of Saddam's tyranny were lost, as was the hearts and minds campaign. The capture of Saddam in December 2003 made little difference. And the phone-camera filming of his bungled execution while he was invoking the name of Allah was a PR train wreck for the West and the new Baghdad government. Few Arabs, even those who hated

Saddam, could condone such an undignified death of a major Arab leader, even if it was done by Iraqi representatives – in the pocket of the USA.

The transfer of power to an interim Iraqi government in June 2004 had not improved matters. In the previous April the US military fought a major battle in Fallujah. In November a second major offensive was launched in the same town. It was described 'as a modern-day Stalingrad with dust for snow'. Many of the men who sold their lives dearly, often in hand-to-hand-combat, were foreign Jihadists. The London *Economist*, often the voice of the British establishment, editorialised: 'The very fact that Americans are having to fight so fiercely inside a major city eighteen months after liberating Iraq from Saddam Hussein, is a sign of how close Mr Bush's Iraq policy is teetering towards failure.' In the USA, *Newsweek*'s columnist, Fareed Zakaria, once a respected hawk, wrote that the president's 'strange combination of arrogance and incompetence' had proved 'poisonous' for American foreign policy.

Conditions in Iraq grew worse. By the end of 2006 US military combat deaths had reached 3,000. Washington ordered a series of troop surges: 21,000 new troops were sent in January 2007; more surges followed and violence was temporarily reduced. Iraqi casualties soon mounted exponentially, however. The highest estimate was in the distinguished British medical journal *The Lancet,* which estimated in October 2004 that 100,000 Iraqis had been killed since the start of the war (though this figure was hotly contested). The country's communities collapsed into an ethno-sectarian civil war of savage proportions. It was not one war, but a patchwork of internecine conflicts. The Kurds strove for more autonomy and the Sunnis, increasingly alienated by a government dominated by the Shi'ite majority, started to look to their own Sunni solutions, often Islamist in orientation; al-Qaeda adherents allied with ex-Ba'athist officers to organise resistance against the Americans and what they saw as Iranian proxies in Baghdad.

It looked like declaring victory and getting out quickly was President Bush's least worst option. His public defence of his last-ditch surge policy rested on two premises, one tragic and the other inaccurate. The former, the inexplicable suggestion that more soldiers needed to fall to honour the memory of those who had already fallen. The latter a need for more time for the Iraqi army to proverbially 'step up to the plate' to defend the Baghdad government. The idea of a truly national and effective Iraqi army was always a chimera. It was more accurate to describe much of the army then as forces on secondment from the Badr Army of Shia militias or the Kurdish

Peshmerga. Both were keen on US training and intent not on stabilising Iraq, but promoting their own ethno-sectarian interests. By the late noughties it was obvious that the best exit strategy was politely asking Iraq's neighbours to avoid getting sucked into a regional war involving the fragile confederation that was supposed to be a unified state. That was one main reason why the Obama administration took so many risks to wrap up a nuclear deal with Iran. Tehran was more than willing to play a short waiting game to see the Americans leave Iraq and so reined in the Shia militias it controlled there.

Al-Qaeda in Iraq (also called AQ in Mesopotamia) began as a small franchise and started to attack US forces within a few months of the occupation. It was initially led by a Jordanian, Abu Musab al-Zarqawi, until he was killed by a US air strike in June 2006. In a portent of what was to come, AQI set out a manifesto:

1. To expel the American occupiers;
2. To establish a caliphate in Sunni parts of Iraq;
3. To organise a 'Jihad wave' that would engulf neighbouring secular states; Fight Israel.

Their methods were a shape of things to come as well – co-ordinated suicide bombings, beheadings of hostages and attacks on Shia mosques and holy places. In October 2006 they actually declared an Islamic state of Iraq in the six majority Sunni provinces of the country. But in the so-called 'Anbar Awakening' Sunni tribal elders, encouraged and paid by the Americans, rose up against the excesses of al-Qaeda. Many of the Sunni tribes and former Ba'athist soldiers were more focused on nationalistic, secular goals, not least of undermining the increasingly sectarian rule of the Shi'ites in Baghdad; some groups were narrowly tribal in their outlook, however. Temporarily, the Jihadist ambitions of the Iraqi al-Qaeda were driven underground. But the increasingly sectarian and anti-Sunni behaviour of the prime minister, Nouri al-Maliki, heading a Shia majority government, was to resurrect the Jihadist goals. He had been in exile for twenty-four years, mainly in Syria and Iran. Closely allied with Iran, despite being cleared by the CIA, he made Baghdad almost a suburb of Tehran. He was also corrupt and notoriously allowed venal favourites to embezzle funds for the large army, generously financed and armed by the Americans. When the time came for the Iraqi army to finally step up to the plate, it simply ran away, leaving its vast array of equipment to the Jihadist enemy.

*The other occupation fiasco*

'There are eleven million mines in this country – almost one for each person living here.' The sergeant's voice booms in the briefing tent at Kabul airport. It is 2.30 in the morning and freezing cold. He also warns of the endemic diseases, including anthrax and cholera. 'Afghanistan has eleven types of venomous snakes and there are scorpions everywhere.' He goes into some detail about a scorpion hiding in an Italian officer's trousers. The sergeant also notes, 'The driving here is terrible. And, by the way, prostitutes are available, but it's illegal. And remember the police are heavily armed. They use RPGs [rocket-propelled grenades] for traffic control.'

The sergeant was briefing fresh troops in May 2002, and I was taking notes while visiting the British-run HQ of the International Security Assistance Force (ISAF), later a NATO force; ISAF was distinct from the US troops fighting in the east, still chasing bin Laden and Taliban remnants. As in Iraq, the Western troops were charged with bringing democracy, reconstruction and peace via training a new national army and police force. The recently installed president, Hamid Karzai, controlled about 10 per cent of the country; journalists dubbed him the 'Mayor of Kabul'. His government had to negotiate with the remaining 90 per cent, which meant using force or bribes, usually the latter.

British troops had done a good job of stabilising Kabul. Many schools, even for girls, had opened. I went on patrol with the Royal Anglians, wearing berets, on its outskirts. Because I stood out from the fit young solders, the locals perhaps assumed I was the interpreter. They asked me on a number of occasions as I walked in line with the British soldiers, Union Flags on their uniform, whether they were Russians. The fact that after six months of occupation Kabul's residents thought that the Soviets had returned was either astounding political illiteracy or the international forces were not as touchy-feely as I had been led to believe. Perhaps Afghans didn't like any infidel foreigners patrolling their streets with guns, even if the troops meant well.

Much of the promised reconstruction money did come, albeit slowly, but it went into ill-conceived NGO projects or into the pockets of corrupt Afghan officials. Banditry, warlordism and drug running were rampant; the anarchy enabled the Taliban to regroup and take over much of the Pashtun south. Production of opium held the Afghan system together; if disbanding Saddam's army was the prime mistake in Iraq, threatening to destroy the opium crop was the disaster in Afghanistan. Ninety per cent of the heroin on European streets allegedly came from Afghanistan. The Brits were supposed to end this particularly malign version of the Common Agricultural Policy. Rather than banning or controlling the heroin supply, some experts viewed legalisation as the only rational route, especially considering the worldwide shortage of morphine-related medical drugs. Instead, occasional attempts were made to destroy a few opium fields in the south. Then the Americans threatened to indulge in mass-spraying which was manna from heaven for Taliban propagandists. Meanwhile drug production and profits soared – and most of it went into the Taliban kitty.

The British, almost broken in Basra, could hardly sustain a two-front war; in exchange for an exit from Iraq, London promised Washington to beef up the effort in the most troubled province of Afghanistan, Helmand. Around 10,000 Britons fought at one time in the south or were involved in training or special forces' duties in Kabul. The Brits never had enough men or often proper mine-protection equipment (although the latter did get better eventually). In the beginning they were too thinly dispersed in 'platoon houses' which on occasion resembled a replay of the Battle of Rorke's Drift. It came pretty close sometimes, but none were overrun. As ever, British generals felt the Americans were too gung-ho – or the more PC word was 'kinetic'. As one British observer, Professor Michael Clarke, noted, 'The Marines are trained to kill people and break things, and they do it very well.' Nevertheless, US Marines had to bail out the British army when it was up against it in the final stages of the Helmand campaign, which lasted until October 2014 when the last British troops left. Britain had fought for thirteen years in its fourth, and presumably last, Afghan war.

As Iraq descended into the sectarian hell of Sunni versus Shia, the internal conflict in Afghanistan raged within the largest Sunni ethnic group, the Pashtuns, who were divided between the anti-Western fundamentalists, many of whom lived in Pakistan or the adjoining tribal area, and the pro-Western, less fundamentalist Pashtuns who dominated the government and the security forces in Kabul. Though the Afghan army had performed better than its totally lacklustre equivalent in Iraq, President Karzai's and his successor's grip on the country was diminishing.

*What did the war on terror achieve?*
The first engagement of the war had not ended well. Despite a series of attempts at elections, Afghanistan's shaky government was continuing to lose ground to the Taliban. American troops were individually often

impressive, even well-intentioned, but to the occupied they looked in their protective gear and armoured vehicles like they were delivering democracy on behalf of Darth Vader. Mobile phones had swamped the country and women were given a few more rights, even in parliament, though little had really changed in political culture, especially outside Kabul. And the Taliban remained popular because they were seen as nationalists fighting infidel occupiers and often maintaining some semblance of *Sharia*-based law and order, while distant Kabul did, or could do, very little. Above all, NATO could not have prevailed in Afghanistan because they were fighting the wrong enemy in the wrong country.

Pakistan had long backed the Taliban and indeed they had helped to found it. Islamabad's rationale was simple – control of Afghanistan was seen as a rearguard defence against its main enemy, India. Afghanistan had nearly always been ruled by Pasthuns – 13 million lived mainly in the south of the country, but 30 million lived in Pakistan. They were divided into sixty main tribal groups on both sides of the British-imposed border. So kith and kin was a major factor – Pakistan had always claimed much of Afghan territory, inheriting rights from the Raj. Most countries have an army; it would be only a minor overstatement to say that the Pakistani army had a country. The most powerful organ in the security forces was the ISI intelligence agency, which oversaw the Taliban activities. Islamabad usually claimed that rogue ISI elements were responsible for misdeeds such as succouring the Taliban. It is true that the intelligence agencies were divided – some officers were more pro-Western nationalists; others were more Islamist internationalists. The end result was a failing, almost rogue state that possessed nuclear weapons. And the West was always fretting about whether or not its 200 nukes were always well guarded. The CIA always feared a Jihadist seizure of nuclear materials for a dirty bomb or the blackmail potential of a complete bomb. Besides its constant meddling in Afghanistan, the ISI also backed insurgencies elsewhere, especially in Kashmir, and turned a blind eye to attacks in India, most notoriously the Mumbai massacres in 2008. It could be argued that Pakistan is possibly the most dangerous country in the world, from a Jihadist perspective, yet it was seen to be a reluctant ally of the West – mainly because of aid and weapons supplies to prop up the government in Islamabad.

The classic example of Pakistani duplicity was its hosting of Osama bin Laden. The arch enemy of the USA was killed by American special forces in May 2011. He was living in a large villa in Abbottabad, only a mile or so from the famous Pakistani Military Academy, the local equivalent of West

Point or the Royal Military Academy Sandhurst – hardly incognito. Now bin Laden may have been pretending to hide in plain sight or senior ISI officials were looking after him as they had done for years. It is just possible that the rogue ISI argument might just be true, but I doubt it. Likewise, the argument that the Pakistanis colluded with the Americans to let them attack the Saudi warlord does not stand up to scrutiny either. There is much debate in Western intelligence circles on the subject, but the most obvious scenario is that very senior Pakistan military officials knew about the whereabouts of bin Laden. He was lightly guarded because he was in the centre of the Pakistani military embrace. That is why the CIA had to organise a secret helicopter incursion from Afghanistan, with fighter escort. It is highly improbable that the Pakistanis knew about this – otherwise bin Laden would have cleared out immediately. The Pakistanis could not be trusted with such sensitive information – the Americans went in solo and clandestinely, and finally got their man. The poor air defence, and being caught out protecting Washington's greatest enemy, were embarrassing to say the least for the Pakistani security services – hence the smokescreen that some US correspondents have taken on trust. Foolish: the whole history of Western security and intelligence relations with Pakistan is that you cannot trust them at all.

For example, Pakistanis and Pakistani territory had been in some way involved in the majority (75 per cent) of domestic Jihadist attacks in the UK, especially the training of would-be *Mujahedin*. It now faces stiff competition from the Islamic State. Perhaps the US billions spent on fighting the Taliban in Afghanistan should have been better spent on neutering the Pakistani threat, not least defanging them of their 'loose nukes'. Originally, US civilian experts and special forces had been involved in protecting them – so the CIA knows, or knew, their whereabouts. Hence the ISI's (justified) paranoia about US intervention. Not least because the Saudis have paid for them and the CIA fears that Riyadh will cash in its chips if the burgeoning conflict with near-nuclear Iran gets any hotter.

If Pakistan batted for both sides, so did Saudi Arabia. It was the epicentre of the Wahhabi creed espoused by al-Qaeda. Riyadh officially, or through individual Saudi billionaires, sent money to a bewildering array of Islamist groups, often nominally for charity or to pay for *madrassahs,* but often the money was siphoned off for arms and terrorist training throughout the Middle East and Asia.

With allies likes these, how could the West hope to win its battles with its Jihadist enemies?

Britain's fourth war in Afghanistan lasted thirteen years, the longest since the Hundred Years' War with medieval France. Five hundred and fifty-four British troops were killed. Military and political leadership were the main causes of this fiasco. The West imposed its own priorities such as gender rights and creating democracy. Afghans were never over-enthused by elections; above all, they wanted security, jobs and food. The conflict started as a limited war to topple the Taliban's support for al-Qaeda, then it shape-shifted into an anti-narcotics crusade, then into a nation-building and humanitarian operation that was sucked into a counter-insurgency campaign, and it finally ended up as a training mission for the Afghan army and police. Sir John Chilcot has spent years on his never-ending enquiry into the Iraq war; Britain, however, needs to know why Clausewitz was ignored in Afghanistan. London had no policy except the perhaps sensible one of keeping in step with the Americans – at least in security co-operation. Yet that long-term safeguard was undermined by the British failures in Basra and Helmand. Richard Dearlove, head of the Secret Intelligence Service (SIS), warned that in Washington 'the intelligence and facts were being fixed around the policy'. Putting so many carts before so many horses was bound to create a debacle. The intelligence was poor and so was the political interpretation. Unfortunately, the British top commanders didn't talk to each either. At the more junior levels the military's version of political correctness is called 'jointery'; the posts are supposed to be 'purple' – a merging of officers in red, light and dark blue. Often the assumption that a naval officer or an air force man or woman could do the same job equally well under fire in Afghanistan or Iraq led to numerous infelicities. Jointery was not practised, however, at the very top levels in the Ministry of Defence in Whitehall. The most senior military man (the CDS, Chief of Defence Staff) might have talked sometimes to the top politicians and very occasionally to intelligence chiefs, but less frequently consulted his single service chiefs. When General Sir Richard Dannatt was made CGS (Chief of the General Staff), the head of the army in 2006, he tried to discover precisely why Britain had entered the war in Afghanistan. He found that there were very few or adequate minutes of meetings with the heads of the navy and air force.[17] They must have met, presumably once a week, but they didn't talk much apparently. Or they told their senior civil servants not to take notes or go for a cup of tea when something important was discussed. The Freedom of Information Act has many exceptions relating to security matters, but it has still discouraged recordkeeping even, or especially, at the top of military and intelligence circles. Short of a major inquiry that can access proper

In the golden age of Islamic culture the Muslim world excelled in arts and sciences, especially architecture. The Dome of the Rock is the third holiest Islamic site, located on the Temple Mount in the Old City of Jerusalem. It was initially completed in AD 691 at the order of Umayyad Caliph Abd al-Malik.

Krak des Chevaliers was one of the most important Crusader castles, held by the Knights Hospitallers until it fell to the Saracens in 1271. Its mighty walls had withstood sieges and the ravages of time. It was one of the best preserved castles in the region, when I last visited in 2008. It has since been damaged during the Syrian civil war. (Credit: Paul Moorcraft.)

Hagia Sophia, the biggest cathedral in the world for 1,000 years, was considered the high point of Byzantine architecture. When the Ottomans conquered Constantinople it was transformed into a mosque and later a museum.

Underestimating Jihad. General 'Chinese' Gordon misread the strength and determination of the Mahdist Jihad and he was killed in the siege of Khartoum in 1885, one of the most dramatic British defeats of the Victorian empire.

*Mujahedin* praying before attacking a Russian-backed government military base near Kabul, 1984. (Credit: author.)

*Mujahedin* doctors giving first aid to a young boy whose fingers had been blown off while playing with a Russian 'butterfly bomb', an anti-personnel device, near Jalalabad, 1984. (Author.)

Author (centre) with *Mujahedin* group relaxing after crossing on foot the Afghan border into the tribal areas, adjacent to Peshawar, Pakistan. 1984. It was good to taste capitalism in the form of a Coca-Cola, after weeks of marching, dehydration, and dysentery. (Author's collection.)

'Doing a Maggie Thatcher.' Author hitching a lift with SFOR British forces in Gornji Vakuf, Bosnia, 1998. (Author's collection.)

Jihadist attack on the Pentagon on 9/11. (US Department of Defense.)

The US Secretary of Defense, Donald Rumsfeld, who supervised the war on terror from 2001 to 2006, possessed an 'adamantine personality'. (Department of Defense.)

Two leading Western correspondents, Lindsey Hilsum and Marie Colvin, amid the destruction of the Palestinian refugee camp in Jenin, April 2002. (Author.)

A British base on the heights overlooking Kabul, April 2002. (Author.)

A lonely British observation post, formerly a Russian OP, guarding an access road to Kabul, April 2002. (Author.)

A British soldier from the Royal Anglians during a patrol on the outskirts of Kabul. The locals asked me if the British troops were returning Russians. April 2002. (Author.)

Hearts, minds and pencils. Female British soldier donating pens and pencils to a girls' school in Kabul, 2002. (Author.)

'Mother of all Battles Mosque', Baghdad, October 2002. The minarets were said to be the same size and shape as a Scud missile. When I attended the Friday prayers, the imam discussed not the imminent war, but relations within families. (Author.)

British armour amid the destruction of Basra, April 2003. (Author.)

The Royal Military Police engage with the locals in a market, Basra, May 2003. (Author.)

Locals complain to a British officer about the occupation, Umm Qasr, May 2003. (Author.)

US Abrams tank in Baghdad, April 2003. (Tim Lambon.)

Osama bin Laden once preferred to 'talk about JCBs not Jihad'.

Abu Bakr al-Baghdadi proclaims the new caliphate on 29 June 2014.

Islamic State propaganda likes to play up the parallels with the Great Arab conquests of the medieval period.

IS parade through their capital, Raqqah, in northern Syria.

IS captured 2,300 Humvees and numerous tanks from the Iraqi army in Mosul.

The IS flag based on the battle flag of Muhammad. The white circle represents the ring-shaped seal, and encloses the three words 'Muhammad is the prophet of God'.

The Islamic State has a lot of hardware, but probably limited access to spare parts and skilled mechanics. Eventually the harsh terrain and over-use will wear down heavy armour that the coalition air forces miss.

IS militants parading through Raqqah.

IS convoy in Anbar province, Iraq. Such operations in daylight are rare now because of coalition air strikes on concentration of IS forces on open roads.

IS beheadings are common. There is method in the barbarity – it deliberately strikes terror in the hearts of opponents, especially the Iraqi army.

The IS message is spreading in Africa. Islamist rebels in Darfur – before the advent of the caliphate. (Author.)

records, the official version of why Britain went so wrong in Afghanistan may never be known. Except for knocking the Taliban off its perch and wiping out or dispersing al-Qaeda, the rest of the war aims, especially nation-building, were like chasing the end of a rainbow.

Iraq, too, had been a lost cause. The fall of Saddam was undoubtedly a bonus for humanity; it was a disaster for the West, however. Most cynics would argue that the best solution for America would be to find a tough military dictator, preferably with a moustache, and certainly a Sunni, and help him run Iraq with an iron hand – yes, just like Mr Hussein. All the American invasion of Iraq had succeeded in doing was establishing Iraq as an all too willing de facto colony of Washington's supposed arch-enemy – Iran.

Iraq had failed the reality test and the audit of war. The state possessed no WMDs and absolutely no link with al-Qaeda even though constant opinion polls in the US showed that many if not most Americans thought that Saddam had nourished Jihadists. He hated them and no hard evidence existed of any connection to any Islamist extremists – despite massive PR efforts by the CIA to suggest otherwise. Iraq was a massive diversion not only from finalising the defeat of al-Qaeda and its hosts in Afghanistan, but was also a propaganda gift to the Islamists worldwide. Although some subtle minds in US intelligence services tried to argue that Iraq had been a flypaper to trap Jihadists in one place and then kill them, the opposite was true. It became a honeypot for genuine hard-core Jihadist foreign fighters and later the centre of the universe for wannabe Jihadists throughout the world, including Europe. Far from draining the swamp from which Jihadists were emerging, Western military action in Iraq had dramatically filled it.

This seems obvious now in the era of the Islamic State. But as early as 2006 the grand old man of American columnists, George F. Will, observed:

All three components of the 'axis of evil' – Iraq, Iran and North Korea – are much more dangerous than they were when the phrase was coined in 2002. The ranks of Islamic extremists have been massively boosted, while American resources have been exhausted in confronting the expanded threat. Worse still, President Bush has lost the war of ideas that, in the end, was the most potent American weapon for battling the nihilism of radical Islam.

The failures – or to be frank – the near-defeat of the British forces in Basra and Helmand have done immense damage to the British armed forces in their longest foreign wars since the end of empire. It is not sufficient simply to blame politicians and intelligence services, although they should shoulder much of the responsibility. Nor is it just a question of no proper strategic thinking. It was a failure of leadership among senior officers in an army which was far too full of chiefs and precious few Indians. The British armed forces are about eight times more top-heavy with generals compared with the Americans. And the Royal Navy was said to have more admirals than ships. In this case, especially in Afghanistan, it was the old British disease of lions led by donkeys. The army was obsessed with cavalier and amateur attitudes associated with the can-do notions of just 'cracking on'. In the next wars – perhaps a cyber one – the British forces may not have the luxury of more than one battle to learn from their mistakes. I comment on the UK forces became I know them much better. I repeat: it is chock full of fighting spirit, but it has been poorly led. Not least by heads of services who often did not have the balls to tell their political leaders where to get off, or in a democracy 'tell truth to power' about operational and equipment capacity.[18] The antiquated structure and thinking in the British army may well not cope with the serious Jihadist challenges of the future, abroad and in the UK.  I have worked with Americans and have usually been impressed by the quality of their officers. Yet, like the Brits, the Americans got a pasting in Iraq and Afghanistan as well, both physically and in terms of reputation.

Of course it cut more deeply than that. In Britain and the USA, war fatigue had set in among the electorate. The fabled 'mission creep' had made these wars longer than the two world wars combined. Even those who returned physically fit were succumbing in large numbers to PTSD, post-traumatic stress disorder, especially in the US. Some never came back alive. My former colleague in the UK Ministry of Defence, Graham Bound, penned a moving book on the personal stories of twenty of the 454 soldiers, Royal Marines and RAF personnel who lost their lives in Helmand. He described the fighting thus: 'IEDs [Improvised Explosive Devices] sown like confetti, gun battles in the poppy fields, bayonets at close quarters; the raging Helmand river flows with blood, sweat and tears.' And the average age of the fatalities was 22.[19]  Bound deals mainly with fatalities, but thousands of British service men and women suffered life-changing wounds, especially from IEDs. The Taliban were very good at targeting commanders of units, from sergeants up to lieutenant colonels.

In the end what was it all for? It is true that the original goal of disrupting al-Qaeda and its leadership was largely achieved. Western troops were soon diverted into nation-building. Yet the original plan of al-Qaeda was to provoke the Western forces to overreact, invade and radicalise Muslims throughout the *Umma*. Thus bin Laden achieved what he set out to do, though he did not live to see the caliphate established. Jihadism is a far more dangerous foe now in the US and Europe than in 9/11 or 7/7.

The kinetic approach did not work and, yet almost by accident, the concept of reform came from within. One of the original beliefs in the CIA was that Saddam's ousting would be the key to unlocking democracy in the region. The opposite happened – sectarian war, terrorism and Islamism took off in a way that not even the gloomiest analysts in Langley or Vauxhall could have imagined. The lucky accident was caused by a very unlikely catalyst.

*Chapter 4*

# The Arab Spring Unsprung

At 10.30 am on 17 December 2010 in the small town of Sidi Bouzid, in rural Tunisia, a female municipal official confiscated the electric scales of a street vendor named Mohamed Bouazizi, for selling vegetables without a licence. She was alleged to have been abusive and slapped him. The 26-year-old vendor did not need a licence and this was the umpteenth time he had been harassed for a bribe by local officialdom. He had to hang on to his job, in an area of 30 per cent unemployment, to help support his widowed mother and family. It was the final straw for him. In utter frustration at 11.30 am he self-immolated with a can of petrol outside the local governor's office – the governor had refused to see him. Bouazizi's was the ultimate protest against corruption and harassment of small businesses. It was not political, but it soon became the most political act in the Arab world, large areas of which were also set on fire by mass protests.

The crowds at Bouazizi's funeral led to protests in authoritarian Tunisia, which fired up national demonstrations; the government fell in the following January. Protests started in Algeria. Each north African country was different in its own unhappy way, but they exhibited a common seething discontent among the masses. Elsewhere throughout the Maghreb protesters burned themselves alive; this domino effect was intended to be political. The most dramatic effects were in Egypt where massive demonstrations led to the fall of President Hosni Mubarak. In March 2011 pro-democracy demonstrations spread to even Syria, one of the most tightly controlled Arab states. The democratic tsunami swept into Libya which was to produce the most dramatic and bloody changes of what was soon dubbed the 'Arab Spring'. In June 2012 after decades of persecution, the candidate for the Muslim Brotherhood, Mohamed Morsi, became the first freely elected president of Egypt. His short rule highlighted the inexperience of the Brotherhood, which was not surprising after decades of working underground or from prison. The government was also deemed sectarian as the large community of Coptic Christians suffered a number of attacks, especially on their churches.

In the following year Morsi was deposed in a military coup and later sentenced to death. The popular uprisings spread nearly everywhere in the Arab world, including Bahrain, which served to graphically symbolise the Sunni/Shia frictions in the region.

The reaction in Western chancelleries was mixed. Historically, especially during the Cold War, the West needed the oil-rich dictatorships for economic and strategic reasons. As Robert Fisk, a well-informed British writer on the Middle East, put it, 'We like dictatorships. We know how to do business with the kings and generals – how to sell them our tanks and fighter-bombers and missiles.' The Cold War was over, however, and the United States had diversified its oil needs, including fracking at home and massive energy supplies from Canada. The Saudis were now useful, but not vital. The original argument had been that backing off from the oil-rich Arab dictators was too dangerous for the West. And yet NATO did not argue that communism should be propped up because Orthodox autocracy or virulent nationalism could flourish in Russia and former satellites if the Wall came down.

Yes, democracy was good in theory, though it could destabilise the dictatorships that were loyal to the West. Egypt was the classic example. Washington did not know how to respond to the rapid fall of Mubarak, the short interregnum of the Muslim Brotherhood and then a military coup. Technically, the US could not do business with a government installed by coup so Washington punished Cairo with a gentle slap on the wrist, by briefly delaying the regular economic and military subventions to the new generalissimo. On the other hand, revolutions from within – apparently demanding secular liberal changes – would undercut al-Qaeda in particular and Jihadism in general. Or so it was thought. Washington remained ambivalent about Egypt. Elections were good, of course, but not necessarily the results. Reasonably free elections had elected an ally of the Egyptian Brotherhood, Hamas, in Gaza. If you gave people the vote, they might just vote the wrong way. Washington was also ambivalent about Libya, which had been courted so recently, personally and successfully by Tony Blair to induce it to give up its rather primitive attempts to develop WMD and also to desist from funding terrorism. Libya had lots of oil, and it was very close to southern Europe. Afghanistan was a long way from the European Union. Now Libya became a concern to some NATO members.

*Libya*
If Saddam had been unpopular with other Arab leaders, Colonel Muammar

Gaddafi was absolutely loathed. He had a deranged genius for insulting nearly everyone and he was dangerously unpredictable, not least in his bad habit of nurturing rebels in foreign countries. In the case of next-door Chad and Sudan, Gaddafi's vast oil wealth allowed him to back *simultaneously* a number of *competing* horses in civil wars. The sheer zaniness of Gaddafi's anointing himself as a 'king of kings' led him to annoy numerous African governments by assembling (and lavishing money on) a horde of legal and illegal royals throughout the continent. He had to pay people a lot of money to deal with him, as he had alienated nearly all Arab and African states. And except for 10 Downing Street he had few friends in Europe. The Libyan dictator's support for the IRA, his alleged backing of the terrorists who brought down the airliner over Lockerbie and sponsoring bombings in West Germany did not endear him to other Western leaders. Strangely, Gaddafi had a well-known obsession with the very winsome Condoleezza Rice, but he also had the hots for a perhaps less glamorous US Secretary of State, Madeleine Albright. Perhaps he just had a thing for powerful female secretaries of state. Other aspects of his weird rule, especially his harems, Ruritanian outfits and personal vanity – he was botoxed up to his eyeballs like a 'sinister Middle Eastern Michael Jackson' – are summarised in Lindsey Hilsum's recent book on Libya.[20] Many outstanding correspondents such as Hilsum initially believed that the Arab Spring would follow the same trajectory as the emancipation of Eastern Europe from the Soviet yoke, and that democracy would bloom even in the arid lands of the Sahara. They were all embarrassed to be proved so collectively wrong.

Protests against Gaddafi's erratic but sternly centralised rule soon turned into a fullscale civil war, initially within Islamist enclaves in eastern Libya. On 11 March 2011 the UN Security Council sanctioned a no-fly zone and NATO started bombing. France and Britain, along with some Arab states, sent in special forces to help with training and to direct air strikes. Instructors from Qatar and the United Arab Emirates trained some groups of Libyans in the Tunisian desert. Jordanian officers were busy in the Nafousa Mountains. About a hundred Egyptian trainers were busy in the east as well as a small team of Italian advisers. The Americans provided a covert unit specialising in intelligence and electronic intercepts. British MI6 and SAS were based around Benghazi and helped to ship Qatari weapons to Misrata. A larger French force was also training and equipping rebels in the west of the country. The uprising against Gaddafi was not exactly spontaneous and self-sustaining combustion.

Britain had just cut its defence budget dramatically and then almost immediately it was sucked into another war in an oil-rich Muslim country, which allegedly had remaining stocks of chemical weapons. Prime Minister David Cameron, a neophyte in foreign affairs, egged on by the far more wily French president, Nicholas Sarkozy, led the campaign to prevent Gaddafi's forces crushing the rebels in Benghazi, in the east. US President Barack Obama officially took a back seat in the NATO bombing, although much of the technical back up, weaponry and intelligence were still provided by the Americans. If Obama was tepid, his secretary of state, Hillary Clinton, was definitely not. The woman tipped to be the first female president was a vociferous hawk. Obama wanted to end the two Bush wars and concentrate on the economy. It was ironic that Cameron, who was pledged to rescuing Britain from its then bankruptcy, entered another war against an Islamic country, with no obvious end game, at the same time as the major public investigation into the Iraq war (the Chilcot Inquiry) had just been completed (though it had not published its findings at the time of writing in late 2015).

The British and French public seemed to support the Anglo-French-led intervention (with the backing of Washington, unlike Suez in 1956). It was likely that Gaddafi would have massacred thousands of the rebels in Benghazi – the Libyan supremo had promised to hunt them down in every alleyway and kill them like rats, hardly a policy of engagement. The UN-imposed no-fly zone was creatively interpreted and extended by Western governments into a no-fly, no-drive, no-Libyan military deployment zone and NATO airpower finally pushed back the government forces. The rebel militias started making real headway in the east and west; they captured the capital Tripoli in August. In September Sarkozy and Cameron flew to Benghazi and posed as liberators in front of jubilant crowds. Cameron called the rebels 'lions'. (Perhaps he didn't realise that a film comedy *The Four Lions*, about incompetent British Jihadists, had been a big hit the year before). It looked like a Western triumph, a repeat of the fall of Kabul – a short sharp air war, with special forces on the ground, to achieve a quick victory for democracy. Or so it seemed, especially when, on 20 October, Gaddafi was caught hiding in a large water pipe by Libyan rebels and summarily executed – much to his surprise. He died believing he was the beloved leader of his people.

Libya, a vast rich country with a population of just over six million, was yet another artificial state delineated by European cartographers. What is now Tripolitania and Cyrenaica, western and eastern Libya, had historically been separate since Roman times and the desert south, Fezzan, was always treated as badlands full of smugglers and tribal bandits. Post-Gaddafi, the country became a collection of fiefdoms; independent militias squabbled, fought and then finally sucked Libya into civil war. The West had seen the rebellion optimistically and naively as nationalistic and anti-Gaddafi. He had ruled the country with an iron fist since 1969 and no tradition of independent political or civic organisations had been allowed. The powerful Islamist undercurrent was unseen by the Western governments intent on destroying the Gaddafi regime. Libya had always contributed a large number of Jihadist fighters to other theatres of war in the Middle East, but Gaddafi had controlled any signs of Islamist discontent at home. The occasional Islamist outbursts led to death or long terms in squalid jails, plus regular torture. Regime change had once again led to the opening of a Pandora's box of Islamist militancy. The honeymoon period for the Western liberators was short. In September 2012 the US ambassador and three other Americans were killed by Jihadists in Benghazi. The British ambassador was the target of assassination attempts. There were repeated attacks on other Western diplomats. This was a replay of Iraq – soon the West was looking for another strongman with fancy uniforms to hold the country together. A prime candidate seemed to be General Khalifa Haftar – he even had the right Arabic name to succeed the Colonel he had helped in the coup of 1969.

Another part of the problem in Libya had also been caused by the West. For example, the many Libyan exiles in Britain were encouraged to go back and join the fight against Gaddafi. Some were Islamists. And yet, unlike later Jihadi tourism to Syria, the British intelligence services turned a blind eye to the exodus of radicals to Libya.

Soon two governments were set up – in Tobruk in the east and Tripoli in the west. In the middle, pro-Jihadist militias stoked up mayhem. The Islamic State soon took over many of them. By July 2014 all the embassies and foreign workers had pulled out, some to operate in safe, but distant, Malta. Besides the Jihadists, the only real beneficiaries from the anarchy were the people smugglers, who sent tens of thousands of asylum seekers to the shores of Italy – when the boats didn't sink. Libya now became the Mediterranean centre of Jihadism and the source of an immigration crisis that was overwhelming the European Union, a crumbling confederation distracted by the upheaval in Ukraine and the financial collapse of Greece. Hardliners in Europe advocated bombing the fishing boats in Libyan ports to control the flood of refugees, but it was Cairo that took action. The new more forceful military government sent in jets to bomb Islamic State fighters in Libya in retaliation for the beachfront beheadings of twenty-one Egyptian Christians in February 2015.

Jihadism was on the march in Libya, a state in which an estimated 27 million weapons were in circulation, although many of them were filtering across the Sahara to the *Mujahedin* in the southern battlefields such as Mali and Nigeria. Fuelled by the triumphalist Libyan Jihadists, weapons, manpower and fervour exploded into Mali and almost took the whole country, until French-led troops pushed them back to their redoubts in the north. Boko Haram zealots welcomed the arms and inspiration from Libya and they expanded their control in northern Nigeria, led by their 'emir', a maniacal figure called Abubakar Shekau. Built around an Islamist core, the insurgents are made up of former bandits from Shekau's own ethnic group. Nigeria's small army of 62,000 (out of a population of 180 million) has been very poorly led and riddled with corruption. In the western Mahgreb an al-Qaeda affiliate attacked a major gas facility at In Amenas, Algeria, and killed thirty-nine foreign workers during a four-day siege.

In Libya the warriors of Allah also had an eye on Mammon: they seized control of oilfields around Derna and the useful working airport at Sirte. (Tripoli's international airport looked like an earthquake zone.) New Jihadist training camps were set up for recruits from the Maghreb. One of them was a young Tunisian student with a passion for break-dancing, before he took up killing. Seifeddine Rezgui slaughtered thirty-eight innocent tourists on the beach at Sousse, Tunisia. Thirty of them were from the UK, the largest slaughter of British citizens since the London transport suicide bombers struck a decade before.

Tunisia was considered the only success story of the Arab Spring, partly because it had peacefully voted out the Islamist government that had been elected in the first flowering of the revolutionary spring. Yet the country, which exported more fighters than any other to the wars in Iraq and Syria, has suffered regular clashes with Islamist extremists as well as two major attacks on Western visitors, leading to a state of emergency and the shattering of the vital tourist industry. The government pledged to build a wall along the 310-mile border with Libya to stop the transit of Jihadists. It would require a regiment of Israeli troops to make it work properly, however.

Chaos, a tsunami of migrants and the rapid advance of Jihadism were not what NATO had signed up for in Libya. Once more, Western military intervention had created an avalanche of unintended consequences.

*The Facebook wars*
Many of the Arab Spring demonstrations were organised by young people

using social media. It was alleged, for example, that US and UK intelligence agencies set up hundreds of social media accounts in order to influence support for Western military intervention in Libya. In Cairo, most of the crowds of optimistic youngsters in Tahir Square believed in the liberalisation of their polity, but it was often the Islamists who mastered the technology. Jihadists believed in returning to the seventh century yet they were avid manipulators of twenty-first-century communications. This had long been the case in the Sunni heartland rebellion against the American occupation in Iraq, for example. Most largescale attacks on US forces were filmed with high-resolution cameras often from multiple camera angles, then expertly edited before being set to inspiring, religious soundtracks. In a few cases the attacks were launched primarily to generate fresh footage. Compilation DVDs were sold in the Baghdad markets for less than a dollar. As the rapid dissemination of the film of Saddam's hanging proved, new mobile-phone technology enabled Jihadist videos to be downloaded easily and circulated. Such films, allied to the graphic images shown on popular Arab satellite television channels, all gave the impression that coalition forces were on the run. Particularly popular, and not only in Iraq, were the slickly produced adventures of 'Juba the Sniper'. In one 15-minute video, for example, the camera follows an American soldier from a distance as he stands near his vehicle and chats with a fellow soldier. Then the sound of rifle fire is heard. The soldier is seen falling to the ground as his panic-stricken comrades swarm around him. Such videos discouraged co-operation with US troops and inspired donations and recruits for the Jihadists. 'One of these videos is worth a division of tanks to those people,' said Robert Steele, a former intelligence officer in the US Marine Corps. Along with its planted material in Iraqi newspapers (regarded with utter scepticism by Iraqis) the American propaganda effort was bureaucratic, unwieldy and ultimately ineffective compared with the small and nimble insurgent propaganda systems that relied on the web and mobile phones for rapid results.

The US had conducted an abysmal propaganda war during the first years of the war on terror. Donald Rumsfeld refashioned the message by constructing the phrase 'a global struggle against violent extremism'. The US secretary of defense quoted Ayman al-Zawahiri, then bin Laden's deputy: 'More than half this battle is taking place in the battlefield of the media. We are in a media battle in a race for the hearts and minds of Muslims.' Rumsfeld said that the US government had not caught up with the twenty-first century as far as media operations were concerned. 'For the most part, the US government still functions as a five-and-dime store in an eBay world.' That was even more true of the UK.

The failed ideological onslaught by the West was associated with the syntactically challenged George W. Bush. The rhetorical genius of Barack Obama promised much to the Americans and to the Islamic community – symbolised by his Cairo speech in June 2009. He also promised to end some of the secrecy at home; it was partly the promise of government transparency that swept Obama into the White House. Yet he soon found that he could not close the detention camp at Guantánamo and that he too had lots of secrets his administration would try to keep from the media. This was illustrated by a media bombshell. The Wikileaks website released in April 2010 a video of a US helicopter attack in Baghdad in July 2007 which killed a number of Iraqi civilians and two Reuters' journalists. Then, in July 2010, Wikileaks published 77,000 raw US intelligence reports covering Afghanistan from 2004 to 2009. Wikileaks was seen as a big ally of the Jihadists by many people in the intelligence world. It was set up by an Australian eccentric, Julian Assange, who also co-operated with the old media, especially the *Guardian* in Britain. Obama had promised transparency, but Wikileaks, and later the highly damaging revelations about US and British surveillance techniques by Edward Snowden, an American intelligence analyst, shook the traditional mindset in both Washington and London. Strategic communications had been forged in a Cold War environment. Those old certainties – stable audiences, clear-cut enemies and supportive domestic bases – were shattered. Instead new media had created a multilayered ecology of domestic and international audiences. Western intelligence had grappled with some aspects of cyber warfare, though not fully with the techniques of influencing the Facebook and Twitter generation. Sheikh Google ruled supreme.

Speed, as Clausewitz noted long ago, had always been a vital component of war. By combining speed and volume, Julian Assange pioneered a method of overloading Western governments, especially in their operations in the Middle East and Afghanistan. He also threatened the surviving print media. The famous Pentagon Papers, for example, released by US defence analyst Daniel Ellsberg in 1971, took twenty-two months to reach the *New York Times*; it was haunted by constant litigation. Wikileaks could launch an instant global news story with little or no legal redress. The tall pale Australian proclaimed a new kind of journalism dedicated to protecting whistleblowers worldwide. Former colleagues portrayed him as a compulsive fantasist and a paranoid, arrogant, workaholic hippy with messianic tendencies. Others described the habits of a tramp aligned with the brain of a chess grandmaster. And yet Wikileaks worked like a wrecking ball not only on previous state media management, but on CIA and MI6 operations everywhere.

Mobile phones and the Internet were fully deployed by the secular youngsters who helped trigger off the revolutions in the Arab world. In tandem strode the new TV networks. Just as the first Gulf War against Saddam in 1991 established CNN, so the Arab Spring buttressed the reputation of al-Jazeera, both in English and Arabic formats. Critics (notably in Egypt) alleged that al-Jazeera was catalysing as much as covering the revolutions. The youths taking to the streets were in many ways the children of al-Jazeera. They were the first generation to grow up with the passionate debates about Arab politics on satellite TV that had displaced the torpid propaganda of state terrestrial channels. Al-Jazeera's rise coincided with the decline of the BBC World Service as a result of cuts in government funding. It was ironic that al-Jazeera was based in Doha, the capital of the tiny but super-rich state of Qatar. The state was ruled by an almost absolute monarchy that had supported the repression of the democracy movements in nearby Bahrain. Another big player was Iran, which set up a London-based English-language station, Press TV. Unlike al-Jazeera, which appeared to play a straight bat in English (if not always in Arabic), Press TV was condemned for peddling downright lies to British audiences, while most foreign correspondents were banned from working in Tehran.

Iran also helped Syria suppress the initial stages of the youth revolution in 2011, by providing technology for blocking satellite phone signals. As in Iran, so too in Syria, cruder methods were also used. Activists were tortured to reveal, quickly, their passwords to Facebook pages and other similar sites that helped to sustain the beginnings of the revolt against Bashar al-Assad. The regime cut off electricity as well as mobile and landline phone systems in many of the initial areas of revolt. Protestors circumvented this by using generators as well as satellite phones smuggled in. All this was small beer compared with what was to come in Syria.

In Islamist-ruled northern Sudan, the government was well-practised in revolutionary techniques. They had successfully staged their Islamist revolution in 1989, and stayed in power. The small student 'Arab Spring' copycat protests in Khartoum were soon quelled with little violence. The ruling party boasted that its 'cyber jihadists' would crush Internet-based dissent. In its 'on-line defence operations' it deployed many young IT specialists who were in this case geeky *counter*-revolutionaries.

*A new dawn of Islamic extremism*

Anarchy had been created in Iraq and chronic insecurity in Afghanistan by the largely unsuccessful military interventions of the West. Then came a light at the end of the tunnel that was in fact the proverbial express train – the Arab Spring. Yet again the West had meddled and created civil war and a space for the Jihadists to spawn. Syria was a little different – the West did not intervene directly for the first crucial years of the domestic civil war. With the partial exception of Syria, al-Qaeda had been contained, though not defeated. Meanwhile, in the war of ideas and media, the West had been completely outgunned. Soon the warriors of the caliphate would become masters of the universe compared with the plodding propagandists in London and Washington. They would prove capable of producing highly emotive videos on YouTube that would seduce young and old throughout the *Umma,* and deftly deploy social media to reach into the bedrooms of disaffected young Muslims to groom them into believing in the paradise of the Islamic caliphate. The Jihadist war was ratcheted up to a much more rapid tempo, in Europe and the Middle East. The 'pure' caliphate had been reborn – it had been the dream of Islamists for generations, if not centuries.

*Chapter 5*

# The Rise of the Islamic State

On 29 June 2014 the new worldwide caliphate was declared, claiming the allegiance of Muslims everywhere: 1.6 billion people, almost a quarter of the planet's population. It was led by Abu Bakr al-Baghdadi, the *nom de guerre* of Ibrahim Awwad Ibrahim Ali Muhammad al-Badri al-Samarrai, born, near Samarra, Iraq, on 28 July 1971. To his followers he was known more simply as Caliph Ibrahim. Also dubbed the 'Invisible Sheikh' because of his low profile, he was particularly secretive about his movements; even when he met his own commanders he would be masked up. This was prudent because of the number of senior Jihadists killed by US air strikes or special forces' operations. In addition, he had a bounty on his head of $10 million. In March 2015 it was rumoured that he was seriously injured and remained paralysed after a US bombing raid.

Details about his private life are few and contradictory; it seems that he was a humble cleric in a rundown part of Baghdad when the Americans captured the city in 2003. He was bright – apparently he obtained a doctorate in Islamic studies. American occupation galvanised his commitment to Jihadism. He was arrested by the Americans in February 2004 and spent some time (possibly four to five years) at the Bucca US internment camp. His length of stay is disputed, but other Jihadists who knew him there claim he was a natural leader in what became an unofficial university of Jihadism, run unwittingly by the Americans. He was eventually released because military intelligence considered him a very low-grade threat. Al-Baghdadi went on to lead a number of insurgent groups, demonstrating his intelligence, organisational abilities and sound tactical skills in planning attacks. His mix of ruthlessness and piety paved the way eventually to the position of caliph, though many leading Muslim scholars have rejected this claim. Nevertheless, in July 2014, he issued a video of his sermon in Mosul: the effect was electrifying for Jihadists worldwide. He asserted his religious, political and military authority over Muslims throughout the *Umma* and urged them to join the only state which was true to the original ideals of the Prophet.

He is rumoured to have had three wives. The story of his meeting one via online dating sounds unlikely. The wives came from Syria and Iraq. One of his wives was allegedly captured in Lebanon along with the caliph's daughter. He is also said to have fathered a son. Some of his actual extended family still live in Baghdad. Importantly, the new caliph claims that his family is originally from the Qurayshi tribe. The Prophet came from this tribe and its members are supposed to have divinely ordained leadership qualities.

This new caliph, originally considered quiet and unassuming, something of a bookworm, and, according to US military intelligence, unthreatening, created a political earthquake in the Middle East. How did he do this?

Since the rise of Wahhabism in the eighteenth century many attempts have been made to revive the caliphate. The Ottoman version was considered corrupt and even apostate, as were some of the earlier successor caliphates that followed Muhammad's death. Today's caliphate claims to represent the purest strand of Salafist Sunni militant Jihadism. Salafists are very divided – some eschew politics and militancy completely – but they are united in their desire to return to the fundamental tenets of the Prophet and his immediate followers, 'the pious forefathers'.

The current Jihadist caliphate originated in a radical group formed in 1999, which pledged allegiance to al-Qaeda in 2004 during the uprising in Iraq. In 2006 it joined other Sunni groups to form the Mujahedin Shura Council, which claimed to set up the new caliphate in October 2006: the Islamic State of Iraq. The Americans had other ideas and, with persuasion, force and dollars, manipulated some Sunni tribes in Anbar province to turn on the al-Qaeda affiliates. They were suppressed though they were not completely eliminated. That was enough for Washington to declare victory and leave Iraq. As the US began to draw down its troops and Baghdad's government succumbed to extreme sectarianism, in May 2010 Abu Bakr al-Baghdadi was appointed leader of the Islamic State of Iraq. He started to rebuild an organisation debilitated by many arrests and deaths at the hands of American and Iraqi government forces. One of the key factors in the movement's resurrection was the absorption of some able ex-Ba'athist combat and intelligence officers, notably Colonel Samir al-Khlifawi. This very able intelligence officer, nicknamed the Lord of the Shadows, played a big part in planning military operations before he was killed, by accident, in early 2014 in a firefight with rival Syrian Jihadists.

Al-Khlifawi, who used a pseudonym of Haji Bakr, was probably the most important single factor in the rise of IS. He was considered a rising star in

Saddam Hussein's intelligence service, based in the air defence force. He was highly able, serious, though not at all religious. Before al-Baghdadi became what some consider a titular leader, Haji Bakr was heavily involved in liaising between the Sunni insurgents in Iraq and Syrian intelligence. Haji Bakr often had meetings in Damascus to discuss the means of ejecting the Americans from Iraq. The clever intelligence officer set about designing – in minute detail – how the caliphate would work. When the Islamists captured large parts of northern Syria he took up residence, with his wife, in a very unremarkable house in Tal Rifaat, north of Aleppo. When rival militias captured half of Tal Rifaat in late January 2014, he was caught in the wrong half – he had refused to move to the heavily guarded IS HQ because of his addiction to living in the shadows. But one of his neighbours betrayed him by saying 'A Daesh sheikh lives next door'. The rival militiamen forced their way in and Haji Bakr, in his late 50s and very grandfatherly in his white beard, fought back with his AK. Outgunned, he was killed and the militiamen had no idea they had eliminated the most capable man in IS. Some of his papers were later smuggled out into Turkey and they reveal a master plan to set up informers in every village, using *Dawah* offices as camouflage in the areas IS planned to capture. These offices were supposed to be for Islamic missionary work; in fact they were the centres of intelligence on everybody of any influence in the town. The closest parallel was the Stasi in East Germany. Meticulous organisation, not just terror, was to be a hallmark of IS success. Before his death, the spymaster had organised a campaign called 'Breaking the Walls': hundreds of veteran fighters were freed in daring raids on government prisons. They also started a wave of car bombings in Baghdad.

Just before the outbreak of the revolt in Syria, I had a conversation in a plush Damascus hotel with the dashing young commander of the country's presidential guard. He was irate that the Americans were so critical of Damascus. 'In the last few months my men have arrested over 2,000 al-Qaeda insurgents who were crossing the border from Iraq. And we are going to keep hold of them. We are certainly *not* helping the insurgency in Iraq.' I had no reason to doubt his word then. President Bashar al-Assad, an anglophile, educated in the UK, and married to Asma, a Sunni who was born and studied in London, was always hostile to Jihadism. Asma was even for a while the darling of women's magazines in the West. Bashar's father, President Hafez al-Assad, was infamous for his persecution of Islamists. So it was one of the paradoxes of the Arab Spring that al-Assad was demonised by the West (like Saddam and Gaddafi) and yet he later became a crucial implicit ally of the war on the Islamic State (after helping it initially – just like Turkey). Al-Assad was of course no bleeding-heart, tree-hugging liberal: his suppression of the first, mainly peaceful, protests against his regime was brutal. Above all, he came to be condemned for his alleged use of chemical weapons against his own people, although some intelligence experts, not all Russians, claim that the chemical agents were planted to draw in Washington to bomb the Damascus regime for crossing Obama's 'red line' – the use of banned weapons. It was strange that the Assad government should deploy chemical weapons in Gouta, a suburb of Damascus, on 21 August 2013, three days after UN weapons inspectors arrived in the city.

I spoke to Gwyn Winfield, one of Britain's leading authorities on chemical weapons, who does not agree with my suspicions of the standard Western line. This is his view:

> The 'who' and the 'why' are some of the most difficult questions to answer regarding Ghouta. Numerous theories have emerged pointing the finger at actors as diverse as Turkey and Saudi Arabia. The most likely, due to the amount of research done on it by individuals such as Eliot Higgins, is that it was Syrian forces. Their continued use of chlorine shows that they clearly lack any moral or ethical objection to the use of chemical agents, in addition to which they were the only confirmed possessor of chemical warfare agents and the means to launch them. The one element that has still to be tackled is the issue of Assad's biological weapons, which are still a lethal working element of Assad's CBRN [Chemical, Biological, Radiological and Nuclear] arsenal.[21]

The presidential guard general whom I had interviewed subsequently defected to London to assist the Free Syrian Army which, although armed and trained by the West and Saudi Arabia, had little success on the battlefields – though in 2015 it made some progress in the south using bases in Jordan.

The civil war in Syria completely changed the Jihadist campaign in Iraq, because it offered so many opportunities for Sunni expansion. It also changed the balance of power between the Sunni and Shi'ite populations in both countries. The Alawites (a creed related to Shia) were just 12 per cent of the Syrian population and in Iraq the Shi'ites were the majority, but now the *regional* Sunni adherents were lining up to form an overall majority. The

Islamic state of Iraq worked with, and often against, various al-Qaeda franchises in northern Syria. It is a complex story, but in essence the Iraqi Jihadists helped create what is commonly called in English the al-Nusra Front, which was committed to fighting the Assad government in Damascus. In April 2013 al-Baghdadi announced that al-Nusra and the Islamic State of Iraq would merge to form The Islamic State of Iraq and the Levant. Nobody had bothered to tell some of the senior al-Nusra leaders. 'Iraqis' and 'Syrians' fell out and the new al-Qaeda boss, Ayman al-Zawahiri, was asked to adjudicate according to Islamic jurisprudence. Al-Qaeda had already complained about the tactical excesses and brutality of al-Baghdadi's leadership. For al-Qaeda to be positioned on the 'liberal left' of any organisation said a lot about IS extremism. Al-Baghdadi, however, refused to accept the intercession by the Egyptian head of al-Qaeda. Some Al-Nusra people, notably the Chechens, came over to al-Baghdadi. The disputes continued about the primacy of removing Assad or consolidating conquered territories; some Syrian Jihadists claimed al-Baghdadi was in the pocket of al-Assad. Sometimes Jihadists combined to fight Syrian government forces and sometimes they fought each other, with the al-Baghdadi troops usually gaining the upper hand. In February 2014 al-Baghdadi formally separated from al-Qaeda and in June he went his own way politically, ideologically and militarily by announcing the caliphate.

*The geo-politics of the Islamic State's rise*
The Islamic State's success could perhaps be the result of al-Baghdadi's neo-Napoleonic genius as a warrior; he was certainly a good organiser, though no modern-day Saladin (yet). Nevertheless, he made the Islamic State (IS) much more powerful than al-Qaeda was at its peak. Al-Qaeda was little more than an idea, its terrorism a rallying cry for Jihadism; its organisation was weak. Bin Laden had corporatised and franchised Jihadist terror, whereas IS is also an idea, though one that has built an army capable of amazing victories just like the Prophet's forces; *and* it is a physical state, a home to summon the faithful to fulfil the endgame prophesied in the Koran. IS poses a very real danger not only to Western interests in the Middle East, but to the West itself. The threat comes as much from regional competition among Muslim nations as the power of IS to attract recruits and funding from neighbouring Arab states.

Firstly, Saudi Arabia and Pakistan have proved much more inimical to Washington's interests than even al-Qaeda and IS. Earlier chapters demonstrated how Pakistan had deliberately sabotaged NATO operations in Afghanistan. Likewise, the Saudis were initially tireless spoilers in the US war against IS. The Saudis and some Gulf Arab states, especially Qatar, poured money and weapons into Syria, much of it intended for the Jihadists. It is true that Riyadh is genuinely concerned about the blowback effect of Saudi *Mujahedin* coming back home to create Jihad cells in its own backyard. The overriding passion of the royal family, however, is the war with the Shia, especially Iran. The Saudi detestation of Shi'ism and Shi'ites dominates everything. Hence the support for fellow Sunni Wahhabis in their battles with Iranian-backed Shia rulers in Baghdad and the Alawite despot in Damascus. The Saudi government dramatically altered course in late 2014, however. Washington did some arm twisting, but the Saudis soon began to fear the IS Juggernaut even more than the West.

The Islamic State began in Iraq and indeed established a so-called caliphate as far back as 2006, though it was the Syrian civil war that provided the real impetus. The Syrian tragedy began as a genuine popular protest against a brutal dictatorship with loud demands for the introduction of democratic reforms. The reality is more confusing, as is the degree of Western involvement in encouraging it. It may have been a democratic internal affair initially, though it became enmeshed in the Sunni versus Alawite clash that soon overflowed into the Sunni versus Shia antagonism in the region as a whole. The standoff consisted of the Saudi standard bearers and their Gulf allies, combined with the Sunni tribes in Syria and Iraq. They faced off against Iran, the Lebanese Shia in the form of the most efficient Arab fighting machine in the Middle East, Hezbollah – as the Israelis found out during their disastrous land incursion into southern Lebanon in 2006 – plus the aggressively sectarian Shia government of Nouri al-Maliki in Baghdad. Behind him stood Tehran and its extensive use of Al-Quds, the special forces of the Iranian Revolutionary Guards. Superimposed on this was the revived Cold War between the US and Russia, nourishing its old ally Damascus; Cold War Mark 2 was whipped up not only by NATO bombing Libya, but by Moscow and its ethnic Russian allies trying to carve out a separate Russian state in Ukraine. The current Middle Eastern turmoil has been compared with the Thirty Years War in Europe in the seventeenth century that ended in the Treaty of Westphalia (1648). It was an ideological schism which brooked little compromise; everyone kept fighting despite the devastation because all thought they were about to win and no *deus ex machina* could bang heads together to make them seek peace. Eventually mass death and extreme exhaustion prompted a deal.[22]

*The course of the war*

The decisive event in the IS war was the capture of Mosul, Iraq's northern capital, on 10 June 2014, after a lightning Jihadist advance. Mosul was Iraq's second biggest city with a population of around 1.5 million people, and it was heavily defended by the Iraqi army. The defending troops, however, ran away, as its officers deserted in helicopters and Humvees; the senior officers were nearly all al-Maliki cronies chosen for party loyalty or adherence to the Shia ideology. The ordinary soldiers threw away their uniforms and escaped where they could, although hundreds more were taken prisoner and executed in public by IS. Modern and highly valuable US equipment, especially tanks and 2,300 Humvees, were captured as well as hundreds of millions of US dollars and other foreign currency in the Mosul banks. The city had been captured ten years before by Sunni insurgents. Nevertheless, the speed of the blitzkrieg constituted one of the most surprising victories in modern military history especially as the IS *Mujahedin* were outnumbered perhaps 20:1 and they were attacking a heavily fortified defensive position. Crucially, the Sunni majority in the city either welcomed or at least condoned the IS takeover, not least to end what was seen as Shia oppression from Baghdad. Many welcomed the flight of the army whose rapacious checkpoints had sucked dry small businesses as well as ordinary travellers. Mosul's inhabitants might not have been looking forward to the strictures of *Sharia* that they knew were coming, especially in a country of compulsive smokers and many whiskey aficionados, but at least they would be bossed around by their own Sunni people.

Not surprisingly IS attributed its triumph to divine intervention, although there was no corroborated sighting of angels in the vanguard. The IS warriors did fight well, but the reason they won was not because they were so good: it was because the American-trained Iraqi army was so bad. And yet IS also pushed deeply into Kurdistan, and got within striking distance of the capital, Erbil. The Kurdish Peshmerga also surprised the West by not living up to its macho reputation. Divided by loyalties to the two main Iraqi Kurdish parties, the Peshmergha had proved themselves good at mountain ambushes, often against Kurdish rivals, but less effective against IS. Ordinary Kurdish male and female fighters, however, fighting for their lives and nationhood, soon rallied and pushed back the overstretched IS troops.

The Obama administration responded quickly by forming a coalition of Western and Arab states to intervene. After all, this was largely an Arab problem and the Sunni versus Shia drivers were entirely Islamic. Saudi, Jordanian and other Arab warplanes were soon in action in real wars for the first time. Nobody wanted to put troops on the ground, however. Weary of ground wars, countries such as the US and Britain confined their support for their allies in Iraq to sending small training units plus equipment to help the Kurds and also to boost the demoralised Iraqi army huddled in Baghdad. IS troops advanced to the capital's outskirts. Iraq's army had stood at 350,000 soldiers; over $40 billion had been spent on it in the previous three years. The trouble was it simply lacked the will to fight. Baghdad was guarded not by the humiliated army and police, but by Iranian-led Shia militias that bristled with the religious fervour to match IS troops praying for martyrdom.

The US-led air campaign did help to slow the sudden IS advance in Iraq. In late September 2014 the Americans extended the air campaign to areas in Syria occupied by IS. The Cameron government, unable to get parliamentary backing, confined air sorties by the RAF to Iraq. Washington insisted that America was not co-ordinating with the al-Assad government, itself fighting IS troops in the suburbs of Damascus. Working openly with Damascus, a regime the Saudis, Turkey *et al* wanted to topple, was not appealing to Western diplomats, and contradicted the Western blurb about Syria.

The West made endless mistakes in Syria, but the most egregious was the assumption that al-Assad would fall quickly, just like Gaddafi. Or for that matter Saddam in 2003. Both dictators had been brought down by Western air power *and* ground troops. In Libya's case it was a replay of the Northern alliance – local fighters allied with Western special forces. Without NATO firepower, the Libyan rebels would have been crushed at Benghazi. The Syrian case was markedly different from that of Libya for one simple reason. There would be no re-run of broad international support, including from Russia and China, for a no-fly zone that was then unilaterally interpreted by NATO countries as a *carte blanche* not just to prevent Libyan air assets being used, but to destroy the Libyan military *en masse* on the ground and in the air by way of co-ordinated, direct assistance to anti-government militias. Anger at this manipulation of the Libyan UN no-fly zone resolution would mean that Russia and China would not agree to any similar UN resolutions regarding Syria. Also, Russia has its priorities in Syria, including its special relationship with al-Assad and tenure of a naval base at Latakia.

Perhaps if the UK House of Commons in London had not voted against air intervention in Syria in August 2013, then the Obama administration would have carried out the air strikes promised after the use of chemical weapons. Al-Assad might then have fallen *before* the Jihadist triumph. Conversely, many left-wing critics in Europe blame Western intervention for the growth of Islamist extremism. Yet, in the case of the al-Assad regime, the West did not intervene – except for a trickle of military support for the Free Syrian Army – and still the Jihadist advance went into overdrive.

The one local player that had the air power and the ground troops in spades was Turkey. It held many of the best cards, because its long borders with IS allowed the massive smuggling of arms, oil and people. Ankara wanted to weaken (or topple) al-Assad and yet also encourage IS to batter the Kurds both in Syria and Iraq. Turkey's highly effective armed forces, if they engaged on the ground in Syria, would probably empower their long-term opponent, the Kurdish PKK,[23] especially at a time when Turkish Kurds were making unprecedented electoral gains in parliamentary seats. The Syrian Kurds (YPG)[24] were also fighting IS with gusto. In addition, numerous militias had sprouted, especially in the north. Syria was fragmenting under the weight of rival armed factions. Turkey, Saudi Arabia and Jordan began to consider seizing border areas as a *cordon sanitaire*, just as Israel had once done in Lebanon (and might do again across the Golan Heights). If Russia hadn't been sanctioned and put into *purdah* by the EU and US, Vladimir Putin might have helped – Damascus still talked to Moscow. Probably a great-power *demarche* may still be the only way of ending the Syrian tragedy, though that optimistic scenario is a long way off and much more innocent blood will be spilt. And even if a Syrian solution is eventually found, it still won't resolve the current IS threat. A united Syria and a united Iraq are dead; Humpty Dumpty can never be re-assembled. Colonial borders will be thrown into Trotsky's garbage heap of history. The success of IS is based on transcending *all* borders – as it prepares to expand worldwide.

*IS reaches out to its brothers and sisters in Africa, Asia ... and Europe.*
There are at least fifty Muslim-majority countries in the world, but probably – census figures are not always sectarian-specific – only four have Shia majorities. The point: in the coming Sunni versus Shia apocalypse the 90 per cent Sunni majority is likely to attract more and more Jihadists. For someone brought up in the post-Enlightenment era in the West the victory of the majority of Shia in Iraq after the oppressive rule of the Sunni minority under Saddam may have seemed a major democratic advance. That is supposed to be the way of democracies: majorities rule. That was the *leitmotif* of Western campaigns against apartheid. If the fall of Saddam is

approached from the mindset of the Muslim majority – that is the Sunnis – and especially those still mired in eighteenth-century Wahhabism – then his ousting by America and the installation of the Shia minority (in the region) would seem unjust, especially to the more orthodox Sunnis who regard the 200 million Shi'ites as apostates. Americans might as well have gone the whole hog and installed a rabbi or bishop as the Baghdad boss.

I am obviously exaggerating the point to make the issue clear to Western readers because, for example, many Sunnis and Shia intermarried under Saddam. It is much less common now, not least because areas are segregated in Baghdad, as a result of ethnic cleansing caused by the current war. Thus, changing governments to match the local majority might theoretically be a good thing within the Beltway in Washington, or in North London, but it is deemed highly offensive by many in the Islamic world (as well as in Belfast). To change the balance of sectarian power in a Muslim country is rare. One of the last occasions was when Saladin, a Sunni, brought down the crumbling Shia-oriented Fatimid dynasty in Egypt in 1171. Adherence to the tenets of the Koran brings with it an understanding of history, so to many Sunni leaders the perceived Iranian takeover of Baghdad was a call to take up arms. Yet to many Shi'ites in the crescent that runs from Iran and the Gulf through Iraq and Syria into Lebanon, the IS Sunni counter-revolution was not only a summons to fight, but both a religious and existential duty to fight to the death.

Morality aside, it may be strategically sensible for the West to stay out of the Muslim version of the wars of religion that nearly destroyed Europe in the seventeenth century. Western intervention usually makes things worse – everywhere. It may be wise for America to butt out of a theological Muslim divide that has raged for fourteen centuries. Let the Muslim brothers and sisters work it out or fight it out. One problem with this argument is the existence and proliferation of nuclear weapons, especially Pakistan's. So perhaps ethics and military strategy might compel the West to assume more than a watching brief.

The Sunni-Shia cataclysm has been rather more academic to the many Sunni Muslims living in Asian and African countries, where Shi'ites are thin on the ground; nevertheless many in these regions have responded with alacrity to the call of the caliphate. Modern Jihadism had expanded rapidly *before* the rise of IS, partly reinvigorated by al-Qaeda's spectaculars. In October 2002 Indonesian Jihadists in *Jemaah Islamiya* used bombs to kill 202 people, mainly Western tourists, on the Indonesian holiday island of Bali. A Muslim insurgency in another part of Indonesia was fought in Aceh.

The long-running Rohingya insurgency in Burma also attracted foreign Jihadists. If ever there was a case of genuine repression of Muslims it has been in Burma. They constitute around 4 per cent of the population, but a movement led by Buddhist monks – supposedly the most peaceful people on earth – has driven 200,000 Muslims from their homes. They created a new wave of boat migrants in the region. It is strange that the pin-up girl of Western humanitarian interventionists, Aung San Suu Kyi, has said almost nothing about Buddhist repression. Muslims have also been persecuted in Sri Lanka, first by the Tamil Tiger insurgents and more recently by the Buddhist-dominated government in Colombo. The most extensive Asian Muslim revolt was in the Philippines; the fighters in the Moro Liberation Front pledged allegiance to IS in August 2014. The long-running war in Kashmir also continues to suck in foreign Jihadists, organised by Pakistan's ISI.

One of the most alluring, and largely unreported, developments in Islamic history took place in the paradise islands of the Maldives. Most people go there on honeymoon to explore each other, not the politics of the Indian Ocean archipelago. Until 2008 its president had been the longest-serving dictator in Asia. Then a young opposition leader, Mohamed Nasheed, won an unexpected electoral victory. I must declare an interest here as Mohamed, popularly known as Anni in the 200 islands, is an acquaintance of mine; he is one of the few politicians I have met who is also a really decent human being. After many periods in jail, including torture, he was considered the Asian Mandela, and became an Amnesty International's 'prisoner of conscience'. I made two films for UK Channel 4 TV with this theme. So Anni invited me to spend the first few hours of his first day in power with him. Many warlords and aspiring politicians had promised me the first interview in the presidential palace when they managed to win power by bullet or ballot, but Anni was the only one who kept his word. In this 99 per cent Sunni Muslim state he won a free and fair democratic election, overturning a dictatorship, without shedding a single drop of blood, and crucially without the presence of a single foreign soldier. One of his first cabinet meetings was held under water – with all the politicians in scuba gear – to dramatise the threat of global warning to his sinking country where the highest ground is six metres. Unfortunately, the idealistic young president was overturned in a 2012 military coup, relatives of the former dictator took over, Islamist extremists started to infiltrate and the black flag of IS has appeared at some demonstrations. The Maldives, though, is perhaps one of the very few Muslim states that could return soon to a Western-style democracy while still respecting Islam.

Elsewhere in Asia the Islamic State was on the march. In early 2015 the Islamic Movement of Uzbekistan signed up to the caliphate. In Afghanistan, the last country that needed more gun-toting religious fanatics, the Taliban were deemed too moderate by some and IS started to make major inroads in the east, especially south of Jalalabad, along the Pakistan border. Better armed and better funded than the Taliban, they did not demand that villagers fed and housed them, although they were stricter than the Taliban, immediately banning cigarettes and burning opium stocks. Some Taliban – especially younger elements – joined the sexy new movement, while other Taliban fighters took on IS. Sometimes Kabul government forces looked on in bemusement, and let them get on with killing each other. Jihadists call large parts of Afghanistan and Pakistan 'Khorasan Province'. Pro-IS insurgents emerged in Pakistan as well as Afghanistan; and Afghan *Mujahedin* were also to be found in Iraq and Syria.

In Africa the picture was more depressing as far as the West was concerned. Jihadists gained control of the Libyan city of Derna and pledged allegiance to the new caliph in October 2014. This was the first city outside the caliphate to swear loyalty to the black flag. Next the old Phoenician city of Sirte, and the former stronghold of Gaddafi, was taken over. IS influence spread rapidly in an anarchic country awash with weapons. IS fighters were temporarily driven out of Derna in mid-2015, but elsewhere Libyan Islamists flocked to the black battle flag of the Prophet. The country was divided into three historical provinces and IS *claimed* authority over Cyrenaica in the east, Fezzan in the desert south and Tripolitania in the west, around the capital.

The most dramatic spread of IS in Africa occurred in March 2015 when Boko Haram activists in Nigeria signed up to al-Baghdadi to become the Islamic State's West Africa Province. Boko Haram had also penetrated Niger, Chad and Cameroon. Nigerian government forces, ill-equipped and poorly led, had proved as ineffective as Iraq's, but a stiffening of Western advisers plus regular troops from the neighbouring states helped to curb the Jihadist advance. This was a rare example of local counter-insurgency forces joining the dots and fighting collectively to a coherent strategy. But like the tearing up of colonial boundaries in the Middle East, Nigeria's old divisions between the Islamic north and the largely Christian south might repeat the Sudanese experience under the pressure of Jihadist atrocities – namely secession.

Elsewhere, in North Africa, IS claimed in 2015 a number of attacks in

Tunisia, especially on Western tourists in Tunis and the infamous beach massacre of thirty-eight holidaymakers. Islamic State was recruiting and training Tunisians in Libya – using 'clean skins', locals with little or no record of activism. Also, thousands of Tunisians had joined the ranks of the caliphate and some could be sent home to cause mayhem. When, in July 2015, the British Foreign and Commonwealth Office – plus similar warnings from other EU states – said another attack was imminent, thousands of British tourists were immediately flown home. This could be the death knell of the vital Tunisian tourist industry, which would badly damage the economy. This in turn plays into IS hands – to bring down the government and create the kind of chaos, as in Libya, where Jihadism can flourish. And it also helps to purge another Islamic country of bikinis, booze and other decadent examples of Western corruption of the Prophet's message. Tunisia also has a long border with Algeria, which had endured one of the most bitter Islamist insurgencies (as well as the most savage anti-colonial conflicts). Unsurprisingly, IS has claimed supporters there too.

On the Arabian peninsula, IS took advantage of the complicated civil war in Yemen, involving Sunni versus Shia, Iranian and Saudi interventions and lots of local tribalism, plus al-Qaeda, to incubate its popularity amid the chaos in the poorest of Arab states. In February 2015 the majority of *Ansar al-Sharia*, an umbrella organisation of Islamist groups in Yemen, broke off their allegiance to al-Qaeda in the Arabian Peninsula to join IS. In the Sinai peninsula some of the Jihadists took the *bayaa,* the oath of allegiance, to IS. The estimated 1,000 to 2,000 Egyptian *Mujahedin* took the name of the Sinai Province of IS. This branch of IS has been murderously efficient, assassinating Egypt's chief prosecutor, overrunning military bases, killing and wounding hundreds of soldiers and attacking (and possibly sinking) an Egyptian naval vessel with a guided missile. A smaller faction of this group also claimed to operate in Gaza. Hamas, not known for its multicultural sensitivities, could either absorb or eliminate them.

Besides a largely rhetorical allegiance of armed groups in the countries mentioned above – some quite large as in Nigeria – perhaps only in Sinai and Libya can it be suggested that the fighters are directly linked to IS control. The caliphate also boasted branches and members in Morocco, Lebanon, Jordan, Turkey, Palestine and, interestingly, Israel among its 20 per cent Arab minority population.

The north Caucasus part of the Russian federation is usually defined as European, though the Islamic State doesn't care for such border definitions. The aspiring emirates of Chechnya and Dagestan had pledged allegiance to

IS, which designated a new North Caucasus *Wilayat* or province. In Western Europe, notably Italy, IS claimed to have infiltrated over 4,000 fighters among smuggled refugees from the Levant and North Africa. They were told to go underground to form attack groups in retaliation for Western air strikes. The numbers claimed seem too high, but Western intelligence agencies took the threat seriously. Part of the IS agenda was to take back the old lands once held by their pious forefathers. Al-Andalus in modern Spain and Portugal was once a jewel in the crown of the Muslim empire. It may be argued that the Islamic administration in lands that are no longer in Muslim possession  was possibly better than it is now, especially in the former Ottoman territory of Greece (in times of Turkish rule, the majority of Greeks were Christian). Yet such an Islamic future for Western Europe is dependent upon IS winning its multi-generational struggle. The murderous attack by two Islamic gunmen on the offices of *Charlie Hebdo*, a French satirical magazine, in Paris in January 2015, suggests that this is, and will continue to be, a long war. And in the end it depends on the ability of IS to recruit new activists and expand its operations inside western countries. To understand how this frightening prospect might happen, it would be useful to look *inside* the caliphate.

*Chapter 6*

# Inside the Caliphate

The Islamic State is an efficient fighting force, but its victories are not purely the result of domestic spontaneous combustion in Iraq and Syria. It has had to trade and deal with outsiders. It is a landlocked state, however, and bigger than the UK, with perhaps ten million inhabitants. It is surrounded by enemies, many of whom are conducting daily drone attacks or air raids by the most modern aircraft. How can IS survive? How does IS operate? How is it financed? What is life like inside the warrior state that wants to go back to the norms of the seventh century, while conjuring with the magic of modern technology, especially their very advanced manipulation of social media?

*The IS mission*
Al-Baghdadi claims descent from Muhammad and so believes that, by returning to pure Islamic roots, Allah will allow the new caliphate to regain its former glory – and lands. He claims he has the right to call on all Muslims to help him do just that, *inshallah*. When the caliphate was proclaimed in June 2014 in a sermon in the prestigious al-Nuri mosque in Mosul, a statement was issued, part of which read: 'The legality of all emirates, groups, states and organisations becomes null by the expansion of the caliphate's authority and arrival of its troops to their areas.' This was not just ripping up the Sykes-Picot borders in the Middle East, it was also a declaration of intent to secure the lands conquered by the Arabs in the seventh to eighth centuries. First the near enemies – the corrupt Arab states – then the far enemies, the West, would be overcome. In the meanwhile, IS would restore Israel to the Palestinian brothers, though Christian Palestinians should not hold their breath. Islamic State has published maps showing the lands once ruled by Muslims – this, of course, includes large parts of Europe. Maps were also produced that indicated new emirates in North America; that would take some time. Man-made borders, just like man-made legal systems, including voting in democracies, are deemed *shirk*, apostasy – for which the punishment is death.

As with the original conquests, it may not always be accomplished by the sword. Many Christians willingly converted to Islam with the arrival of Allah's warriors in the Middle East, North Africa and Europe. They might have appreciated the better law and order, or the simple purity of the new faith, or perhaps they just decided to pay less tax. Muslims believe that people do not 'convert' but 'revert' to Islam. According to the doctrine of *fitrah,* all humans are born with an innate desire to worship the true God. So when non-Muslims see the light, they are returning – reverting – to belief in Allah. IS is founded, as we have seen, on the most extreme version of Islam, a mix of militant Salafism and Wahhabism. Those who do not agree with its millenarian worldview – including many eminent Muslim clerics – are regarded as apostates, deserving of the same rough justice as Shi'ites, Jews and Christians. The roots of IS are debated – some scholars emphasise the connection with the twentieth-century Muslim Brotherhood; others stress the eighteenth-century Wahhabi influence. It should be said, however, that many in the Muslim Brotherhood are horrified by the IS phenomenon. The textbooks used in IS-controlled schools are Wahhabi religious textbooks from Saudi Arabia. Many of the IS judges are Saudis who follow Wahhabi practices. The core philosophy of IS is precisely symbolised by its flag, a variant of the battle flag of Muhammad. It shows the seal of Muhammad within a white circle. Written above it in Arabic is 'There is no God but Allah'.

Despite its reliance on other Islamist traditions, IS likes to emphasise its purity in its return to the seventh-century morality. It condemns some of the later caliphates and the Ottomans for deviating from the faith. Anyone who follows secular law is a disbeliever, which would include the Saudis. Only the IS caliphate has the authority to call for Jihad. First, by force or persuasion, Muslim societies must be purified, and then the non-believers elsewhere will be reverted or conquered. This leads IS into surprising byways: Hamas fighters are regarded as apostates, who have no right to wage Jihad against Israel – Jerusalem will be re-conquered in due course by IS. Unlike al-Qaeda, IS espouses a strong apocalyptic belief in the imminence of the end of days. IS will defeat 'the army of Rome' (presumably the Americans) in the north Syrian town of Dabiq in a final climactic battle between believers and unbelievers. This at least should enable US intelligence to avoid being caught unawares again. The problem is the prophecies, in the *Hadith,* are not clear as to precisely *when* this will happen. IS interprets the prophecies to mean that only four caliphs will succeed al-Baghdadi before the final Armageddon. Whether this means that four sure-sighted CIA drones can bring on the apocalypse is as unclear as Christian scholars' frustrations with interpreting today's politics in the light of St John's Revelations. IS takes the end times vision very seriously. Its main recruiting and propaganda magazine is called *Dabiq*. So it is not only dangerous, but perhaps even foolish, for unbelievers to mock these messianic beliefs. If your opponents believe them, best to take them at face value. The same mistake was made by the British in Sudan when they completely misread and underestimated the local messiah, the Mahdi, who inflicted the greatest humiliation of the Victorian empire at Khartoum in 1885. Caveat scoffers.

In view of the strict beheadings policy of IS, it might be better to leave the criticism to Islamists, especially Salafist and even Jihadist muftis. They accuse IS of being *Khawarij* or heretics. 'They have existed since the very early period of Islam and they will continue to cause strife in the Muslim nation until the end of time when they will join forces with the False Messiah,' according to some Muslim scholars. Other hard-line Islamists, including Saudi imams, regard IS as anti-Islamic imperialists. By driving a wedge between Muslims, they are doing the work of, or are even in the pay of, the usual suspects – 'Zionists, Crusaders and Safavids' (Iranians). In late 2014 a group of Islamic scholars from around the world penned an open letter to the new caliph. 'You have misinterpreted Islam into a religion of harshness, brutality and torture … this is a great wrong and an offence to Islam, Muslims and to the entire world.' Saudi imams have also added nuance to the critique. They said that IS warriors were executing people for violating *Sharia* law, but they themselves were encouraging women to migrate to its territory, travelling without a male guardian or even against his wishes. They stopped short of suggesting it was *haram* for women to drive in the caliphate. Some but not all Islamic scholars in the West have also roundly condemned *Daesh*, the rather pejorative Arabic acronym for IS. Authorities in the caliphate are very touchy about their nomenclature. I have used 'Islamic State' because that's what they call themselves (in translation).

One of the most eminent Western scholars of the early Islamic period is British historian Tom Holland. In his writings he has made the relevant point that IS is *very* Islamic. When they smash the statues of pagan gods, they are strictly following the example of the Prophet. When they boast they are the shock troops of a would-be global religious empire, they are precisely emulating the early caliphs. When they execute non-Muslim enemy combatants and take their women as slaves or impose unfair taxes on

Christians, this is what the early Muslim chronicles of the conquest gloried in. Since *all* Muslims believe in regression to the ideals of the Prophet, it is very difficult to call IS 'unIslamic'. They are extremists in their behaviour, but not in their beliefs.

*Conspiracies and truths*

A large number of Muslims no doubt believe that Allah is the greatest supporter of IS. If some Muslim critics, however, claim IS is guided by Mossad, Washington and Tehran, then that may be the least of the conspiracy theories. Turkey is mainly in the line of fire, not least because it has a long border with IS, and Ankara is capable of policing its borders much more effectively than it does. Numerous reports have circulated of Turkish intelligence agents supporting IS. Extensive trade in people, oil and weapons has gone on across the border. It has been dubbed the 'Gateway to Jihad', especially when so many Western would-be Jihadists – including three generations of one British family from Luton – transited the country, until NATO and especially British intelligence kicked up a fuss. Certainly in the early days of the IS revolution, Ankara was very helpful, even with treating IS wounded fighters in Turkish hospitals. The Turks might just have been hospitable to fellow Sunnis, though the evidence adds up to intentional support of armed opposition to the Damascus regime that Turkey definitely wanted to remove. Or did, until the West started to rethink its policy of ousting al-Assad. In late July 2015 Turkey entered the air war against the Islamic State to hit IS targets inside Syria near the Turkish border. Ankara also launched air raids against PKK bases in northern Iraqi Kurdistan. Critics assumed that Turkey was far more interested in undermining the Kurds rather than IS. That is the reason it agreed with Washington to set up a so-called 'safe area' on its border – to curb Syrian Kurds' desire to set up their own self-governing enclaves.

Qatar was also in the frame for supporting IS. The small, very rich country had always tried to punch above its weight – one of the reasons for launching al-Jazeera in its capital, Doha. As with the Saudis, the argument for the defence is that *private* benefactors *in the past* backed al-Nusra and IS, as well as continuing to support the Free Syrian Army, on Washington's advice. This is a little like the standard Pakistani defence that *rogue* ISI officials *may* have backed the Taliban *in the past.* Qatar had very publicly supported the Muslim Brotherhood in Egypt until the military coup. That is why Cairo's new military government singled out al-Jazeera journalists for harsh prison terms. Doha had long been a haven for exiled Islamists and

Jihadists and the reason it was the venue for the endless peace talks about ending the war in Darfur. The Saudis have pumped billions into preaching Wahhabism in *madrassahs* (religious schools) around the globe and have paid for Salafist insurgencies from the Philippines to Afghanistan. The Americans knew all about Saudi money funding the Free Syrian Army, but could never sufficiently *prove* that Riyadh directed that some of those arms should go to the various Jihadist groups fighting al-Assad.

One of the most counter-intuitive accusations is that al-Assad was supporting IS. His main political platform has always been that he was a bulwark against terrorism, especially al-Qaeda types. This held little water at the beginning of the rebellion, but then it became a self-fulfilling reality. An EU enquiry reported that oil was bought directly from IS and that government-run plants provided power to IS areas. But Baghdad still paid government salaries, sometimes, to its officials in IS-run areas. A parallel is the fact that the Sri Lankan government paid salaries to teachers and doctors in the zones administered by the Tamil Tigers during the long civil war in that country. More persuasive is an analysis of combat between IS and the Syrian army – attacks are far less – both ways – than al-Assad's onslaught on other rebel groups. The US government accused Damascus of organising air strikes to support an IS advance on Syrian opposition positions around Aleppo. The Syrian government has thus been accused of being the 'air wing of IS'.

If al-Assad really wanted to create an enemy scapegoat to justify Western acceptance or active support, then he has achieved this goal at a very high price. Vivid pictures of the massacre of hundreds of Syrian Alawite soldiers by IS in May 2015 in recently conquered Palmyra were even more obscene against the backdrop of the magnificent ruins of the Greco-Roman and Persian civilisations that made the city a UNESCO heritage site. What will be left after the Islamic State's cultural vandalism is a terrible thought. Meanwhile, perhaps 300,000 Syrians have been killed, four millions have sought refuge outside the country and even more are internally displaced. If al-Assad was callous enough to help create such a monster as IS then he deserves all he gets if IS storms his palace in Damascus – although he would probably be sitting comfortably in a secluded dacha outside Moscow by that stage. Yet al-Assad has proved a great survivor – the longer the IS war goes on, the more the West will need him – if his once-capable army doesn't disintegrate or, more likely, retreat to an Alawite homeland along the Mediterranean coast around Latakia.

Another counter-intuitive proposition is the allegation that the US has connived to indirectly support IS by arming and training so many Free

Syrian Army men who promptly joined al-Nusra and IS. Rand Paul, the US Senator for Kentucky and Republican presidential contender, claimed that Washington's hostility to al-Assad and the initial threat to bomb government forces were aiding and abetting IS. The CIA was aware and probably helped the transfer of much of Gaddafi's arsenal en route to rebels, Islamist and 'moderate', in Syria. Iranian leaders have sometimes made similar allegations that US troops did nothing to stop the IS killings when they were present at the fall of Ramadi. American troops were there as advisors and trainers; taking part in combat again in Iraq could have led to all sorts of diplomatic, let alone military, wrangles. The Arab street is always full of rumours (and sometimes ham-fisted US psy-ops propaganda). Al-Baghdadi was supposed to be Jewish, working for Mossad. And political gossip circulated in what passes for the chattering classes in Tehran that Obama had created IS to contain Iranian power. Ah, people will always believe what they want to believe – the basic principle of propaganda everywhere.

*Running the Islamic State*
Islamic State propaganda tries to create an impression of heaven on earth for observant Sunni Muslims, whereas Western media portrays a slave state run by hypocritical holy fascists, full of beheadings and arbitrary justice. The truth lies somewhere in between perhaps, although the execution of captured journalists has prevented very much independent reporting. The caliphate survives on brute force *and* good governance. And the latter is appreciated after the years of warlordism, especially in Iraq. For a brand new country, the size of Pennsylvania, under constant blitz from jet fighters and drones, IS has managed to create a viable administration. Indeed, its thoroughness is exhibited by its annual survey, something along the lines of a company report, listing its achievements.

Caliph Abu Bakr al-Baghdadi is the equivalent of an executive head of state. He has a cabinet of advisers. His two deputies administer IS territories, Iraq and Syria respectively. Twelve *Walis* or governors of conquered provinces advise the caliph. Beneath the main leadership council are sub-committees dealing in military, intelligence, financial, legal and media matters. Another committee acts as a moral guardian to ensure that all decisions are in accordance with *Sharia*. The Iraqis are said to dominate the organisation, with some Syrians objecting to this domination. Even ardent Syrian Jihadists have complained, *sotto voce*, about Iraqi 'occupation'. On the other hand, Turkmen, the third largest Iraqi group after Arabs and Kurds, are said to be influential, even though historically they had suffered discrimination because of their Ottoman connections. Presumably the governors reflect the local ethnic backgrounds of their provinces to ensure the loyalty of local Sunni tribes. IS imagines itself as an embryonic universal state, but the localised tribal instinct is still strong in Arab culture.

Figures for inhabitants of the state vary though ten million is the average guesstimate. The de facto capital is in Raqqah, in northern Syria. The infrastructure is partly run by former civilian workers of the al-Assad government, provided they take the oath of allegiance to IS. Water supplies are obviously important. The IS capital has been supplied with electricity and water from the nearby dam. This is presumably a target for coalition air strikes, especially as IS has deployed water as a weapon of war elsewhere. It closed the gates of the Nuaimiyah dam in Fallujah in April 2014 causing flooding and water shortages in Shia settlements to the south. Two can play at the water-denial tactic. Before the current war with IS, Turkey's so-called 'neo-Ottoman' policy invested in major dam-building projects, including one called the South-eastern Anatolia Project (or GAP to use the Turkish acronym) that could mean that the amount of water extracted from the mighty Tigris and Euphrates rivers could be so great that they no longer reach the sea. In a few decades, if IS survives, it might run out of water – if Turkey is still an enemy.

The IS administration also tries to provide basic social services such as schools and health facilities. Food is partially rationed, but equally distributed, apparently. Taxes are collected in a way that is regulated by *Sharia*, unlike the rampant extortion and corruption of the previous administrations. Not all foreign volunteers become cannon fodder; some are tasked with helping the administration (though Brits have complained about latrine duties). Courses for women teach basic nursing and domestic duties so they can become 'good wives of the Jihad'.

The Islamic State is a new entity with many untrained administrators. It cannot control everything, so it has tried to leave loyal local councils and bodies largely alone. The many informers will soon tell the emirs if things go astray. Away from the very local administration, IS generally rules with a rod of iron – it has a world to conquer and discipline is vital. A UN human rights report said that IS 'seeks to subjugate civilians under its control and dominate every aspect of their lives through terror, indoctrination, and the provision of services to those who obey.' IS makes no secret of the punishment of those who *don't* obey. It films beheadings of prisoners of war and also punishment of floggings for minor offences such as not fasting during Ramadan.

Amnesty International has released detailed accounts of ethnic and religious cleansing, especially of Alawites, Christians, Yazidis and Druze. Arabisation as well as religious motives seem to be at play. The UN has reported incidents of Arab Sunni clerics being killed for refusing to pledge allegiance to IS. Christians not murdered in the immediate military advance are given three options – in the same manner as the original Arab conquests: convert, pay the *Jizya* tax, or death. Saudi-style religious police enforce the *salat* prayers, the obligation to pray five times a day. Female religious police enforce a strict dress code regarding modesty, especially veils. Women are encouraged to stay at home and go out only when necessary, veiled, and for any journey, with a male guardian. Music is banned and smoking, including hookah pipes, is *haram* (though some front-line fighting cadres smoke in private). IS has restored traditional punishments – execution – for witchcraft, often interpreted as 'fortune-telling', once a popular diversion. *Hadud* punishments, not uncommon in the Islamic world, mean amputations – for theft, for example. Adultery will result in the Koranic punishment of stoning. IS is definitely not a paradise for gays – several videos have been made of IS troops throwing them from tall buildings.

From the Western perspective, the questions will inevitably be: what do you do for fun in IS? It is clear that some young fighters, both locals and foreign, are energised by the Jihad. Some *Mujahedin,* especially on the social media propaganda, are seen as heroes. And they can have four wives. Some of the child soldiers would presumably not be ready for four wives or indeed four mothers-in-law. Allegedly, young pre-teen males are indoctrinated at religious camps, where they are said to practise beheadings on dolls.

Another diversion for bored *Mujahedin* could be a visit to the slave markets. Thousands of Christian and Yazidi women have been enslaved, according to the testimony of a lucky few who survived and escaped from IS. For a society that is super-anxious about the behaviour and dress of women, the regular rape of captives is peculiar. In *Dabiq,* specific Koranic authority for enslavement of non-Muslim captives is quoted in detail. The magazine also threatened to sell US first lady Michelle Obama into sexual slavery for a third of a dinar. Some *Mujahedin* engage in temporary marriages and then pass on the female slaves/wives to fellow fighters (provided they are not pregnant). Female slaves are generally treated like mere cattle. Four wives and an array of concubines are also good for the birth rate – to boost IS population and to replenish the martyrs killed in battle.

Added to slavery and genocide, IS has been guilty of what has been called 'cultural cleansing' – its destruction of pre-Islamic heritage, including the bulldozing of the thirteenth century BC Assyrian city of Nimrud. It is a tragedy that IS controls numerous wonderful historical sites, many now destroyed. The destruction of so much memory and history from the past of the whole of mankind, while unforgiveable, must pale alongside the scale of human killings in the litany of war crimes.

These crimes are portrayed as Koranic dictates to new recruits to IS. Training in *Sharia* is an important element of affirming group loyalty. Training varies according to an assessment of the new soldier's loyalty and capability: it can vary from two weeks to up to six months. Inside the training camps the recruits receive a mixture of religious, military and political instruction, usually from the same five-man team of veteran Jihadists. Depending on the exigencies of the local military situation, recruits in training can be sent to man roadblocks, but very rarely to the front lines. Arabic is also taught to non-native speakers. After they pass out from the IS boot camps they will be supervised and can be flogged for infringements, especially if they express reservation about minor issues such as beheadings. They can be sent back for more religious indoctrination. Just like evangelical Christianity, Islam is taught in a very simple, direct and lucid way, but sometimes arcane secrets are revealed so as to impress recruits with the power and depth of the IS ideology.

*Where does IS get its finance?*
The Islamic State is rich, far wealthier than al-Qaeda. Some of the money comes from looting. When Mosul fell the central bank was relieved of around $430 million cash in US dollars. Lots of gold also went into the carefully recorded IS coffers. With all the precious metals, IS announced its intention to mint its own gold, silver and copper coins similar to the currency used by the Umayyad caliphate. Another ready source of income is oil. The warrior state perhaps earns up to $1–2 million per day from oil sold illegally via Turkey. At one stage it was operating around 350 oil wells, but some have been 'degraded' by coalition air strikes. In April 2015, when Tikrit was recaptured, IS was said to have lost control of three large oilfields. It is also alleged to sell energy, gas and electricity, to the Syrian government.

Another important income stream comes from selling ancient artefacts via Turkey and Jordan for the European, American and Asian markets and allegedly on eBay. Cuneiform tablets, for example, worth hundreds of millions, have been spirited away; large statues have gone as well, but they are more identifiable abroad as well as rather heavy to ship. Presumably IS archaeologists check out what can be sold before they bulldoze the priceless heritage of Mesopotamia. IS may have made about $200 million a year from its sideline as an art dealer.

Sometimes IS looks more like a mafia gang with beards, not least in their income from kidnapping for ransom. Western hostages have been relieved of their heads, though some European governments have paid out a lot of dollars for hostages returned intact. A more subtle form of religious extortion is applied to the pious in the Arab world. Official donations from Saudi Arabia and Qatar may well have declined, but private donations remain very profitable for IS. Some money goes direct via the *halawa* network; other money comes in directly with foreign fighters. More arrives via 'humanitarian charities' that raise money online as well as via traditional methods such as collecting tins.

The Islamic State has extorted money from businesses in its area of control in the beginning; then it switched to the more conventional form of governmental extortion, taxation. The tax system works rather well when a government indulges in crucifixion. Christians, pious Muslims as well as Syrian government employees all tend to pay their taxes promptly. In Western terms, IS appears to behave like the Mongol hordes, or perhaps latter-day Nazis. Like the Germans, however, IS is often punctilious in its methods, not least about relying on religious mandates. For example, *Ghanaem* and *Faiae*: these principles refer to seizure of assets. *Ghanaem* allows the right to seize property if the owners have tried to defend their property. *Faiae* refers to property or even towns if the owners/inhabitants succumbed peacefully. Careful readers will recall that this debate exercised the early Arab invaders and led to many debates in the chronicles of conquest because it made a great deal of difference to the booty and slaves that could be acquired. The distinction is still important as some property cannot be seized in the case of peaceful surrender. In particular, women – who are viewed as property by IS – cannot be taken in the case of *Faiae*. It is worth looking at the implications of the financial principles in more detail, not least for their implications for Muslims outside IS.

The Islamic view of taxation
It would be inaccurate to discuss merely the gangster side of IS finances; the religious aspect is important. It applies especially to IS, but also to money raised in the Islamic diaspora. *Zakat* is a tax ordained by the Koran. It is one of the five pillars of the faith. Along with the *Shahada*, bearing

witness to the uniqueness of Allah and the position of the Prophet as his messenger, the observance of the five daily prayers is another pillar. Then comes the Ramadan fast, and finally the *Haj*, the pilgrimage to Mecca if the Muslim can physically or financially manage the trip.

*Zakat* was an integral part of *Sharia,* though it fell away in modern times as secular taxation was introduced in many Muslim countries. So going back to the original system is important to fundamentalists. The first Muslim civil war was fought over this tax; the first caliph felt that without this source of money Muhammad's mission of Jihad could not be accomplished. The tax was levied on saved money, also agricultural goods, including all kinds of crops and some livestock. The tax, proportionately applied over a year, was based on savings, not income. Property and transport, from horses to aircraft, remain exempt. The rate of tax on animals is detailed, as befitted a society where camels, cows and sheep were very important sources of wealth. The money collected had to be spent in eight specified ways, not least to help the poor, to convert non-Muslims and to help free slaves. All rather noble, but it also mandated money to be spent on soldiers for the Jihad.

The principles were carefully applied by the Taliban in Afghanistan, a largely agrarian society. *Sharia* judges applied the laws respectfully (usually), especially compared with the corrupt practices of the Kabul government. The taxes on opium of course were very useful for the fighting funds. The more the *Sharia* judges spread to settle non-tax disputes the more efficiently and willingly the *Zakat* was paid. This method was also applied in the tribal and border areas of Pakistan, where the official government system, where it existed at all, was totally venal. So when IS applied the religious model to its territories it was more generally accepted than the previous rapacious methods, not least because it was specifically sanctioned by the Koran.

The way *Zakat* is spent is ordained by the Prophet himself. Islam also encourages voluntary giving (*Sadaqat*), though the spending guidelines of charitable funds are not strictly mandated. It can be spent on orphans or mosques, and it can be donated publicly or secretly, though the Koran encourages secrecy so the generosity is for God's pleasure, not neighbours' praise. This money is usually kept away from the state, often given directly to the recipient. Though *Sadaqat* is voluntary, sometimes it is given as a penance, for example breaking the Ramadan fast. Like the Catholic medieval practice of selling indulgences, the system is used extensively in the West to collect Jihadist funds. It is a means of washing away your sins, pleasing God, the local imam, and giving the *kuffar* a kick in the butt. It is a tempting combination for people in Britain who can't or won't risk the trip to Syria. The Koran mandates money for Jihad via *Zakat*, but encourages in addition voluntary payments for *Mujahedin.*

Right from the start, contributions to the military effort, whether weapons or animals, were encouraged. In addition, the practice of *Tajheez al-Ghazi* – equipping the warrior – created a method of being a 'proxy Jihadist'. In early Islamic times wealthy men and women would provide clothes, weapons, armour and horses for the *ghazi* (warrior) going off to war. People in Luton or Bradford or New York cannot usually provide camels, swords and shields, but they can donate the *Tajheez* money. This income flow is a key form of under-the-radar funding as it is usually in cash. This system previously paid for foreign fighters to go to Afghanistan, Bosnia and Chechnya. The amounts given to each Jihadist depended on the costs of travel and sometimes on how much an AK costs in the respective arms bazaars.

*Can the caliphate survive?*
The West is wrong to suppose that a state partly based on religious terror must inevitably implode. History affords many examples of regimes based on terror surviving and even thriving. Evil isn't always destroyed. The guillotine was the symbol of another regime obsessed with beheadings and yet the French conquered most of Europe. The Bolsheviks ruled by terror, as did the Chinese Communist Party for decades. Pol Pot's attempt to emulate the Chinese ended finally in defeat, but only after a ground invasion by the highly disciplined Vietnamese army. In more recent times the Taliban managed to control 90 per cent of Afghanistan until it was dislodged, for a while, by US power and a ground invasion by the Northern Alliance. It is true that IS continues to fight on multiple fronts and sometimes appears overstretched in holding back its many enemies, local and international. Yet it has proved capable of adapting quickly, especially to air attacks.

It is also state building quite effectively. The state has attracted from ninety countries over 20,000 foreign fighters (including 6,000 from Europe) to replenish its battlefield losses. And it has won over many locals with its dramatic curb on the previous banditry. After so many years of turmoil the locals relish being able to travel without being robbed. Evidence exists of venality on the part of some commanders – who are sometimes publicly punished – but mostly IS enforces a strict law-and-order policy. The IS government attends to administration by and large fairly; justice in the *Sharia* courts is usually swift and generally seen as effective, by believers.

ID cards have been issued and even guidance on preserving fishing stocks. The chances of IS survival and even success depend on not just military prowess, but in the longer term on some acceptance, if not enthusiastic endorsement, by the people it governs.

The Islamic State could be defeated by external military means, or perhaps survive and expand. Nevertheless, the emergence of a sovereign state with embassies and international airports is highly unlikely, not least because IS doctrines reject such pagan ideas as membership of the UN and the diplomatic community. The Taliban, with a similar ideology, did in the end boast embassies, most notably with two of the three countries that recognised the Emirate of Afghanistan, Saudi Arabia and Pakistan.

The Islamic State could still implode because of its own internal, let alone international, contradictions. The lands it holds are generally poor (except for oil) and its inhabitants are relatively few in such a large area. If it collapses it will not disappear, but morph into another version of Jihadism. The caliphate has been so hyped as the fulfilment of God's word, however, that its demise would be a crushing blow to the Salafists who support it worldwide. The preceding modern Jihadist movements were based on cell structures so it was easier for them to go underground and mutate into more virulent strains. The caliphate is different – it is very unlikely to form a government in exile as defeated European states did when overrun by the Nazis in the Second World War. Al-Shabaab suffered a major reversal caused largely by foreign armies, but managed something of a comeback, as did the Taliban. The Islamists in Mali were severely thrashed by French-led troops, but have also managed to retake territory. The point bears repeating: if IS is defeated then God's word is wrong, or at least the IS interpretation of Allah's word. It will be hard to imagine the concept of the caliphate recovering. It is almost a century since the last caliphate gave up the ghost – a replay may take another century.

Facing such a religious catastrophe, the true believers of the Islamic State are likely to fight long and hard to ensure the survival of a territorial rather than a virtual caliphate. Running a state is much tougher than running an insurgency. The ideology might prosper, but not necessarily administrative solutions to the practical problems of balancing the budget, inflation, supply shortages and export restrictions – all the severe challenges of running a state in wartime that even advanced countries found hard in the Second World War. Even in peacetime, the neighbouring Arab states have not excelled in governance. The peculiar blend of highly selected verses from the Koran, Arab nationalism, tribal affiliations, anti-Shia diatribes, allusions to Crusader history and prophetic warnings of impending Armageddon might not be enough to stave off the anger of a starving, isolated, exhausted and diverse population.

The Islamic State's two major successes have been military and propaganda. Few foreign Islamists will come to fight and live in a state that is about to expire. Meanwhile the clever propaganda has created the image of continuous battlefield achievements while the truth – in the summer of 2015 – is that IS is just about treading water. Most of the caliphate's weapons came from the West, captured from the Iraqi army or gifted via the Free Syrian Army. How will the larger assets, such as the tanks, be maintained? Who will sell spares to IS? Where can the trained mechanics come from?

The more desperate IS becomes on the front line, the more it will pump up its propaganda. An example of Islamic State's flair for publicity happened in November 2014 when it managed to publicise the simultaneous oaths of allegiance from Jihadist affiliates in Yemen, Libya, Egypt and Algeria. This gave the impression that IS wanted – the inevitable and rapid expansion of the caliphate. Except for Libya, the IS advance in these countries was negligible in hard military terms, however. You would not have realised that from the media coverage. Until the West gets strategic communications and a convincing counter-narrative in place, IS will continue effectively to spread its own message.

*Spreading the word*
Looking at the Koranic roots of the IS tax system, the Sharia courts and the religious indoctrination of new recruits are reminders of the depth of intensity of the faith that underlies IS. It is easy for Western secular audiences to see just medieval barbarism and snuff movies, yet the leaders of IS are often devout men who genuinely believe they are doing God's work. Serious historical method underlies what appears to be madness. The savagery is often calculated. No wonder the Iraqi soldiers were so inclined to run away in their tens of thousands from Mosul. The Iraqi forces have not been driven out of conquered cities; rather, they simply drive out when they can. Trained Western soldiers would have fought, but if they started losing they would also be tempted to retreat, in a more orderly fashion than the Iraqis, but no one would want to tarry and be taken prisoner by IS. Just as the Koran proclaims, spread fear and your enemies will run away or the city will surrender without a fight. That happened all through the Arab conquests and it is happening today.

Likewise, the passionate sense of mission reaches into the homes of the

Muslim diaspora. The propaganda, in many languages, is very slick. IS runs a radio network, but its most successful propaganda is on social media, especially Twitter, and its hashtag campaigns. Western intelligence interception of social media from IS has been useful in all sorts of ways, including calculating the co-ordinates for drone strikes. IS has prevented some of its people from connecting to the Internet via smartphones and personal laptops, and allowed limited use to a network of vetted Internet cafés. The Western counter-narrative should play this up – many young Muslims might give up their home comforts to travel to Syria or even their lives, but never their smartphones. Also, Twitter has closed down some Jihadist accounts, but they re-open under different guises a few hours later or the next day. IS uses other social media sites very effectively, as well as YouTube. That is why IS press-ganged a hostage journalist, John Cantile, to present a more Western-oriented approach to the news. Many Jihadist wannabes in the UK have fallen hook, line and sinker for IS propaganda, and regard news from the likes of the BBC as mere lies. This is one major reason why the danger on the home front is mounting, partly because Dr Google has been displaced by Sheikh Google.

*Chapter 7*

# The Home Front

In a world of globalised commerce and global media, globalised terrorism should not be surprising. The initial threat was from al-Qaeda sending its warriors to attack the US and Europe. More recently the threat has come more from *within* the West. Many Muslims in Europe have been radicalised by tragedies in the Middle East, especially highly publicised dramas such as Israel's retaliation against Gaza. Thousands of European Muslims have recently gone out to fight, initially against al-Assad, but then got sucked into the holy war waged by IS. Many Western-born Muslims have been killed, but many more have come back. Some have been disillusioned, though a dangerous and committed minority has returned to wage Jihad at home.

In Britain the congregation of would-be and virtual Jihadists has changed since the 1980s. At first intelligence agencies had to concentrate on overseas influence, especially training in Pakistan. That country was an ingredient in 75 per cent of attacks and planned attacks. The key link was with radical 'hate preachers' using mosques in the UK. Now it is much more informal; Jihadists use private homes and above all the Internet. The process of indoctrination is similar, however. First, young Muslims take on board the extreme ideology, then they merge it with a strong sense of grievance. Finally, they are mobilised by members of a likeminded group or a single incident at home or abroad to decide to travel on the path of Jihad. In the case of some it can be an individual decision to launch a 'lone-wolf' attack by picking up bomb-making skills on the Internet. The psychological steps of embracing an ideology, developing grievances, real or imagined, plus the group- or self-mobilisation can be found in thousands of cases of British Jihadists. It can take months or years, though in some cases the radicalisation-to-action process can be as short as three weeks. Now the Islamic State has provided a vast religious home for these radicals.

Islamic State has achieved so much more than al-Qaeda. Its ability to hold territory and create the longed-for caliphate has added great lustre to its appeal. It operates within three concentric rings: maintaining and expanding its conquests in Iraq and Syria; establishing affiliates and franchises throughout the Islamic world, especially Libya; and encouraging terrorism in the Western world. The West has not mastered a counternarrative to match the Jihadist message. Welcoming, mistakenly, the Arab Spring was not a substitute for a coherent military strategy and political narrative. As ideological extremism has expanded so has terrorism, especially in Europe.

The multiple crises in today's Europe in some ways mirror the chaos in the international system that permitted the rapid advance of the Muslim armies in the seventh and eight centuries. One of the biggest crises is immigration, partly caused by Western interventions and the subsequent Jihadist-induced carnage in Arab lands. It is deeply ironic that IS is calling for Muslims to heed the call to join the Islamic utopia, when millions of Muslims are fleeing IS depredations and the general catastrophe that passes for political life in the region. Only a small proportion of Muslims trying to smuggle themselves into Europe, mainly via Libya, are likely to be IS operators. Most are desperate economic migrants. The dangers of uncontrolled mass immigration/asylum-seeking are more a political challenge than a security matter; nevertheless, IS penetration cannot be ignored. It is much easier, however, for a British or French Jihadist to fly comfortably from Turkey rather than spend money on training a non-EU citizen and then to risk the perils of the Mediterranean in a clapped-out boat. Nevertheless, the political fallout from immigration into the EU has been poisonous. Rows over sanctions against Russia, the prospect of a British exit and the continuous Greek tragedy have also enfeebled Europe. The multiple crises are feeding off each other. Eurosceptic parties, often anti-immigrant and anti-Muslim – from Denmark to Spain – are on the march. Europe is struggling to keep even its single currency afloat and it has little time to forge a coherent response to the Jihadist threat. In a crisis the entire ethos of the European Union is generally to find a fence to sit on.

France, with its five million Muslims, has suffered constant Islamist terror attacks. The most dramatic was the *Charlie Hebdo* massacre in January 2015. The French used to deride the British for their class-conscious and racist rule in Africa compared with their own assimilation policy. Yet the French were often very discriminatory, except that they called their colonial subjects 'Monsieur' while they did it. The French have created Arab ghettoes in their slum *banlieues* of the big cities, which often erupt into mini-intifadas. The French also enforce a rigid post-revolutionary policy of separating church and state, which has led to all sorts of strange bylaws, such as banning veils and *burqas* with veil in public places. Such a law, while perhaps sensible in certain places, such as for teachers in schools, doctors in hospitals or tellers in banks, would offend not just libertarians in Britain. Telling people how to dress smacks of IS absolutism. The French, with their long colonial experience of North African violence, have not always been as good at counter-terrorism as their Anglo-Saxon allies.

Nor has the US assimilation model been an unbridled success for the Afro-Americans, a large number of whom have embraced Islam, not least via Louis Farrakhan and his Nation of Islam. Nonetheless, the USA has suffered from less home-grown Jihadism, partly because of the small proportionate size of the Muslim population. Density, especially in the UK Midlands, is *a* factor in ghetto-based radicalisation. In a US population of 320 million, Muslims comprise around 2.5 million, which is less than 1 per cent, compared with five million Muslims in a French population of 66 million, about 8 per cent. Many of the worst attacks have been in London and Paris, and the most right-wing reactions in Holland, areas of concentrated immigration. London is a famously liberal city; nevertheless economic absorptive capacity – the ability to integrate millions of aliens and provide them with a good life – must eventually impact on religious and political radicalisation. Thomas Malthus was famously proved wrong, but common sense suggests there must be a population limit somewhere. And the more people, the more difficult and expensive it is to maintain surveillance of dangerous radicals.

For decades, French intelligence agencies chastised their British counterparts for allowing so many Jihadist plotters to live unmolested in London – in what they dubbed 'Londonistan'. The unwritten understanding was that they could do what they wanted so long as they didn't break any British laws, not least about planting bombs on their home turf. Even Islamists I knew well, for example in Khartoum, used to complain that London was a hotbed of Jihadist sedition. There was a time not long ago that if you wanted to talk to exiled leaders of various Islamist fronts from Pakistan, Afghanistan, Egypt or Timbuktu, you could meet them for a coffee in a council flat in Tooting or Dagenham, or the back of a shop on the Edgware Road, to hear their litany of complaints about the countries they had left. They might add a sideswipe against the Americans, though they rarely complained about their gracious hosts. When I first started meeting London Jihadists in 1984, in exchange for their help they might ask for a ticket home, or occasionally the price of a black-market RPG to take back as well. Now it is much more difficult to meet dedicated Jihadists in the UK. They often despise contact with *kuffars* who might be penetrating their secrets, though sometimes long-established local leaders of, say, the Muslim Brotherhood, usually Palestinians, are accessible and can be charming in their near-perfect English. Perhaps now fearful of deportation, these usually comfortably off, professional people always emphasise their democratic aspirations. And you meet them in their smart offices.

Britain, with its three million Muslims, became the European centre for the most extreme of Jihadist exiles and hate preachers. Often they and their families were subsidised by the state. When some were eventually brought to trial it would cost an extra few millions. Because of human rights' legislation, partly based on European law visited by default upon Britain courtesy of its membership of the European Union, these preachers could rarely be deported, except after years of police, MI5 and legal effort. A notorious example was the former imam of London's Finsbury Park mosque, Abu Hamza, an Egyptian. He became the Islamist whom the media loved to hate, almost a pantomime villain, especially because of his two hooks for hands and one eye (caused by a mishandled bomb exploding in Afghanistan). At one time Hamza was living with his large family in a £600,000 council house and claiming benefits. Yet five of his sons repaid British hospitality with convictions ranging from bomb-making to armed robbery. In total, Hamza cost the British taxpayer nearly £3 million, including the legal costs, though not including the massive amount of intelligence time and money. After an eight-year battle he was deported to the US where he received a life sentence for terrorist offences, with no chance of parole. Mohamed Emwazi, better known as the head-chopping 'Jihadi John', who murdered a number of British hostages in Syria, was connected to Hamza. Emwazi was raised in London and educated at university there. Another notorious preacher was Abu Qatada, a Jordanian. After years of fighting deportation back home, he was finally returned in 2013. He was tried and released. The links of these preachers to Jihadist attacks were usually well known to MI5, yet proving it in open court was often counter-productive because of the risks, for example, of compromising sources or surveillance methods. Britain in effect allowed a host of young men to be turned into wannabe fighters for Allah by the presence of these and other preachers. The Jihadist cell linked to the June 2015 atrocity in Tunisia also had London connections.

In the beginning many of these preachers were tolerated because personally they genuinely did not want to 'shit on their own doorstep', to use the vernacular, but also because Britain was not on their respective organisations' target list. The renaissance of Jihad focused at first on the near enemy in the Middle East. Various factors such as fresh Jihadists with universal goals, the advent of satellite TV, especially al-Jazeera, and increasing Western military intervention all generated a revived international consciousness. Also, the locally based Jihadists had not achieved much in the Middle East. The tough secular dictatorships in Iraq, Syria, Egypt and Libya did not go in for long expensive trials – they executed or jailed suspected Jihadists. Al-Qaeda, however, did not invent spectaculars against the far enemy, especially the US and Europe; the PLO had done a lot of pioneering terrorism in the West, most infamously at the Munich Olympics. And, in a reverse flow, Britons had fought in their hundreds in Kashmir to support separatists and Islamists fighting the Indian army. A smaller number had fought in Afghanistan and Bosnia. None of these British volunteers then wanted to attack the home base. British Jihadists expected to come back, if they had survived their foreign battles, to a quiet life, albeit one with more street 'cred' for having fought for the oppressed brothers and sisters abroad. They had done their bit almost as a rite of passage.

Obviously 9/11 was a game-changer for attacks on the far enemy who – thanks to globalisation – wasn't that far away anymore. Al-Qaeda intended to provoke the West into waging a crusade in the Middle East and thus to polarise Muslim and Christian communities in Europe and Arab lands. After the American revenge in Afghanistan in late 2001, British-born bombers moved in to action – targeting English shopping centres and London nightclubs. The domestic Jihadists who bombed the London transport system on 7/7 used the Anglo-American invasion of Iraq in 2003 as a partial pretext.

Mohammed Saddique Khan, one of the four 7/7 suicide-bombers, was a well-respected community leader in Beeston, West Yorkshire. Popular with local Muslim youths, he had run a small Islamic bookshop and had a wife and a young child. Speaking in a strong Yorkshire accent, the message from the grave on his farewell video said:

> Your democratically elected governments continuously perpetuate atrocities against my people all over the world …. We are at war and I am a soldier. Now you too will taste the reality of this situation.

The 2005 bombings killed fifty-two totally innocent people, including several Muslims. This spectacular, the highest casualty count since the 1988 Lockerbie atrocity and the first suicide bombings within the UK, came the day after Britain had won the bid for the 2012 Olympics, and this success was partly based on London's multi-cultural reputation. 7/7 caught the British intelligence agencies largely by surprise. The peace agreement in Northern Ireland in 1998 had brought some respite to MI5 and Special Branch who had been focused for decades on the IRA; many experienced intelligence officers were made redundant. Previously, 9/11 had caught the Brits unawares as well as the Americans. Then the various British agencies had few or no Afghan specialists, or even an operational 'Afghan desk' and very few Arab linguists.

When they did lumber into action, British intelligence concentrated on Brits helping terror networks abroad, not al-Qaeda organising domestic attacks. One of the main concerns for MI6 became the exodus of hundreds of British Somalis to support al-Shabaab in the decades-long civil war in Somalia.

In late 2003, I left the UK Ministry of Defence to launch a personal crusade and a commercial magazine about homeland security. It was called *Resilience*. Unfortunately it did not prove very resilient as it lasted only two issues, partly because of my deficient business acumen perhaps, but mainly because of a lack of awareness of the imminent dangers. A sister magazine on CBRN, run largely by my colleague Gwyn Winfield, later cornered a world niche market. Both Gwyn and I were convinced that Britain, in the aftermath of 9/11, was not taking homeland security seriously – outside London. We wrote and broadcast about all sorts of homeland security matters from inadequate civil defence, poorly paid and poorly trained airport baggage handlers and the fancy airport security machines that were badly manned or sometimes mere placebo deterrents as well as the lack of preparation of some emergency services. We understood that Britain could not replicate the vast sums spent on homeland security in the US, but the UK spent little money, and was not co-ordinating properly. In particular, we were concerned about transport security. In the first issue of *Resilience* I wrote about the dangers to the London transport infrastructure. I was attacked in the media for scaremongering; a few days later Jihadists bombed the train network in Madrid, with mass casualties, more than the subsequent transport bombings in London.

Four bombs, on three underground trains and one red London bus, and the failed attempt to reprise the atrocity two weeks later, changed the foreign intelligence focus. Since 7/7, although only one person, Drummer Lee Rigby, has been killed in Britain by Jihadists, the mood and security responses have changed dramatically.

In 2006 intense Anglo-American counter-terrorist work prevented the downing of seven passenger planes flying to the US from London, in a plot using liquid explosives. Thousands of people could have been murdered in the air and on the ground. Imagine seven Lockerbies in one go. At least forty big and small actual plots, as opposed to vague aspirations, have been thwarted in the UK since then. Flying has now become a tiresome exercise because of the (sometimes) necessary if always undignified security checks for all travellers from Britain. All must be checked; liberal Britain has not allowed advance profiling – the very successful Israeli method – although in practice it does happen here. Britain also tried to crack down on the financial flows to Jihadist causes. If Abu Hamza cost the state £3 million, then Osama bin Laden and his acolytes have cost the British taxpayer billions in airport security, let alone the intelligence and military costs. If bin Laden wanted to bleed the Western economies, he partly succeeded, although he did not do quite as much damage as greedy bankers. Western counter-terrorist forces have probably now captured or killed nearly all the 9/11 plotters. The West, however, was again taken by surprise by the caliphate just as much as it was blindsided by 9/11.

Nevertheless, more spending on MI6, MI5 and GCHQ had prepared much of the groundwork for defence against IS at home. One important advance was joining the dots – especially between the police and its Special Branch component and the domestic counter-terrorism intelligence chiefs. Special counter-terrorism units were spread around the country – not just centralised in the Metropolitan Police's SO15 Command in London. The police Counter Terrorism Command, known within the Met as SO15, was formed in October 2006, with the merger of its two predecessor units: the Anti-Terrorist Branch (SO13) and Special Branch (SO12). They could now work in unison in the Midlands, for example, where there were concentrations of Muslims. Local police knowledge could help to find the unofficial informal networks that were often based in private homes and businesses, not in the mosques. They had to look at big plots and lone-wolf self-starters. When bin Laden was killed in 2011, a revenge attack on the 2012 London Olympics was fully expected. Long before he was killed, bin Laden had told one of his bodyguards that, after his expected assassination, 'My blood will become a beacon that arouses the zeal and determination of my followers'. Extensive measures were put in place to ensure a successful Olympiad.

Jihadism has ebbed and flowed over 1,400 years. Al-Qaeda is no longer the main domestic threat, although its chief offshoot, Al-Qaeda in the Arabian Peninsula, was involved in serious bomb threats in the West until very recently. Many of its leaders, especially Anwar al-Awlaki, an American-born imam, are no longer with us. Al-Awlaki, who once preached hellfire for the unbelievers in the Falls Church mosque in Virginia, was killed appropriately enough by a Hellfire missile from a US drone in 2011. Al-Qaeda's challenge to the West has dwindled, partly because its leaders have been wiped out by US forces, and partly because many of its members have absconded to join IS. In fact, the more 'moderate' post-bin Laden al-Qaeda is now considered a potential or actual ally by some Western and Arab intelligence agencies. Some cynics are calling the new potential Jihadist allies the 'moderate beheaders'.

The threat to Britain has changed, but the Jihadist world view, rare in the 1990s, is now common among Muslims in Europe. Perhaps as many as 2,000 Britons have gone over to IS, and around 4,000 from the rest of Europe. Include Muslims from outside Europe and that adds up to an estimated total of 20,000 foreign fighters in the IS ranks. Thousands of European Union citizens, from Britain and across the European continent, have received full Jihadist military training no different from that available in Pakistan and Afghanistan, training that would have included familiarisation with a variety of weapons and explosives and a range of terrorist tactics. They would also have undergone sophisticated and increasingly triumphalist Jihadist political indoctrination, including the need to take the battle to the belly of the beast, the western 'Crusader' states. Many of these European citizens would then have taken an active part in the conflict in Syria and Iraq. Many who do not go for a Jihadist tourist trip and migrate permanently are in touch with stay-at-home British Muslims who may share the passion, but won't risk life and limb. Al-Assad's brutality in suppressing dissent, together with condemnation by opportunistic Western governments and their calls for regime change in Syria, fired up these people. *Jabhat al-Nusra*, the al-Nusra front, an al-Qaeda affiliate, is getting support from members of the anti-IS coalition, partly because it says its aims are purely local: getting rid of al-Assad and installing *Sharia* in Syria. And al-Nusra has a proven track record of aggression when it decides to fight IS. Some of the British Jihadists who are understandably enraged by the horrors inflicted by al-Assad are said to be prepared to fight there, but *not* at home. Probably about 15 per cent of returnees remain active Jihadists who admit to counter-terrorism officers that they want to continue the fight in the UK. Of course many returnees remain schtum. Short of locking up all returnees, it is sometimes hard to decide whether those who bonded together in Syria will not bomb together in England.

Except for psychopaths and well-trained specialists, most people don't like killing or witnessing it and suffer traumatic flashbacks, sooner or later. Mohamed from Bradford or Ahmed from Cardiff may come home exhausted, thinner and probably demoralised, even though few untrained Brits who don't speak Arabic are put in the IS frontline. Even though some of the foreign Jihadists may have been cleaning latrines or perhaps later manning roadblocks, most will be glad to get home to a place where they can get a signal on their smart phones and somewhere they can charge their iPads, and even get regular meals and a shower. These people can help counter-terrorist experts in the de-radicalisation programmes. The same officers, however, must be sure they can weed out the truly committed Jihadists who will bomb at home and send out their friends, brothers and even parents to Syria.

*Why?*
Most Britons who have not studied the history of Jihad constantly ask why do young, second- or third-generation citizens, many well-educated products of a British liberal society, want to join what appears to be a medieval death cult? Many Britons, and not just feminists, particularly ask why so many intelligent young girls, often from middle-class homes, want to become Jihadi brides? If I had a single definitive answer I would be in the running for a Nobel Peace Prize. There are as many reasons as travellers to Syria. Amongst the young men, many go for passionate religious reasons, some go for adventure. So you can simplify by saying they are either believers or 'gangstas'. The same can be said for impressionable young girls, the 'caliphettes'. Some are devout – most teenage girls want to fixate on something that explains the meaning of the universe. Some are attracted by the grooming on social media – especially the young *Mujahedin* who preen for the girls. They can be paraphrased as believers or Beliebers. The social media is a Wild West for IS, which sends up to 100,000 tweets a day.

Some sociologists have emphasised the typical hormonal factors among young people, although you don't have to be a Muslim to be a dangerously unhappy teenager. Young Muslims do often lead cloistered social lives, however, whereas young non-Muslim men and women can join gangs, get drunk in a pub and fight at football matches, as well as indulge in unbridled sex, drugs and rock 'n' roll. Most Muslims can't. The politics of sexual frustration is part of the explanation, therefore. Some wannabe Jihadists are attracted to the apparent James Bond lifestyle. A poorly educated unemployed Muslim living in awful conditions in Bradford might want to travel to improve his life chances, just as many young men rushed to join the colours in 1914, or were attracted to fight in the Spanish civil war in the 1930s or maybe take a gap year to help deprived kids in Africa. Today's bored and frustrated young Muslims – if they are not distracted by the sexual grooming sets in many English cities – can aspire to join a warrior caste, which entices hordes of young Jihadi brides. Or, if they are brainwashed to become suicide bombers, pull a host of virgins in paradise. The young women, mostly 15-18, can aspire to be one of the four wives of the posturing young blades brandishing AKs they see on the Internet. They can square all this with their conscience – especially leaving home and rebelling against their parents, a delicious teenage combination – by entering a perfect Muslim life in the caliphate. IS propaganda plays on the sufferings of Sunni Muslims under al-Assad and Shia-dominated Baghdad. They can also appease their consciences by offering to help the suffering of the internal refugees. Females tend to go in groups – they reinforce each other's juvenile views. Men also tend to travel in packs, which sometimes involve schoolmates or even whole families.

This idealism is not restricted to young Muslims. The same kind of faith inspired Zionism then and now. Many extreme Christian sects would migrate too. The most law-abiding of them all, for example Jehovah's Witnesses, would move *en masse*, if their elders told them to form a territorial 'new world', in anticipation of the imminent Armageddon. Jonestown and its massacre were unusual, but many mainstream American evangelicals wait for the Rapture and a few move to, or regularly visit, Jerusalem to anticipate Christ's Second Coming.

Add to this the sense of oppression and self-justified rage that inspire many young Muslims who feel alienated from the job market in particular and British culture in general. Many claim they are constantly discriminated against. MI5 refers to this as 'blocked mobility'. A variety of psychological, familial, cultural and social motivations are at play. Packaged by neighbourhood, prison, mosque and the Internet, these motivations may prompt the Jihadist adventure. Many even in prosperous families are tempted; Jihadism is not simply a product of financial deprivation. As Lenin suggested, most revolutionary leaders are likely to come from the middle class, not the oppressed proletariat. Class, education and family wealth are often irrelevant to idealism and the search for faith or adventure.

*The dangers of denial*
Just as most Arabs in the Middle East believe in the conspiracy theory about

9/11 – that it was a CIA/Mossad confection – likewise many British Muslims adhere to theories that play into a sense of victimhood. A BBC poll of 1,000 British Muslims conducted not long after the *Charlie Hebdo* massacre in Paris in January 2015 found that 27 per cent had sympathy for the motives of the perpetrators. One Muslim responded on BBC Radio 4 about the cartoons thus: 'If they hadn't poked fun at our Prophet, no one would have died.' An NOP poll, taken before IS was set up, reported that 68 per cent of British Muslims thought that Britons who insulted the Prophet should be prosecuted. Jailed, not killed. In a poll for the Policy Exchange think tank more than a third of British Muslims said they thought that apostates – those who left the faith – *should* be killed.

Often seemingly modern Muslims share these views and they also believe that their communities are under attack. You just have to listen to the BBC's Asian network's phone-ins to hear how many Muslim callers either deny the criticisms of IS or allege that it is a CIA plot to discredit all Muslims. When criticised for these paranoid views, many Muslims will play the race card. Polls indicate that half of British Muslims will admit to wanting *Sharia* in Britain and many use existing *Sharia* courts for non-criminal issues, even if they don't formally advocate the ISIB, the Islamic State of Ireland and Britain. Just as Jihadists are often very Koranic in their behaviour, so too many British Muslims will condone the Jihadist worldview, even if they do not support terrorism to sustain that caliphate.

In many mosques non-violent Muslims get sucked into the Jihad network. Although some moderate imams have driven out the Jihadist recruiters some remain, but they work more discreetly. Recruitment is done now through informal networks and less often in the mosques. But even the more covert recruiters may also work as *Tajheez* co-ordinators. Many family heads will confess that they have families and businesses to look after, though they will pay 'charity' money as ordained by the Koran. Some of this cash will go to pay for Jihadists to travel to Syria. Little old ladies will also ease their consciences by handing out money in the form of various penances, for example breaking the Ramadan fast. Around £2,000, always in cash, will be collected for the travel expenses of each aspiring Jihadist. And the most trusted of them will take perhaps £10,000 for the commanders of the unit the recruits are making for. Some of this funding is an open secret in the communities and it is considered *haram* to betray what is going on to unbelievers, especially the police.

Islam is immensely divided in the UK, though there is a strong sense of local cohesion to the sect or clan and nationality of the families' origins.

Many families subscribe to the so-called 'myth of return' – that they will go back home to the Indian sub-continent at some stage, perhaps to retire to the homes they have bought in their native towns and villages. And many regularly visit their extended families, not least to choose nice unspoiled spouses from 'back home'. In tight Muslim communities children will go to private faith schools or Muslim-majority state schools where they may interact very little with any Christian locals who still live in the area. They will grow up in a family that is imbued with a different culture; a different language is spoken in the home. The mother and, almost certainly, the grandmother will not speak much English. They may deal with the benefits system or NHS via a younger English-speaking family member or the courts via a translator. They watch satellite TV in their own language. For all intents and purposes many live entirely separate lives from native British-born non-Muslims. This is the result of the disastrously failed and highly dangerous multi-cultural experiment, born of the politically correct 1970s.

Trevor Phillips, once the arch-guru of multi-racialism and former chairman of the Commission for Racial Equality, recently confessed that

> while a beautiful theory, in practice, multi-culturalism had become a racket, in which self-styled community leaders bargained for control over local authority funds that would prop up their own status and authority. Far from encouraging integration, it had become in their interest to preserve the isolation of their ethnic groups.

He also lambasted a whole range of issues related to Muslims, from female genital mutilation to the emasculation of children's education in the Trojan Horse scandal (see later) and the blind eye turned to widespread electoral fraud by Asian Muslims. Denial of these cancers in society was partly because of the political correctness demanded by the apostles of multiculturalism.[25]

Non-Muslims also practise a form of denial, partly because of the intrinsic nature of a democratic society. It has been unofficial practice based on a form of political correctness to say that the IS atrocities have nothing to do with Islam. 'Islam is a religion of peace' was the mantra. This position changed when David Cameron tackled the subject head-on in a watershed speech in Birmingham on 20 July 2015. The domestic intelligence services and indeed anyone who had been involved with security understood that politicians felt that they had to play the game in order to avoid inciting more divisions in society. The best that can be said about the political establishment behaving in this way was that it was a form of 'noble lie', that the assumption was based on a British public that was a 'lynch mob in waiting', as writer Douglas Murray put it.[26] This obfuscation has allowed Jihadism to thrive in Britain and France. Not naming the beast, the inherent danger in our Western societies, does no favours to Muslims. It is perhaps the ultimate Islamophobic act not to name the threat and deal with what it is, not just for the 'Christian' majority, but for Muslims themselves. It takes the pressure off Muslims to reform the negative and dangerous traditions in their own communities.

By naming and shaming the beast within, a fifth column to be frank, the government's new approach – forging anew a concerted military and political strategy – helps to create a narrative that allows Muslims to integrate better into British mainstream, without losing their faith. It has been patently absurd to insist that individuals who kill cartoonists for blaspheming Islam while shouting 'Allah Akbar' have nothing to do with Islam. The violence associated with IS has *everything* to do with Islam, the worst kind of Islam, yes, but Islam nonetheless. No religion is peaceful, but Islam is specifically not. The Koran, like the Bible's New Testament (although rarely the Old), has many passages proclaiming peace, yet Islam is not primarily a religion of peace. For many hundreds of years the most devout of its followers have been practising a bellicose Jihad that is encouraged throughout the Koran. IS is merely following the rules, to the nth degree.

Hiding behind the noble lie not only discouraged Muslims from trying to reform, it also stored up anger in the broader community. The British public is not as stupid as politicians believe. Voters can see for themselves what is happening on their TV screens or iPads. The growth of right-wing parties throughout Europe has partly been a reaction to the noble lie. The United Kingdom Independence Party (UKIP) frightened the hell out of the now ruling Conservative Party by taking nearly 4 million votes in the May 2015 election, more than the left-of-centre Liberal Democrats and the Greens combined. UKIP says it is not racist, although it is de facto an anti-immigration party, and many immigrants from outside the EU are Muslims, mainly from the Indian sub-continent or Africa. Some MPs in the Conservative Party and the intelligence services have long feared that public opinion would overtake the politicians' officially anodyne line, especially if Jihadists repeated 7/7. Then many of the 1,740 mosques in the UK could be firebombed. It may not be a lynch mob, but large sections of public opinion are seething with an inchoate mix of racism, Islamophobia and anti-immigrant sentiments, plus more coherent concerns about overcrowding in schools, housing and the NHS, all of which could erupt into major violence nationwide as occurred, for different reasons, in 2011. This is exactly what Islamist extremists want – to polarise communities, boost the sense of Muslim victimhood and prompt more migration to IS and more lone-wolf 'knights' to bomb the *kuffars*. This is the worst nightmare of the security services. Until the prime minister told the truth to the British people, this was a highly probable outcome of another Jihadist spectacular in London. It may still be.

In modern times Britain has been tolerant of religious minorities. Some Jews might disagree; they sometimes blame the recent rise of anti-Semitism in Europe on the increased number of Muslim immigrants. The last significant religious disturbance in the UK was the anti-Catholic Gordon riots of 1780, which was confined to London. The religious complexion of the UK, however, has changed more in the last few decades than in the previous three centuries. Islam is the fastest growing religion in the UK, mainly due to immigrants and their high birth rate, but also to conversion. It has doubled in size in about fifteen years. The Pew 2014 Global Attitudes survey said that 26 per cent of Britons had unfavourable attitudes towards Muslims in the UK (presumably it is much higher now regarding Muslims *inside* the caliphate). This is half the negative views in Spain, Greece and Italy. That this should be so relatively low following 7/7 is an impressive comment on British tolerance. Brits were not generally prepared to condemn a whole community for the actions of a few extremists, no matter how murderous. But this was before the mass rape and abuse of young white girls by Pakistani gangs was revealed throughout Britain, but most notoriously in Rotherham, where more than 1,400 cases were recorded by the police. It was also before the slaughterhouse antics of Jihadi John. The fact that he spoke in a London accent was a PR disaster for British Muslims; it also angered the Americans whose security agencies seem to be more concerned about the enemy within Britain than the indigenous intelligence agencies sometimes appear to be. Previously this could be translated as mad, bad *individuals*. The departure of hundreds of young Muslims in groups to fight for IS raised the question of *community* loyalty, however. Lumping together Rotherham and IS *et al* may be misleading and unfair. Many Muslims will argue, with some reason, that these sorts of crimes are not sanctioned by the Koran.

Because Muslims are so divided by language, creed and national legacies, they have never managed to form effective national bodies. Most of the community leaders are useless windbags. To allay the concerns of the non-Muslim majority, Muslims must find better ways of expressing their outrage and hostility to what is being done in their name. More important, they must jettison their sense of denial and *from within* start dealing with these crimes. Obviously local communities must – with alacrity, conviction and enthusiasm – work with the police and security services to point fingers, name names and not hide behind the convenient excuse of community loyalty. Loyalty to Britain must transcend all else, although in individual cases – regardless of faith – it is usually difficult to turn in your own son and daughter. Recognising the problem early, and at least hiding passports or asking the state to cancel them, might be a start. They could shift schools or mosques. Better to move to another town rather than have your son sacrificed as a suicide bomber.[27]

*The toxic by-products of denial*
A full survey of how political correctness has undermined relations with the Muslim community in Britain would require a separate book. I list just a summary. The fact that the police were too afraid of being called 'institutional racists' (after the Stephen Lawrence Inquiry) held them back from pursuing the obvious racial/religious dimensions of Pakistani grooming gangs in over thirty cities, but most infamously in Rotherham where *The Times* tirelessly investigated. If white women are described as 'prostitutes' in some Islamic schools and Muslim elders ignore what is happening under their own noses and if the police and local councils are afraid to act then you will get 1,400 children and young girls gang-raped and forced to take hard drugs in one town. Thousands of lives have been ruined – it is not only in Syria and Iraq that young people's futures are being wrecked, because of their traumas, even if they physically recover. Local *Sharia* courts don't do anything about such crimes, although often they abuse women's rights, especially in family matters. Many immigrant Muslims, who cannot speak English, feel they have no choice but to obey Islamic jurisprudence. For the same reasons, not one single case of female genital mutilation has been successfully prosecuted in UK courts. It is a cultural atrocity and not just a Muslim one, but thousands of Muslim women are sent back to hellholes such as Somalia to 'visit relatives', though in reality to undergo the most barbaric surgery, often with little or no modern medical oversight. Many such operations are performed in the UK. Until recently the police were reluctant to take any action, regarding it as a domestic issue. It is not: it is a serious crime against young girls, who may

literally be scarred for life. I won't go into detail about the serious repercussions of the many botched operations that can affect functions from sex to urination to childbirth. Most organised religions are a conspiracy against women, but this is one of the worst manifestations. And it is not sanctioned in the Koran; it is a cultural factor. I helped to make a TV documentary on this subject in Africa over twenty years ago, though very little has changed in Britain since then.

For similar reasons the police have been sometimes reluctant to move against honour killings of young women who marry outside the Muslim faith; likewise schoolteachers and police have often ignored young girls who suddenly disappear from school to go back to Pakistan for a forced marriage. In schools where Muslims are in a minority teachers may enforce the legal responsibility to check on such lengthy absences, but in Muslim-majority schools they may condone or ignore the practice. In the 1980s a pioneering Bradford head teacher called Ray Honeyford wrote a series of articles in a spirit of trying to protect the children in his care: not only girls who were forced into marriage in Pakistan or Bangladesh, or boys who came into the classroom exhausted by lengthy lessons in the madrassah and who were being brought up to believe that their home was elsewhere and they owed no loyalty or gratitude to Britain. They were growing up as Muslims who happened to live in the UK, rather than as British people who happened to be Muslims. They did not want to be integrated into the *kufffar* society. Honeyford was forced out his job by his politically correct superiors.

The Trojan Horse scandal in a group of schools in Birmingham proved his case, rather too late. In 2014 whistleblowers tipped off the Department of Education that Salafists were trying to subvert six state schools. It was alleged that boys and girls were separated, extremist preachers were hosted, a negative view of unbelievers was taught, especially about the loose morals of white women and so on. The main allegation was that a Jihadist viewpoint was being inculcated. Teachers and governors who objected were forced out. An official enquiry by Peter Clarke, the former police anti-terror chief, concluded that there had been efforts to 'introduce an intolerant and aggressive Islamic ethos into some schools'. The secretary of state for education, Nicky Morgan, argued that the teaching of British values was as important as maths or English. She warned against schools that 'don't subscribe to our fundamental British values, try to hijack our education system, radicalise our children and break those societal bonds'. She said in early 2015 that this sort of teaching creates the conditions for the *Charlie Hebdo* massacre in Paris.

Just as the hate preachers had radicalised the mosques, they also worked on rallying and isolating Muslim youth in schools (and universities). Children were taught to empathise with the brothers and sisters around the world, but especially in countries where the Crusaders and Zionists were subverting Islam and killing Muslims. They were led to believe that the assimilation ideals of their parents' generation were a betrayal. Under a series of Labour and Conservative governments, religiously segregated areas were accepted – ironically at the height of the anti-apartheid frenzy in the Western media. Segregated areas were tolerated or even encouraged under the banner of diversity in Britain. Police averted their eyes and soon a distinct rule of law developed for many Muslims.

An example of this was the acceptance of systematic electoral fraud on a massive scale within constituencies containing significant Muslim immigrant communities. Widespread postal voting fraud in Oldham, Burnley, Kirklees, Slough, Walsall and Birmingham was reported to police who refused to act for the simple reason that nearly all the complaints were related to Pakistanis and Bangladeshis. The most egregious example of corruption was in what was dubbed the 'Islamic Republic of Tower Hamlets' in east London. Police found many excuses not to act as the local mayor constantly and effectively played the race card. Eventually a private prosecution forced an enquiry and the mayor was sacked, and all the ruthless and dishonest practices were laid bare. Another noted Muslim pocket borough was Bradford West, which had voted for the flamboyant Respect MP George Galloway. He played the local Pakistani clan chiefs at their own game – often leaders in Kashmir had much more influence than Bradford bigwigs. When Attorney General Dominic Grieve, Britain's most senior law officer, complained that voting frauds were nearly all associated with British citizens of Pakistani heritage, he was forced to withdraw his remarks and apologise, even though the political class knew they were true. Eventually, the police began to investigate and to prove the accusations. Perhaps the postal voting system should return to its original intention – allowed only for people proved to be abroad during the election or unable to actually walk into the polling station. If a voter simply can't be bothered to go to the poll, or can't read enough English to distinguish the name of the politician his community has told him to vote for, then maybe he or she shouldn't vote at all. Local councils spend a fortune in immigrant areas on numerous pieces of paper and online information in a complex array of languages. The same is true of hospitals with multi-language computers for patients' access. Perhaps all this money would be better spent on paying for immigrants to learn English. That is just one aspect of teaching British values – speaking the language. (I write as a Welshman who was very concerned with maintaining Welsh, the original language of the British Isles before mass Anglo-Saxon immigration.)

Many other issues could be listed. For example, the police often fail to crack down on Muslim militias who 'police' their own enclaves, stopping Muslim shops selling alcohol and cigarettes, or harassing non-Muslim women for wearing allegedly improper dress. One of the most expensive aspects of Asian immigration for the health service is the practice of marrying first cousins, usually via arranged marriages. Half of Pakistanis marry their cousins. On average such consanguinity causes up to thirteen times more likelihood of genetic defects in babies; the cost of care, sometimes for life, is a heavy burden on the NHS. Such inbreeding also damages the future gene pool.

Not all the above issues relate only to Muslims. Honour killings, marriage to cousins and female genital mutilation extend to other cultures and faiths. The politically correct avoidance of addressing these social problems has a unique effect on Muslims, however, because of the determination of many to isolate themselves from *kuffars* and the resulting chronic security threat. Sikhs and Hindus do not threaten a universal and violent Jihad.

*Counter-terrorism*

Although the police have often ignored the social aspects of Muslim exclusiveness, the security agencies have not. The government's official approach is to 'contest' violent extremism. It is not aimed solely at Jihadism. MI5 still has to worry about the various breakaways from the Provisional IRA as well as far-right activists. The far right also wallows in conspiracy theories, for example that Islamists are on the point of taking over the UK. Most of the time and money, however, is concentrated on the Jihadist threat because of its many current examples of terrorism in the UK. The counter-terror strategy is officially based on four areas:

- Pursue: to stop the attacks
- Prevent: to stop people becoming terrorists or supporting terrorism
- Protect: against terror attacks
- Prepare: to mitigate against the impact of attacks if they happen.

Protect is the most active element in persuading young Muslims not to engage with extremism. *Non-violent* extremism is seen as a gateway to

Jihadism. A whole range of local authority personnel can recommend someone to the Protect programme, which is run largely by the police. The idea is never to arrest, but to help persuade. Referrals to Protect in many counties with large Muslim concentrations are doubling or even trebling every year – the small number of dedicated police officers is almost overwhelmed. The Prevent approach includes what is called the Channel Programme. In 2013-14 about 4,000 Britons, including 1,450 children, who were considered in danger of radicalisation were processed, although only 20 per cent would actually be judged likely to become violent terrorists. The numbers in Channel have doubled over the last two years. Channel, however, had around forty workers, mainly British Muslims, who conduct a series of one-to-one counselling sessions; they try to bring back the youngsters from the brink of active extremism, before they actually fly to Turkey. Some of the effort has also been put into those who had returned from Syria or those who had tried but failed to get there, despite some politicians calling for the returnees to be locked up and the keys thrown away. That is the way to create martyrs.

The counter-terrorism officers have searched for trusted imams to rehabilitate returnees – this is much more convincing than well-meaning police men and women, social workers or aged community leaders, and certainly better than politicians sermonising in Westminster. Despite, or because of, being the very beating heart of Wahhabism, Saudi Arabia did have some success in their intensive use of imams to de-radicalise Saudis returning from Jihad overseas. (They could also afford to bribe them with nice houses and large stipends in exchange for good behaviour.) In the UK the vast majority of returnees have not been charged or even arrested. Sending them to prison – especially as it is almost impossible to prove what they might have done in Syria – will radicalise them further, and the prisons, even more. That is the view of British intelligence agencies. Making them Prevent missionaries – under careful supervision – and the threat of prison, or removing their passports if they were not born in Britain – could be an inducement. They would not be extensively paid (except for expenses) unless they were persuaded to work for MI6. Sometimes their idealism can be folded back on itself to help Britain. It is stupid to jail a potentially good intelligence asset, especially the more adventurous type, who has not been broken or brainwashed by his time in Syria. Penetration of IS is only possible by a Muslim, especially if he can speak Arabic and has some combat experience. The handful of returnees who can be trusted to go back, would be well paid – if they survive. And their skills should be retained and a suitable job found, just as Britain (eventually) provided sanctuary for the Iraqi and Afghan translators for the British army who wanted to settle with their families. For all those Muslims from home and abroad who serve Britain loyally proper respect (and payment) should be given, although returning agents will receive their tax-free accolades discreetly.

Police arrest about one person a day on average on terrorism charges. The very effective 'jointery' between MI5 and the police (and occasionally the special forces) so far has saved the country from another 7/7 spectacular. The other emergency services have also put in a great deal of effort to learn from the many weaknesses displayed in the response to 7/7. Nevertheless, the IRA cliché is also true of Jihadism: 'You have to be lucky every time. We have to be lucky only once.'

Prevent is not the only scheme – after the 2005 bombings the government spent perhaps as much as £80 million on 1,000 projects in concert with nearly a hundred local authorities. The idea was to allocate money to various Muslim groups who were deemed hostile to extremism. The theory of getting more Muslims to do the heavy lifting was a good one, but quite often the money went to the wrong people, even to imams who called for Jihad or attacks on democracy and even British forces. Even when the money did not fall into the wrong hands, some of it was wasted, in the usual manner of do-good money donated to NGOs and charities. The government funded and then withdrew support from 'Tell Mama', a hotline that was designed to record and then ask police to respond to serious abuse or assaults on Muslims. Counter-terrorism officers had decided that some of the alleged attacks on Muslims discussed on the hotline were exaggerated and were likely to poison relations with the wider community.

Often, Muslim communities do not want to engage with Prevent or Channel. They have alleged that reporting to the police could lead to arrests and damage to job prospects. Prevent police officers carefully avoid arrests, unless faced with an obvious crime and do not flag up the counselling so no future employer can discriminate against the Muslim youngster. Some schools have been reluctant to engage with Prevent, especially the kind of schools outed in the Trojan Horse enquiry; nor have they been keen to recommend other government anti-radicalisation strategies. Maybe such schools should be closed. Maybe *all* Muslim faith schools should be closed. Maybe the French model should be adopted and end *all* faith-based schools funded by the state, including Christian and Jewish schools. If parents want to pay for extra religious education on the weekend, that is up to them. Such a policy would be unfair on the numerous Catholic and Church of England schools in what is still nominally a Christian country, especially when no Methodist fundamentalists have planted bombs, or no Anglican bell-ringers have set up AK-wielding militias and no armed wing of the Catholic Church has called for a crusade to regain the lands once controlled by the Vatican.

Counter-terrorism has to focus not only on individuals suggested by Prevent or schools. Ofsted should be toughened up to avoid the previous fudge and complacency in dealing with recalcitrant governors and teachers in some Muslim-majority schools. Also much radicalisation takes place in prisons; one obvious solution is to avoid concentrating Islamists in or two prisons and thus obviate the Jihad university status the Americans provided to Iraqi insurgents in detention facilities such as Camp Bucca. Universities have been soft on Islamist extremists too, especially not booting out firebrands visiting or running the student Islamic societies, despite the potential infringements of free speech. Forced separation of women and men at college audiences should never be allowed on campuses. The Charity Commission is also clamping down on charities funding IS in the name of helping Syrian refugees.

A full account of the counter strategies against the 'virtual caliphate' would require a technical detail that is frankly beyond this writer as well as beyond the perimeters of the Official Secrets Act. Edward Snowden, the US IT specialist working for American intelligence, may have been a heroic whistleblower to the *Guardian,* but he dramatically undermined Western surveillance of numerous terrorist organisations and risked many brave agents' lives. The political debate about the limits to surveillance in a free society has been endlessly rehearsed in the US and UK. In Britain the work of GCHQ has been vital in uncovering plots to bomb and attack citizens at home. The separate work on taking down the Jihadist websites is a daily game of whack-a-mole. They pop up again the next day. As Jihadist and paedophile grooming has proved, the Internet can sometimes be the agent of the devil. Many of the big boys in the game, such as Google, are US organisations. Despite lobbying, carrots and sticks and pressures on their tax base, leviathans such as Google can do far more to tackle Jihadist penetration. It is easier to close down the Jihadist-leaning TV stations, however. IS has been very adroit in its use of social media for recruitment and general PR, but it has not yet moved into the most crucial area of cyber war. If North Korea can do it, then IS could soon aspire to bring down networks in the UK. This may be the shape of things to come, if IS is not destroyed.

The Muslim extremists constantly complain that the West is at war with

Islam; certainly IS is at war with the West. Maybe we should take them at their word. If Western military responses need to be restrained, its ideological narrative should not be. We are fighting a war; the resources deployed in the successful Cold War should be used again. For example, the propaganda work of the BBC World Service and Radio Free Europe can be reprised.

\* \* \* \*

The government's naïve attempts to use good radicals against bad ones has not worked that well. 'When there are no enemies within, the enemies outside cannot hurt you,' said Winston Churchill. Effective counter-terrorism in Britain should strive to remove these dangers, although the threat will linger for a generation or more, even if IS is totally eradicated. Projects such as Prevent are a sound idea, but they need able partners in the Muslim community. All Muslim communities must step up and provide leaders who want to co-operate with the new government strategy being developed under the Cameron plan.

Muslims need to take action and to lead. A number of mosques have not even tried to reform. A prominent mosque in Cardiff next to my *Alma Mater* was attended by the first British Jihadists to make an IS propaganda video. And some groups linked to Jihadist preachers, who stay just within what they see as the right side of the law, continue to spread hate. Counter-terrorism's strategy is obviously to try to control the origins of the domestic threat rather than deal with the aftermath of an attack by British-born terrorists. Looking for early signs of conversion to extremism – and separating the symptoms from the normal aberrations of moody teenagers – can be exasperating for a close family, let alone the mosque or even vigilant security personnel or social workers. And it is difficult to gauge when the espousal of radical extremist views leads to putting the beliefs into practice with bombs at home or joining IS. Going from self-justified rage to the bomb or gun can be a rapid or slow process. The 'pre-Jihadist' phase of complete belief in fundamentalism is sometimes obvious – young zealots usually want to share their newly discovered notion that God has put down a special ordained path for him or her that they must follow, on pain of eternal punishment. The second is a profound contempt for the decadent West in general and British sham democracy in particular. The third phase may be an absolute conviction of victimhood, that Muslims are uniquely maltreated by British authorities and by other religions. This self-induced sense of victimhood, no doubt coloured by a string of personal slights, real or imagined, can be a virulent driving force. The fourth stage is the acceptance of a conspiracy that glues the other factors together: a combination of Zionists, Americans, London politicians toadying to Washington, and shadowy world government organisations all trying to destroy the one true faith – that the caliphate is risking all to defend. Besides, this was all prophesied in the holy writings, so it must be true. The next step – a chat to a few people he knows who are in touch with the *Mujahedin* and voila! a ticket to Turkey. Some find the money by stealing from their parents or sometimes with the encouragement of the parents, even though later some Muslim families will swear total ignorance. Lying to *kuffars*, especially in their deceitful media, is sanctioned by the Koran, notably in the noble case of Jihad.

Facing this sort of attitude, Cameron's talk of a full-spectrum response, both on the battlefields and at home may cut little ice. The best way forward may be for Muslims to reform their own closed and closed-minded communities. What can they do to solve what is essentially a Muslim problem that has been visited on all the unbelievers?

*Reform*
Many British Muslims regard themselves as modern worshippers of Islam and are convinced that they are the opposite of the medieval version of what is pumped out by fanatics in the Middle East. The reverse may actually be true.

On New Year's Day 2015 a small man called Abdel Fattah al-Sisi did what no other leader of the Muslim world has ever done. He was frank about what was wrong with Islam. It helped that he was the president of Egypt and so was unlikely to be locked up or knocked off. The quiet, gentle and studious Abdel grew up in the mixed Gamaleya district of Cairo. In those days of greater toleration little Abdel would hear the church bells ringing and see Jews walking to the synagogue. A devout Muslim, his time at an army school led to his lifelong military career; he later studied at staff colleges in the UK and US. The so-called 'Quiet General' had also been a senior military intelligence officer, the kind of man the Western agencies liked dealing with. Nevertheless, he was not an American patsy – Washington condemned his coup against the Muslim Brotherhood who had allowed persecution of Coptic Christians.

He gave his major speech at the Al-Azhar University in Cairo, probably the most conservative, if also venerated, university in the Islamic world.

And his audience mainly comprised imams. In a speech that was largely ignored by Western media, he called for a religious revolution in Islam.

> We are in need of a religious revolution. You, imams, are responsible before Allah. The entire world, I say it again, the entire world is waiting for your next move because the Islamic world is being torn, it is being destroyed, it is being lost. And it is being lost by your hands.

He talked of IS as a mutant strain of Islam. He also said, 'We need a modern, comprehensive understanding of the religion of Islam rather than relying on a discourse that has not changed for 800 years.'

Other Muslim leaders who have called for minor reform, for example of Pakistan's apostasy laws, have been assassinated. The Jihadists, of course, claim that their return to the seventh-century doctrine is totally pure; they insist that instead of reforming they should arm for the inevitable clash of civilisations. The West and Islam cannot co-exist, they claim. And more and more people in the West are coming to accept this Manichean inevitability as well. The separation of church and state emerged in Europe after the devastating religious wars of the early seventeenth century and was partly responsible for the rapid material advances: science and technology were untrammelled from the likes of the Inquisition. The separation of church and state was also crucial to the development of Western democracy. But Islamists argue that church and state must be fused under *Sharia* law. *Dawla* – the basis of the caliphate – means an actual Islamic state, though the word is not mentioned in the holy texts. Some Islamists, for example the Muslim Brotherhood, claim that an Islamic democracy is possible. In Egypt they have contested elections, but – with the partial exception of Tunisia and Turkey – in the Middle East Islamic democratic victories usually mean pulling up the democratic gate behind them.[28] They stay in power, as in Iran or Sudan. It would be hard to imagine an opposition party contesting a free election in the Islamic State.

In the case of Egypt, the democratically elected Muslim Brotherhood government was overthrown after one year in office in a military coup led by al-Sisi. It is therefore odd that such a clarion call for reform should be made in Egypt with its long history of totalitarianism. The concept of *Ijtihad* – questioning and re-interpreting – is fundamental in the Koran, not blind faith. When Muslims did this a millennium ago they managed to achieve a golden age in science and the arts. Then followed the dark ages of sclerotic intellectual development in the mosques and in many aspects of political and social development. Islam missed out on the major stepping stones in Western progress from the Italian Renaissance, the Enlightenment and the religious reformation in Northern Europe and later the Industrial and scientific revolutions. The Arab world was slow to catch up with Silicon Valley.

Religious obscurantism in Britain should not come as a surprise. Just a handful of the 1,700-plus British mosques follow a modernist interpretation of the Koran. In the USA, more than half of all mosques describe themselves as adhering to interpretations of the Koran that adapt to modern life, not the conditions in Arabia in the seventh century. In Britain the obviously male-dominated mosques make the decisions – perhaps a quarter of mosques do not allow women on the premises, or severely restrict their movements and naturally enforce separate worship. This is not because of the influence of the traditional culprit, Saudi Arabia. The Saudis provide money and many of the textbooks for religious schools, but the Wahhabis control only a tiny number of mosques. The largest single influence is the Deobandi, who control nearly half of all mosques. Who are they?

They are a revivalist movement within Hanafi Islam. Established in 1887 during the Raj, they spread throughout British India and Afghanistan (where they helped later to nurture the Taliban's ideology). Its origins stem from hostility to Western influence and especially British rule in India. Besides controlling around half the UK mosques, it produces in its seminaries about 80 per cent of the home-grown imams. Deobandi religious debates are often legalistic and sometimes centre around such minor social issues of whether believers should wear ties, even to work, or compromise with Western dress in general, or how many miles a woman can travel, even to the mosque or hospital, without a male guardian. Discounting the veil would be far too revolutionary. So integration is not at the top of the Deobandi bucket list. The whole impetus of the movement was to avoid the corrupting contagion of the West. The furthest its most liberal members will go is to advocate politeness towards non-Muslims, but friendship is discouraged. (To be fair, this is what many Christian sects, such as Jehovah's Witnesses or Plymouth Brethren, also believe. They quote scripture: 'Bad associations spoil useful habits.') In short, British Muslims should not blame foreigners for illiberal attitudes – they need to look at themselves, especially if they should even consider David Cameron's call to welcome the delights of British society. Just as the extremes of Catholicism were muted by adjusting to a liberal society, it may be that in time the same kind of gradual reformation might happen to British Islam.

Unfortunately, the defeat of IS requires prompt action, not decades or even centuries for Islamic theopolitics to evolve.

On the other hand, one of the most prominent reformers (and critics) of Islam, Ayaan Hirsi Ali, is optimistic. Born a Muslim in Somalia, she underwent female genital mutilation and a forced marriage (her family says an arranged marriage) before fleeing to the West. In Holland she progressed from cleaner to MP and finally ended up teaching at Harvard and married to one of Britain's most eminent historians, Niall Ferguson. The producer of a short documentary she worked on in Holland, Theo van Gogh, was assassinated by a Moroccan refugee, living on Dutch state benefits, who also threatened to kill Hirsi Ali. She now lives under twenty-four-hour protection. Hirsi Ali has written a powerful book entitled *Why Islam Needs a Reformation Now.* In it she writes that despite its largely negative outcome, the Arab Spring shows that 'ordinary Muslims are ready for change'. I would argue that economic desperation and lack of human rights were more a factor than a desire for religious reformation, however. More convincingly she argues that the majority of moderate Muslims are sickened by the massacres of Boko Haram, the murder of 130 schoolchildren in Peshawar by the Pakistani Taliban and the shopping mall killings in Nairobi by al-Shabaab.

Hirsi Ali divides Muslims into three groups: firstly, Jihadists whom she calls Meccans; secondly, the silent majority who are devout but abide by the rules and abhor violence – she calls these Medina Muslims; and, thirdly, she groups a minority who are modernisers and dissidents like herself. She believes that the West should help the dissidents in the same way that it did in the Cold War. Central to her thesis is that Islam is inherently violent. She advocates a reform of Islam that would entrench the conventional five pillars – belief in one God, prayer, the *haj*, fasting and giving alms. She would, however, make five major amendments, including getting rid of Jihad, *Sharia* and ending the death cult that puts a premium on martyrdom to reach paradise. Whether she becomes another Martin Luther or instead ends up on an IS chopping block is an open question. She is being rather hopeful expecting that Islam, so resistant to change and modernisation, would swallow such big changes. Nevertheless, her optimism is infectious. She insists that women are leading the reformation in Islamic society. That is why Islam has produced a Malala Yousafzai as well as an al-Baghdadi.

Hirsi Ali has lost much credibility among Muslims and non-Muslims alike because she has been accused of lying, not least about her status in Holland that led to her being kicked out of the Dutch parliament by her own party. She has also been castigated for allying with American neo-conservative attacks on Islam, as well as needlessly inflaming Muslim sensitivities. She said, for example, about Islam: 'When a *Life of Brian* comes out with Muhammad in the lead role, directed by an Arab equivalent of Van Gogh, it will be a huge step.'

Nevertheless, although she admits she is now an atheist, her views on reform are interesting. Hirsi Ali believes that IS cannot offer anything except death and destruction for the stagnant economies and polities of the Middle East. She says poetically that 'a return to the time of the Prophet is a venture as foredoomed to failure as all attempts to reverse the direction of time's arrow'. But perhaps the most poignant quote in the book is her repetition of Malala's words about the Taliban: 'They are afraid of books and pens. They are afraid of women.' She concludes by suggesting that perhaps the Muslim reformation will succeed in some places initially just as the Protestant revolution seduced only parts of Europe. The Internet, she argues, will do for the Muslim Revolution what the printing press did for the Christian reformation.

In one respect Hirsi Ali hits the nail right on the head. Muslims cannot be de-radicalised unless Muhammad is also de-radicalised as well. To reform and to modernise Islam means recognising that the stories told about the Prophet are largely fictions often deliberately concocted by Muslims dealing with the particular political and social contexts of the seventh and eight centuries. It took Protestant churches a few centuries to accept the same arguments for re-interpreting the Bible and the Catholics are beginning to catch up. The Inquisition stifled the career of perhaps the world's greatest scientist, Galileo, who argued that the earth went around the sun. A well-known Saudi imam, Sheikh Abdul Aziz bin Abdullah, gained notoriety for issuing *fatwas* about women drivers, both Saudi and American, though he was most famous for issuing a *fatwa* denouncing as atheists all those who argued the earth was round. The government in Riyadh told him to wind his neck in when a minor Saudi prince went up on an American space shuttle. Modernisation must mean tolerating criticism in a liberal society. The 1989 Iranian *fatwa* issued against Salman Rushdie because of his novel *The Satanic Verses* convulsed the Islamic world and helped to radicalise many British Muslims. More recently, cartoons have fuelled rioting and Jihadist revenge killings. If Muslims don't have enough confidence in the strength of their religion (or in Allah to punish such sins) then they should leave Western liberal countries and emigrate to authoritarian Islamic countries that will punish such artistic transgressions. The alternative is to stay and conform with the norms and laws of the societies they have chosen to live in, or change those norms by parliamentary means. At best, it will take a generation or two for a modern version of Islam to take hold in Britain. Meanwhile the Islamic State carries on killing in Mesopotamia and grooming gullible Muslims in Europe. Western intelligence agencies are struggling to keep up, and they won't until they address the elephants in the room.

*Chapter 8*

# Elephants in the Room

I have touched on intelligence failures throughout the book. It might be useful to look at a few major themes together. All major spy agencies make big mistakes. Political spying is often about tactical brilliance and strategic myopia. Even before the intelligence disasters of 9/11, the Americans had missed the preparations for Pearl Harbor, for example. Nobody in the Western intelligence agencies was prepared for the Warsaw Pact's invasion of Czechoslovakia in 1968 or the collapse of the Shah of Iran in 1979. Worse, during the end of the Cold War nobody noticed that the USSR was about to collapse, though – to be fair – the Russians weren't up to speed on that either. Part of the reason was that in major Western intelligence agencies the James Bond image is completely wrong. Intelligence officers in the West do some political spying – keeping up with the gossip – but they don't go under cover. They simply hire people, natives to the country, for money these days. The concept of spying for ideological reasons as during the Cold War is passé. Many of these people then lie for money, as did Curveball, the secret and bogus Iraqi source for the bull about Saddam Hussein's alleged WMD. The German spooks who were handling Curveball told the CIA it was probably rubbish, but the Americans wanted to believe it. Nevertheless, at the operational level the US agencies and the British have done an excellent job of stopping most of the planned attacks by Jihadists since 9/11. It is the strategic vision that is lacking.

It used to be different, especially in understanding the Middle East. T. E. Lawrence knew what was happening a hundred years ago and the latter-day American equivalent, the CIA man Robert Ames, knew what was up until he was killed in the Beirut bombing of the US embassy in 1983. In the specific case of sound understanding about the Arab world the cutbacks in Whitehall have almost extinguished the Arabist as a species. A hundred years ago T. E. Lawrence could advocate a pan-Arab state with knowledgeable fervour. If the post-war treaties, instead of dividing up the Ottoman empire in the Sykes-Picot arrangement, had instead created the

Great Arab state, perhaps the world would have been a better place. The pervasive anti-Semitism in the region may not now exist. Perhaps nor would the general backwardness of the Middle East. Perhaps that is the result of terrible leaders and bad governments and not the default position of anyone who believes that the Koran is the word of God. Arabists may be few, but it is still no excuse for the frequent lack of history displayed by Western political leaders, from the invasion of Suez in 1956 to the recent fiascos in Iraq and Afghanistan.

Sometimes it is useful to reflect on history and the lessons it provides. Islamic hegemony flourished on the Iberian peninsula for hundreds of years. What rolled back Islamic control of Spain? As anyone who has watched *El Cid*, the 1961 historical epic film, a romanticised story of the life of the Christian Castilian knight Don Rodrigo Díaz de Vivar, will know, riding at his side into battle against the Almoravid rulers of southern Spain were their fellow Muslims, rulers of some of the other smaller Islamic states that had allied with Christian kingdoms. The reality is that the Islamic control in Spain was only brought to an end by a concerted policy of divide and conquer. Similarly, history teaches us that the Crusader kingdoms and principalities established by Western Europeans in Asia Minor and the Holy Land were also picked off one by one through similar tactics on the part of Saladin's successors. The lesson for the current war against the Islamic State is clear: victory depends on working with and within Muslim communities.

*Shooting Four Elephants*
1. Despite its reputation as one of the best in the industry, British intelligence is playing catch-up with regard to Islamic State and the potential and actual threat it poses to the national security of the United Kingdom. It took the British security forces and intelligence services decades to effectively contain Irish republican terrorism within the United Kingdom and Europe. After thousands of deaths, thousands of bombings – including London spectaculars that caused billions of pounds of damage – the British authorities managed at best to force a stalemate on the gunmen and bombers of the Provisional IRA. In thirty years of counter-insurgency within its westernmost province, the British security forces (and the Northern Ireland government) made virtually every mistake in the book, starting with internment without trial. They detained Republicans and not Loyalists and did not cooperate with the Irish government as they had successfully in the 1950s. The British state was run ragged trying to contain a few hundred dedicated PIRA gunmen and bombers emanating from within relatively

small communities. The gunmen were generally averse to committing suicide in the commission of their crimes and the terrorists were white, Western and, despite propagandist projections, their first language was English. The British state is now faced with acts of terrorism being committed by racially diverse Muslim militants of any one of three dozen different nationalities, culturally different not only from English society, but also to other Muslim communities and speaking languages that would take several years for any British intelligence officer to master, even if they had the time, inclination or ability to do so.

It was bad enough a decade or so ago when the nearest ideologically charged young Muslims in Bradford might get to Jihad would have been playing the baddie in the 'Call of Duty' computer game in their bedrooms. Merely watching them, monitoring gossip inside and outside of some mosques and preventing any attempt to access pro-Jihdist websites stretched British intelligence and security officers to the full. The position today is infinitely more problematic. There are hundreds of young British citizens, and thousands of EU citizens who have participated in full-spectrum on-the-job terrorist training in countries such as Egypt, Tunisia, Libya, Somalia and Syria and have returned home.

2. The elephant in the room with regard to a coherent British counter-terrorist response to Islamic State, and certainly one which David Cameron for his own electoral reasons would not wish to address in the lead up to the United Kingdom's referendum on EU membership, is that no effective national security and counter-terrorism policy can be put into place as long as Britain remains a member of the European Union. At present Britain does not control its own borders. The UK is legally obliged to allow any EU citizen into its country and EU citizens have a right to stay within the United Kingdom. It can be argued that Britain's borders are those that delineate the European Union, which is to say the borders of Greece, Italy, Spain etc. Over 137,000 migrants attempted to cross the Mediterranean in the first half of 2015. Inevitably many, if not most, of these migrants will be Muslims from countries devastated by Western military intervention and subsequent inter-communal and sectarian violence. The EU is committed to accepting and absorbing tens of thousands of these migrants who are to be shared out across Europe on a mandatory basis. While Britain may well refuse to accept its quota, the simple reality is that the thousands of 'refugees' and 'asylum seekers' who are accepted by countries such as Finland and Slovakia (not known for being the targets of international terrorism) become EU citizens

by naturalisation several years down the line and will then have automatic and unfettered access to the United Kingdom. Any realistic terrorist threat assessment must assume that a number of these new EU citizens freely able to travel to and reside in the UK may well be terrorist sleepers, supporters or sympathisers. The well-publicised Mediterranean phenomenon aside, the European Union receives 626,000 asylum applications per year. The British government is itself constrained in its approach to asylum seekers in any instance by European law. Security concerns may be overridden by European human rights and civil liberties legislation, legislation more applicable to living in Lichtenstein or Poland than dealing with tangible threats posed by national and international terrorism in the twenty-first century.

And just as Britain is simply unable to police its own borders it is similarly hamstrung in drafting and implementing its own anti-terrorism legislation. Several British laws aimed at countering a terrorist threat within the UK have been struck down and overturned because they conflict with European legislation and European human rights conventions. British security legislation is often being rendered null and void by European judges of questionable quality, often appointed because of politically correct judicial activism in countries unaffected by terrorism.

It could be said that the European Union may have kept the peace in Europe (and certainly within its member states) for fifty years. It may now pose a threat to that peace, most certainly within Britain. Losing control over which flavour potato crisps may or may not be eaten by the British public may be a price worth paying for membership of the European Union. Losing control over one's borders and who is allowed unfettered access to visit and reside within the UK, and being unable to enact legislation the British parliament deems necessary to contain a clear, present and growing terrorist threat, is a price Britain cannot continue to pay.

3. Another massive elephant is bellowing in the room, namely the British government's double standards with regard to Jihadist terrorism. The UK, largely as a result of its war against the PIRA and other republican and loyalist terror groups, has some of the most draconian anti-terrorist legislation in the world. This body of law was substantially added to in the wake of 9/11. By the end of the first decade of this century it was illegal for a British citizen to as much as look at a Jihadist website, let alone download anything from it or, heaven forbid, try to visit Pakistan for any purpose related to Jihadism. Dozens of young Pakistanis were prosecuted, convicted

and jailed for crimes along this spectrum. Then came the British-led intervention to topple the Gaddafi regime in Libya and a clear contradiction in British government policy. While it was illegal for a young Briton of Pakistani descent to as much as look at a Jihadist website in his own bedroom, the British authorities turned a blind eye to the hundreds of young Britons of Libyan descent (and sometimes their dads and uncles) travelling from Britain to undergo Jihadist military training and political indoctrination in training camps in western Libya and eastern Tunisia that were replicas of al-Qaeda camps in Afghanistan and Pakistan. These British citizens then went on to fight with Islamist militias against Gaddafi forces, militias which often enjoyed close air support from British and NATO aircraft. The right-wing *Daily Mail* found itself running articles with the headline 'Why do so many Libyan rebels seen on TV speak with British accents? The answer lies in Manchester' and reporting on the 'Untold numbers of British Libyans' from Edinburgh, Manchester, Birmingham and London who had come to Libya to fight. The *Daily Mail* actually identified some of these fighters and published photographs of them with automatic weapons. Anthony Loyd, a reporter for *The Times* of London, met a British-Libyan fighter from Manchester carrying a surface-to-air missile. The BBC, Channel 4 and *Daily Telegraph* also reported on these British fighters in Libya. When asked in Parliament in mid-2015, however, if the British government was aware of any British Libyans who took part in overthrowing Colonel Gaddafi and whether any of them had since returned to the United Kingdom, the government stated that they 'do not hold any information on this matter'.

If the government was actually unaware of the fact that possibly hundreds of British citizens travelled from Britain for military and terrorist training to engage in Jihadist violence in Libya in 2011 then it is an *intelligence* failure of epic proportions. It may well be, however, that the reticence on the part of the government to acknowledge this Jihadist tourism is because the untried British coalition government turned a blind eye to it for short-term political advantage – the overthrow of Gaddafi. This would be a *political* scandal of epic proportions. The latter explanation, crass short-term opportunism would explain why the British government continued to turn a blind eye – or may even have encouraged – a similar flow of British Muslims to participate in the Syrian civil war.

The facts speak for themselves. The Syrian civil war began in 2011. Writing in February 2013, the US Army's Combating Terrorism Center noted that 'Since the start of the Syrian war, British police have arrested and charged *three* men for their roles in a terrorist conspiracy linked to the conflict'. (Emphasis added). That is to say, from 2011 until early 2013, the British government had detained only three men for Jihadist activities in Syria.

The report also noted that:

> The most striking aspect about the Syria-UK connection is its similarity to past events. Not only are there shades of Bosnia in the ease with which Britons can join the war in Syria, but there are also similarities in the structures that have nurtured the conflict. Longstanding London-based preachers have returned to join fighters on the front lines, convoys run by Muslim charities take food and supplies while hosting events at which they criticize the lack of action by the international community, and young men are taking time off from their ordinary lives to join the fight.

All the above applied to the uninterrupted and unimpeded flow of British Muslims to fight in Libya, a natural extension of which was a redeployment of these fighters and others to the Syrian conflict. The British government somewhat naively thought that the Syrian government would fold as quickly as the Libyan regime (another intelligence failure – or merely wishful thinking – on the part of Whitehall as anyone who knew of the Syrian army's reputation could have told them). The American Combating Terrorism Center also very accurately pointed out that the 'fallout from Syria has the potential to have negative repercussions in the United Kingdom for years to come'.

A cynic might argue further that the only reason the initial three Britons referred to above were arrested was because the British government's hand was forced. They were arrested only after two journalists, one British and one Dutch, escaped from their captors in Syria and made it to safety in Turkey. The journalists had been taken captive and mistreated by a group of mostly foreign Jihadists in mid-2012. Once free, they publicised the fact there were almost a dozen British Jihadists – nine of whom 'had London accents' – in the group of fighters that had kidnapped them. The journalists identified one of the Jihadists as a National Health Service doctor. This man, Shajul Islam, a Briton of Bangladeshi origin, was subsequently detained in October 2012 when he returned on a flight from Egypt with his wife and child. His co-conspirator was similarly a Briton of Bangladeshi descent.

To summarise, apparently the British government was unaware of the fact that hundreds of young British Muslims had left the country to undergo what can only be described as Jihadist military training and gain hands-on experience in the Libyan civil war, despite it having been extensively covered in the British media. It has publicly stated that the government holds no information on this phenomenon, apparently not even newspaper cuttings by British newspapers of record. From 2011 until well into 2013 it appears to have been similarly inept, detaining only three people because they had unhelpfully kidnapped a British journalist who told the British police – and all this before the declaration of the caliphate that galvanised not just young British men, but also their sisters and whole families. It is a classic case of 'blowback', the unintended consequences of a covert operation that are suffered by the government that initiated the project.

Al-Qaeda itself can be seen as the ultimate example of 'blowback'. Western governments encouraged thousands of Muslims, in this case almost all from Arab countries, to serve Western foreign policy by successfully engaging in Jihad against the Soviet invaders in Afghanistan. These young triumphalist Jihadists (one of them Osama bin Laden) then returned to their homes in the Middle East and festered politically. Many were drawn to continue Jihad on a road that led directly to 9/11. Two decades later this formula was repeated when the British government, amongst other European governments, used young Muslim citizens in their countries to overthrow or try to overthrow Arab governments in Libya and Syria for reasons that are still unclear. Many have similarly returned home to fester. Some, a tiny minority of those who have been exposed to Jihadist training and ideology, are being criminalised by a reluctant government. In the 1980s and 1990s, Western governments left several Middle Eastern governments with the legacy of their foreign policy in the form of thousands of disgruntled young Jihadists. The Cameron government has managed to do much the same thing, except that the disgruntled young Jihadists are now returning to Britain's cities.

The most benign way of describing the British government's on/off approach to Jihad tourism by young British citizens is that it is sending out mixed signals. It can also be described as a colossal intelligence failure or simply the opportunist and naive blundering of a government in pursuit of a short-term political objective: the overthrow of the Gaddafi government, a short-term objective with unforeseen and horrific long-term consequences for Libya, North Africa and Europe. The end result is the fact that the United Kingdom now faces an unprecedented threat to its national security.

4. Fighting the last war. However much we pay lip service to the dangers of fighting the last war, it is self-evident that this is precisely what we are doing

with regard to the Jihadist war we may or may not realise we are fighting. We are spending billions of pounds building aircraft carriers (and probably sharing them with France), and buying attack aircraft while we have been outflanked by Islamic State's asymmetrical Internet and social media blitzkrieg. At a time when it should be re-equipping for a battle that will need to be fought by very different means within the heart of Europe, NATO is busily focusing its intelligence capabilities on re-learning Russian, demonising Vladimir Putin, counting tanks and engaging in military exercises on NATO's border with Russia. It would be far better to work with Russia, not fight it. Instead, the West should form a joint coalition against Jihadism. That is but one option in dealing with the caliphate.

*Chapter 9*

# Future Options

So what does the future hold for the inevitably long war with Jihadism? Prediction is risky in a world that is probably more unstable than in the 1930s. As Harold Macmillan allegedly said when asked by a journalist as to what influenced his policies, 'Events, my dear boy, events'. As I write this, in late July 2015, Turkey has just entered the war against the Islamic State (and the Kurds). And in the previous week agreement was reached between the great powers and Iran on a nuclear deal in exchange for the gradual removal of sanctions. Iran was tired of its pariah status and, above all, wanted to return to the world community. It has trumpeted its desire for 'dignity'. Understandable, but it shouldn't have spent the last four decades hosting terrorists around the globe. An even more respectable and therefore active Iran would terrify Saudi Arabia and Israel, let alone Republican and neo-conservative politicians in the US. Iran has often been unpredictable – despite the Sunni-Shia divide described in detail in this book, Tehran has frequently bucked the trend and backed, for example, Sunni Hamas and supplied it with rockets and other weapons because it suited Tehran's geopolitical ambitions. A more assertive Iran, especially if it cheated on the nuclear deal and continued to develop its nuclear weapons' capability, could stampede Saudi Arabia into cashing in its Pakistani chips and a move to a parallel nuclear status.

This begs an answer to a central conundrum in this book. The West has relied on two allies in the war on Islamist extremism – Pakistan and Saudi Arabia – that have done the most damage to the American-led campaign against Islamist extremism. Yet if Washington were to completely withdraw its diplomatic love from Islamabad and Riyadh, plus its copious weapons supply to the Saudis and endless cash to fuel Pakistani corruption, both Muslim states could collapse. As it is, Pakistan barely functions as a state and the Saudi superstructure is a house of cards. The implosion of both countries would hardly lead to democracy. As in most Islamic dictatorships, the likely results will be anarchy and then a Jihadist Islamo-fascist government, especially in Saudi Arabia, the epicentre of Wahhabism.

Various – mostly extreme – scenarios have been suggested for Pakistan. It was created by Caesarean section from the Raj. That was the first partition, then Bangladesh broke away in another bloody partition. The US could defang Pakistan of its loose nukes, and the far more powerful and responsible India could help with another partition. Kashmir could be re-united under Indian suzerainty or even UN guardianship. The Pathans could be re-united – doing away with artificial colonial borders again. A great power *demarche* could finesse some promises of good behaviour from the enlarged Afghanistan (actually returned to its original territories). Baluchistan rebels have long fought for independence – give it to them. This would leave a rump state of Pakistan – no longer a military threat, but perhaps a disaffected big Gaza, though the even more powerful India could ensure it stopped supporting Jihadism. None of this is likely to happen. Nevertheless, it does suggest a direction of travel to remove the long-running Pakistani threat.

Saudi Arabia is another artificial creation, partly the product of romantic British Arabists. It persecutes the minority Shia, does not allow any chance of equality of citizenship to the many foreigners who keep the country running, and most of all deploys its vast oil wealth to fund what many American analysts see as Islamist 'nutjobs' around the world. Its human rights record is abysmal, not least its public executions, whippings of dissenting bloggers and victimisation of women. It does not allow homosexuality or Christian churches (despite its tens of thousands of Christian guest workers), although I am not conflating the two issues. It has partly slipped its umbilical dependence on Washington and is acting as a free agent in the war in Yemen, though it helped the US in its coalition building against IS. Arab history has suggested that royal families are not very durable; yet any kind of republic in Saudi Arabia or, say Bahrain, would almost certainly be ultra-Islamist. Maybe in the short to mid-term, the West has no choice but to deal with the dictators it knows – again. Dreams of Arab democracy are just that. It is about time that the West gave up its belief that Western democracy works outside a small number of mostly cold northern Protestant states and accept that it hardly ever works in the hotter polities of Arabia and Africa. Not a worldview that the UK *Guardian* would embrace, but nonetheless generally true. Personally, I can't bring myself to believe that Arabs are not ready for democracy, though my job is to work with geopolitics how they are, not what they should be.

I have considered some of the intelligence issues and domestic reforms in Europe, the home front. Here I want to analyse the major options for dealing with IS in the international arena. The scenarios follow an arc from a soft- to hard-power response; some might interpret it along the left-to-right spectrum.

*Surrender/defeat.* It is unlikely, though possible, that the caliphate will repeat the original imperial expansion after the death of Muhammad. I can't speak for God. Personally, I am not that keen on reverting, but advantages could accrue. A united Islamic Europe would probably not suffer from the perpetual tragedy of Greeks not bearing gifts. Muslim rule previously did better than the Greeks themselves and taxation might work better with cigarettes and alcohol removed from the tax base. The former fascist countries of Spain, Portugal and Italy might possibly accommodate themselves to Islamo-fascism. If the UK is renamed the Islamic Republic of England, Wales and Ireland, Scotland might finally achieve its independence as a socialist republic free of *Sharia* law. The Scots would fight to the death for their whiskey. The rest of Britain would behave as their fellow citizens did in the Channel Islands and as the French behaved during the Nazi occupation: 10 per cent actively resisted, 10 per cent actively collaborated and 80 per cent kept their heads down.

Yes, endless nit-picking about *Sharia* laws could keep lawyers busy and financially happy. Islamic lawyers are notoriously fractious – the debates on whether it is *haram* for women to wear a bra could fill a book. I have always tried to follow the legal debate on smoking. As a regular visitor to Khartoum I was shocked to find recently that smoking shisha pipes in public had become illegal. I felt sorry for the young people. They can't dance in clubs and, of course, alcohol is banned, so young men indulged in the traditional Arab custom of smoking pipes in cafés. I would join them, chat and smoke (another of my addictions, backgammon, is unfortunately uncommon in Sudan). An Islamist government minister explained to me that it was banned in public because they were sure that naughty youngsters were mixing cannabis with ordinary tobacco. They were allowed to smoke pipes at home, however, because it was assumed that parents would not allow cannabis use. How quaint. One advantage of an Islamic Europe governed by *Sharia* would be the banks. Islamic jurisprudence has displayed great imagination in getting around the fact that Muslims cannot charge interest on loans. Historically that was seen as a (useful) failing of the Jews. It is interesting that the Islamic banking industry did not suffer like their Western counterparts in the big crash. Part of the reason was the underground *halawa* network that funds so much genuine commerce and illegal money laundering for the Jihadist cause. It might also be because they are more moral, and certainly less greedy. Obviously, I am being somewhat tongue in check here, but Islamist victory must be considered as a logical possibility, even by atheists.

*Compromise.* Appeasement has a bad name, yet it was the dominant approach in the mid-1930s. Winston Churchill was one of the prominent exceptions and he was wrong on nearly everything else in this period, especially about clinging on to empire. Nevertheless, he was proved correct in debunking appeasement. But most politicians and intellectuals – with the trenches of the Great War still seared into their consciousness – thought that Wilsonian liberalism was the best way to proceed. If Hitler had been sane, it would probably have worked. Nearly every single war has ended in some sort of peace treaty. The Second World War was an exception – the Nazis had to suffer unconditional surrender (though the Germans control Europe today). Most insurgencies end in a deal – the British pride themselves on ending the thirty-year latest round of the Irish 'troubles' with the Belfast Agreement. Imperial history teaches that nearly every terrorist, if they avoided assassination and/or survived colonial jails, ended up on the winning side, sometimes in government. Kenyatta, Begin, Mugabe – the list is endless – terrorists/freedom-fighters turned prime ministers. In modern times, one of the few examples of an outright military victory over a prolonged insurgency was in Sri Lanka, when government forces completely defeated one of the most effective guerrilla organisations in the world, the Tamil Tigers, in a climactic last stand in May 2009. The Tigers had refused all peace deals and overreached themselves.

In other words, maybe the best way of dealing with IS is eventually to recognise its claims to the territory it holds or will hold. This is not necessarily self-flagellating liberal angst about our guilt for colonialism and its awkward borders. It works in *realpolitik* terms too. As with the gamble on Iran's respectability, sometimes bringing rogue states in from the cold can work. It hasn't so far with North Korea, nor is it easy with IS whose ambitions are boundless and won't recognise formal diplomatic protocols, let alone borders. The West did, however, deal with the Ottoman caliphate for centuries, despite its expansionist goals. Likewise, the West did lots of deals with the USSR, despite its universal ambitions. The Cold War analogy might not hold in this case as the USSR was in terminal decline, whereas Islam is resurgent. The West made President Omar al-Bashir a pariah, but then utilised his diplomacy to end Africa's longest war, in South Sudan. Then he became the first sitting head of state to be indicted by the International Criminal Court for alleged war crimes in Darfur. And yet despite US sanctions, al-Bashir acted as a peacemaker in independent South Sudan and in other regional conflicts. The West is now courting this Islamist leader to assist in securing Libya's borders.

If the Islamic State survives – possibly a big *if* – then applying standard diplomacy might tame it. Treating it like Israel could bring benefits. The Jewish Agency was allowed to encourage *aliyah* – emigration to the homeland – even under the Nazis (for a while in the mid-1930s even the Gestapo got in on the act, and made a nice profit). Likewise, *hegira* to the caliphate might be a safety valve for lots of disaffected and idealistic young Muslims in Europe. Letting them go, encouraging them to migrate, might obviate some home-grown terrorism. Allowing them back is another issue.

When discussing the question of appeasement, it must also be realised that the European Union, a wannabe superpower, is by instinct and practice wedded to compromise, the half-brother of appeasement. The EU would be instinctively drawn to striking a deal, if possible, with radical Islam.

*Status quo.* This is the normal template for Western politicians, especially in Britain: muddling along in the same old way. This may be a recipe for disaster or at least the extension of the current conflict with Jihadism for an extra generation or two. Jihadists think long term – back to the Prophet and forward to the inevitable triumph of Allah's will on earth. Inevitably, democratic politicians are short-term thinkers, more concerned with keeping their seats and staying in power. Until another 9/11 happens – as per Macmillan's dictum – Number 10 Downing Street and the White House will tend towards the status quo, with occasional military tweaks or bellicose slogans. That gives the advantage to IS. The status quo, if not outright appeasement, is the likely and understandable option for European politicians currently overwhelmed with pan-European crises in Greece and Ukraine. The Greeks' endless failure to get to grips with their economic woes, because of a fatal mix of their own mañana, bankers' manipulation and Brussels bureaucrats' elevation of political goals above economic sense, could destroy not just the euro but also the EU. That might appeal to some Eurosceptics, but European diplomatic and military unity, as part of NATO, is necessary to fight Jihadism's threat to Europe. Some hard thinking and decisions on priorities might force the West, post-Putin, to re-engage fully with Moscow, because it will be needed to find a solution to the imminent existential threat to its ally, Syria, and to join in a bigger, more aggressive coalition on the war against Jihadism – another logical future option.

*Full-spectrum intervention.* It was brave of David Cameron, flushed with the surprise election victory in May 2015, to use the term 'full-spectrum' response to the 'existential' threat of IS. Many in military and intelligence circles in London and Washington were waiting for such a rallying cry. Finally, the Tories agreed to meet the NATO goal of spending 2 per cent of GDP on defence, although the government was accused of 'cooking the books' by including elements of the intelligence and overseas aid budgets. The NATO alliance has become a very large welfare state where America pays and the European countries draw endless benefits.

Previous full-scale invasions did not work. Over 150,000 US troops in Iraq struggled to contain a much smaller Jihad/nationalist insurgency waged by both Sunnis and Shi'ites. And the British and American publics – at the moment – will not tolerate another ground invasion. It is tragically likely that a major spectacular – perhaps a Mumbai-style assault in London or, God forbid, an attempt at a 'dirty' bomb in Manhattan – could change opinions. The inevitable overreaction will polarise Muslims versus the rest. That kind of antagonism is exactly what Jihadist propaganda feeds off. So better perhaps to devise a new form of intervention now before domestic opinion is inflamed.

Although more Western troops, as trainers, special forces etc., will inevitably be needed, an invasion with divisions of NATO troops is not required, even if it were politically feasible. Expanding the current coalition is one route. Getting Russia on board will take time, but Turkey's very recent air intervention could be a turning point, provided it does not alienate the Kurds who are doing much of the effective fighting. Ankara's permission for the US to use the large and modern Incirlik airbase is a major bonus for the US Air Force. The longer the IS war the greater the empowerment of the Kurds throughout the region, unless Turkey maintains its two-front war of using air attacks on IS to cover its main effort against the Kurdish PKK. Turkey could benefit short-term by seizing some of Syria's territory – part of it disputed in the past – not least to prevent the emergence of a statelet run by Syrian Kurds. Longer term, the continuing chaos and fragmentation of next-door Syria and Iraq will destabilise not just the southern provinces of Turkey, it could poison the whole polity. Turkey's powerful army could seal the border with a reasonable degree of effectiveness. The endemic smuggling in the region will have to be curbed – and Ankara persuaded by the EU and arm twisted by the US into agreeing that helping to end the IS trade routes is beneficial to Turkey's position in NATO. The Kurds in Iraq are dependent on Western military support; they can also be persuaded to toe the Western line, not least because they hate IS. And the newly resurgent Kurds in Turkey are being helped on their road to democratic participation by lots of quiet Western assistance, not least from Britain, although the Turkish air raids on the PKK bases in Iraq's Kurdistan could re-ignite the civil war in Turkey that cost 40,000 lives.

Israel has been busy in the IS war too, and not just fortifying its position in the Golan and protecting the Druze community. Jerusalem knows that it has to keep a low profile, but its highly efficient intelligence assets can be used to even greater effect by the West, provided Prime Minister Benyamin Netanyahu does not slide into a long sulk because of the deal over Iran. This game-changing nuclear deal should encourage Tehran to rein in Hezbollah in Lebanon. Able fighters, they have suffered heavy casualties in the Syrian civil war. The key player is al-Assad. Should he stay or should he go? What if he were knocked over by the proverbial bus or, more likely, be 'accidentalised' in a vehicle crash? Were a real peace summit in Geneva to be revived, his departure might be part of a final settlement. The future shape of Syria is likely to be decided on the battlefield, however. IS is trying to create a big religious super state; ironically, it has inadvertently created the conditions for the Balkanisation of the region. Iraqi Kurds, Alawites and Shia in Iraq might all end up with smaller independent homelands. None of these new states can be mapped yet. If IS is defeated, Iraq is likely to become three separate states or a confederation of three states at best.

All wars end eventually. It is too early, however, to finalise a redrawn map of the Middle East. The priority should be the destruction of IS, or strict containment, as soon as possible. So the first step is to boost the coalition. The Arab states should increase their almost non-existent military contributions on the ground – it cannot be just NATO trainers. Training whom? The Peshmerga programme can be doubled. The Iraqi army is a waste of good training time and money, but has to be involved for political reasons. The new Iranian respectability could allow the secret US-Iranian programmes on the ground to be more visible and larger. The Iranian Revolutionary Guards commander, General Qasem Soleimani, has been a very able strategist and his use of Al-Quds special forces as trainers and fighters has produced results on the battlefield. The Shi'ite militias can fight, though they need more training on how to take prisoners and then treat them well. The Free Syrian Army is possibly a lost cause. Nevertheless, their training should be boosted and their deployment quarantined to stop them defecting. Although it will take time, improved training and vetting should prevent so many joining the Islamists; once it becomes clear that IS is losing, FSA defection will plummet.

Private Military Contractors/Companies (PMCs) could be added to the force structure. Despite the bad reputation of some American outfits in Iraq, they can be very effective as well as politically useful – you can get the same effect without putting British or American soldiers on the ground. And their tough and often effective intervention can always be deniable by London and Washington. The Nigerian government deployed a South African outfit to help sort out Boko Haram. The ex-apartheid soldiers were usually successful in a mercenary role in Africa, although twenty years after Mandela came to power most of the pot-bellied white warriors are past it. The more recent South African companies have employed younger former communist guerrillas with the apartheid veterans providing the officer corps. Colonel Eben Barlow sorted out the drug-crazed, arm-chopping rebels in Sierra Leone in 1995. He renamed his Executive Outcomes as the slightly less sinister Specialized Tasks (Training, Equipment and Protection). A British media hero, Colonel Tim Collins, is the CEO of New Century, a PMC that is training in Afghanistan. The UN hates what it calls mercenaries, but UN peacekeepers from the developing world are often corrupt, inefficient sexual predators who join UN forces often as a financial scam. Some are good soldiers, such as the Nepalese, of course. Exclude the UN, and Western PMCs do work when they are properly led, like most military organisations.

Air power must be better co-ordinated and the Britain's Royal Air Force should increase its widow's mite and also be allowed (legally) to bomb Syria as well. Obviously more special forces will be required on the ground for FAC duties – forward air control – and for search and rescue. So instead of invading, more of the same, albeit much better co-ordinated, will help. Sealing porous borders is the key: to pound IS and cut off its supplies. This policy also demands ending remaining financial support from external Arab funders. The Gulf states and the Saudis are increasingly alert to the dangers of their previous subvention of the Jihadists. And this new aggressive coalition policy cries out for US leadership. Obama won't do it, but his possible successor, Hillary Clinton, is much more a foreign-policy activist. Maybe Hillary could do to IS what Maggie did to the Argentineans. The 2015-16 presidential election fight in the US is partly about America's future role in the world. To use Obama's words, 'nation building at home' takes priority for some, while other contenders prefer the more forceful balance between classic realist interventionism and 'offshore balancing'. All have recognised the basic lesson of Vietnam, as well as Iraq and Afghanistan: others will always fight longer and harder in their own country than even the best US combat troops with the best of intentions. It may require a Republican president in the White House to use more force against IS, without thousands of ground troops. Obama's current policy of offshore balancing is really 'other people's armies' or, as Richard Nixon called it, 'Vietnamisation'. Currently, the US is leading from behind. Perhaps that is correct and the only way to make Arab allies lead from the front.

The mounting tempo of Western involvement will depend on the political will, which should not wait for the kick start of a domestic terrorist spectacular. Britain has pledged to increase its defence budget, but it lacks manpower. More Britons are joining IS than plugging the hole in the reserve forces which are supposed to fill the gaps in the Regular Army. This is nonsense – Britain is militarily overstretched so the Army should go back to the 100,000 plus before the recent peacetime cuts, rather than being the same size as the New York police department. David Cameron talks big about fighting IS, but the RAF can spare just eight Tornados to drop 5 per cent of the coalition's bombs. The Tornados, despite the re-fits two years away from museum service in theory, are a generation behind the F-22s they fly alongside. And Britain has sent just forty old heavy machine guns to the Peshmerga. Overseas aid can legitimately be spent in a war-prevention role. Aid is the new colonialism. NGO workers in Africa now outnumber the imperial administrators of the last century. The idea of ring fencing the DfID (Department for International Development) budget – and not the defence provision – makes no sense when Britain is effectively at war. It is all very well for prime ministers to keep saying we need more special forces, but they forget where they come from. Britain's SAS and SBS are respected worldwide, especially by the Americans, but to generate elite forces you need a large army as a recruitment pool. If selection can be two or three out of a hundred from already tough, trained soldiers often from the Parachute Regiment, then it is counterproductive to reduce the British Army to the size it was in peacetime 200 years ago. Sometimes only fifteen new recruits per annum reach the exacting standards of the two main special forces. The two key elements of the special forces directorate, the SBS and SAS, are traditionally undermanned. They rarely reach the optimum size of 450-500 men each. Now the lack of troopers has become serious. The allied Special Reconnaissance Regiment and Special Forces Support Group are also under-strength. Thirteen years of fighting in Iraq and Afghanistan, as well as training missions in Africa and South America, have taken a heavy toll in lives, wounds and general burnout. Ramping up the coalition is only one option, however. If Britain is going to war, then the wholehearted intervention abroad strategy might also have to merge with elements of other future options.

*An Arab solution.* The success of domestic counter-terrorism in Europe depends on local Muslim involvement and probably leadership. The same could be said for the chaos in Iraq and Syria. These are essentially Arab problems, so let them fix them. The West has tried and failed. The previous option involved beefing up the Arab-Western coalition and they may still need some Western support if they go it alone. The fall of al-Assad had been predicted for years, and while it now looks as though the old Syria is finished, al-Assad might nevertheless be part of what comes out of it. When the Damascus dictator retreats to his new bunker-state around Latakia (or an isolated dacha outside Moscow), who will take over in the capital city? The Islamic State? None of the Arab coalition led by Saudi Arabia wants that. The moderate alternative, the Free Syrian Army, is getting nowhere. In early July 2015 Ash Carter, the US defence secretary, stunned the US Senate when he admitted that out of the planned 5,400 men, the Pentagon had trained just sixty FSA fighters. On top of that the US Army had re-trained fewer than 3,000 Iraqi army personnel. The strategy of training new boots on the ground is so insignificant that IS could be in Riyadh before it was operational. The muddled West has been fighting the wrong war, very half-heartedly, possibly with the wrong allies.

In addition to the Syrian army, which has lived up to its reputation as tough and no-nonsense, only two other armies are doing the business in Syria: IS and the al-Nusra Front. Sometimes they have fought each other and sometimes they have co-operated. Al-Nusra is an al-Qaeda affiliate and so the West won't work with them (officially). Yet it appears that Saudi Arabia, Turkey, Qatar and the Gulf Emirates are doing so. It is the 'moderate bcheaders' option. Al-Qaeda originally sprang from the Wahhabi tradition ensconced in Saudi Arabia and, so long as al-Nusra is persuaded with arms and money to take on IS, the enemy of my enemy is my new friend. Saudi's tentative new alliance with al-Qaeda extends to Yemen. There the Saudis are prepared to back AQAP in its campaign against Iranian-backed forces. To Riyadh, Iran is the supreme enemy and Washington is perceived as cosying up to Tehran over the nuclear deal and in Iraq.

The US still has a $25 million bounty on Ayman al-Zawahiri's head, but the al-Qaeda chief is adapting to the new conditions. Al-Qaeda has been moderating its behaviour in both Syria and Yemen. It is not beheading, raping and pillaging, or at least far less than the really nasty IS. Al-Qaeda and the Saudi-led group want to topple al-Assad and keep his mentor, Iran, out of the region. Al-Nusra has joined a new grouping called the Army of Conquest, an alliance of rebel groups in northern Syria and the Saudis are helping it. It has to be noted that the new model has all the hallmarks of a standard American insurgency design. This grouping is made up nearly exclusively of Syrian volunteers – most Syrian rebels, including Islamists, don't like the swaggering dominance and behaviour of IS foreign fighters, be they Iraqi or British. Al-Qaeda is said to have tempered its international Jihad in favour of *national* Jihad. This might be an expedient tactic or a genuine strategic decision, but an al-Qaeda government in Damascus may be the least worst option for the Americans and their allies. That is what many Arab intelligence officers believe. They have persuaded Abu Mohammed al-Julani, the al-Nusra/al-Qaeda boss in Syria, that trying to run and rebuild a devastated Syria will be challenge enough for decades. He has said he will not use the new mini-caliphate in Syria as a base to attack the West. Al-Qaeda has a strong following in Syria, Iraq and Yemen and one form of Jihadist is likely to seize Damascus. The Israelis or Jordanians or even the Americans could hold it, briefly, but won't. The Saudis and Israelis are new best friends so they will work together on who takes over Damascus. Ultimately, the Saudis may be correct in believing the only way of bringing down IS is from within the Jihadist movement.

*The Garrison State.* The previous case for more forceful intervention by the West (if not the Arabs) could entail considerable blowback from terrorism on the home fronts. If it becomes widespread then a garrison state strategy, or parts of it, might be deployed. American strategist Edward Luttwak famously advocated such a strategy regarding Africa – that it should be ring fenced except for trade in vital minerals and no Western, or UN intervention, should be allowed. All external meddling has tended to make things worse and often delayed the resolution of internal conflicts that sometimes needed to be fought out to reach a resolution. Luttwak, a brilliant military historian, has frequently got his predictions wrong. Moreover, this was a theory that obviously ignored all the humanitarian factors. This 'leave-them-to-it' concept can be extended to include the Middle East. Except for protecting Israel, and perhaps preventing Iran completing its nuclear weapons' programme, the American government should leave the region to sort out its own sectarian wars. Such hard-ball concepts, allied to war-weariness of failed intervention in Muslim countries, and earlier Vietnam, plays into the legacy of isolationism in American thinking. Throw in new developments in energy supplies, including fracking, and the need for Arab oil would be drastically curtailed. It is valid to argue that Britain or the West should never intervene in Islamic countries, except under the UN aegis for obvious humanitarian purposes such as alleviating natural disasters. Most of the problems are man-made, so a strong case can be made for keeping out of any imbroglio. Clearly, intervention in Iraq and Libya made things much worse. The anti-Saddam crusade was particularly pointless, and although the stated desire to save lives in Benghazi was far more understandable, the cynical way in which the intervention was initiated was very questionable.

If Europe fragments or is further weakened following the bitterness caused by austerity in general and in Greece in particular, prompting not just a Grexit, but a British exit as well, the isolationist mood in Britain may well intensify, especially if Jihadist terrorism is added to the mix. Britain could tighten up its very flabby border and immigration controls, and it could eject obvious terrorist suspects who have hidden behind human rights legislation to stop them being returned to their own countries for trial. Freed from restrictive European Union legislation, Britain could dramatically tighten its own laws. Britain does not properly monitor who comes in and who goes out, so often the authorities have no idea how many dodgy immigrants, terrorists, or bogus asylum seekers are in the UK.

In the summer of 2015 daily televised scenes of migrant chaos at the Calais entrance to the Eurotunnel displayed not only massive traffic jams in Kent, but also massive political chaos in Westminster as well as the customary rows in Europe. The migrant base near Calais held 5,000 migrants; nicknamed the Jungle, it contained an improvised shop and clinic as well as a little shanty office that offered advice on how to seek asylum in the UK. In the last week of July 2015 alone, 150 illegal immigrants managed to sneak across on trains or trucks. Once inside Britain they had very little chance of being sent home. Hundreds of thousands of desperate migrants, in Europe, on the Mediterranean, or waiting in Libya, were trying to make for Britain, partly because they could speak some English as well as their belief that the streets are paved with gold. Few solutions have been offered to the migration crisis except humanitarian absorption that will exacerbate the security and political dilemmas. One wealthy philanthropist suggested a new 'Migrant Nation': buying fertile land maybe in depopulated Russia,

Kazakhstan, the Scottish Highlands, or perhaps an island in the Philippines. The model would be Liberia or Israel. In this new state all would be equal and full citizens. This is a nice try, but it won't fly. A better idea might be for the Greeks to cancel their debts to Germany by selling them a few islands. These islands could become a new mini-state, especially as they are convenient to the migrant flow. Germany could then provide jobs for the migrants with extensive construction works in the new Migrantistan. This sounds like crazy science fiction, but the current mayhem around the French side of the Eurotunnel is reminiscent of the 'swarming' scenes in the sci-fi film *World War Z*. Migrantistan would also be more humane and voluntary than the realist option: bombing the boats in the migrant ports in Libya, Western re-colonisation of the country and the erection of large internment camps to send back the huddled masses to their countries of origin; difficult in the case of Eritrea's slave state, though not Africa's supposed superpower, Nigeria. And, *inshallah,* Syria might be pacified meanwhile.

In Britain, internal monitoring must be improved as well. A few years back, the approximately 2,500 people in MI5 were doubled, but even with the sensible dispersion of police Special Branch to regional offices to work with MI5, the domestic security systems were run ragged trying to keep tabs on an estimated 2,000 Islamist terrorist suspects. The 2,000 suspects are now probably 4,000. Do the maths. For a watch on a very high-profile suspect, it takes three shifts of watchers plus phone surveillance etc. That could be up to fifty people, though twenty to twenty-five could be normal for a VIP Jihadist. Multiply 2,000 by twenty-five and you need 50,000 trained and very patient watchers. MI5 had just 5,000 personnel and many were office bound. So pouring money into overseas aid, until recently spent in China and still in India, with its proverbial space programme or (former Royal Navy) aircraft carrier when we didn't have one in service, seems asinine. So Britain must spend more on its own domestic and overseas intelligence agencies. MI6, or formally the Secret Intelligence Service, is also understrength. These are reasonable measures, but a full garrison state will demand more and more security, and more infringements of the civil liberties for which we are supposed to be fighting.

One way of improving British counter-terrorism is to recruit more women. Females probably make better spies because they are better listeners, more patient and less needlessly macho. This was proved by their outstanding if largely unheralded performance in the Special Operations Executive during the Second World War. Stella Rimmington became the first female 'head of shed' as Whitehall would put it when she was made

Director General of MI5. Eliza Manningham-Buller, a counter-terrorism expert, later followed this precedent. The agency's 'operational department' needs more watchers ('mobile surveillance officers') and has advertised for them. With the rise of the Jihadi bride syndrome, extra women, especially if they are of Asian descent, would be a bonus. So would Arabic linguists. They should not have obvious distinguishing features such as tattoos, if they want to get out of the office. And they want multi-taskers, i.e. women, who can 'watch, plan ahead, drive, communicate to your team and make decisions while you're doing so'. Driving and talking – a female speciality – is very handy. Driving and reading a map is perhaps a less common female skill, however, as MI5 seems down on sat-navs. They have to be patient and observant for long hours of inactivity and then be ready to rush into action. It's not James Bond, but the pay is good and generally the agencies are excellent employers. End of advert.

If more Muslim inhabitants of Britain become radicalised then encouraging the extremist minority to emigrate to IS will not be enough, especially if IS brain-washes more stay-at-homers. Britain introduced internment in Northern Ireland and in colonies such as Kenya and South Africa. It didn't work in the colonies and was probably counter-productive for security in Ireland. Arguably, the largescale internment of Japanese in the US during the Second World War did work, as perhaps the internment of some Germans and British fascists at the same time in Britain also proved effective, in some cases. If Britain does move on to a serious war footing, then a whole raft of unpleasant measures, from detention without trial to press censorship and even rationing, as in 1939-45, might have to be introduced. Nobody would want that, even if the so-called fifth-columnist argument were dangerously valid. In short, adopting a more robust policy to destroy IS sooner perhaps will avoid more casualties and much harsher domestic measures later.

*Mix and match*
Probably, an untidy mix of these future policies will be deployed. No surrender definitely, and internment very unlikely, but a combination of coalition-building, plus a joined-up strategy of much more kinetic activity on the ground and in the air, and maybe even the offer of a deal to recognise IS, will materialise over the timespan of a decade or so. Or maybe the Arabs may surprise everybody, especially themselves, and inflict the *coup de grâce* on IS. It will take time so the more the government explains the seriousness of the situation and the British people respond, above all in the Muslim

communities, then there should be less blowback for the necessary stronger intervention. IS is a much bigger threat than al-Qaeda. The war on terror lasted a decade, largely failed, and instead morphed into the current war with IS. If IS cannot be destroyed, and I think it can be, then a more pusillanimous response could be recognition of IS. If that is what a large number of Muslims want maybe they should get it. It is a maxim of counter-insurgency that it is 20 per cent force and 80 per cent psychology. We should not be afraid of using force robustly when we have to, but even more the 80 per cent hearts and minds must be used, especially at home in Europe. For too long, political correctness has prevented British authorities from recognising and then addressing the problem. We must all stand up against the evil of IS, and, most of all, European Muslims who have often kept quiet among the too-silent majority.

# Conclusion

The IS threat both to the Middle East and Europe is very real. The Jihadist warriors have conquered surprisingly quickly large parts of Iraq and Syria by military means. In modern Europe this is unlikely to happen on the model of the rapid Arab conquests of the seventh and eighth centuries or the later Ottoman advances into the heart of Christendom. Nevertheless, the terror attacks on Europeans and Americans are likely to increase in intensity and extent – from Tunis to Paris to New York. The initial Arab conquests were the result of their targets' weaknesses as much as the power of Islam. The Byzantine and Persian empires were almost defenceless because their initial strengths had been ground down by war and political fractiousness. Today, Washington is not leading and Europe is in political and economic disarray, as NATO attempts fitfully to guard its eastern borders from Russian revanchism.

A re-conquest of Europe is unlikely in the foreseeable future, though an expanding caliphate in the Middle East could portend endless war and terrorism. Jihadism began in the seventh century and has returned in fits and starts since the death of Muhammad and Osama bin Laden. Over 1.6 billion Muslims believe in the faith and many millions also believe in the Jihadist interpretation of that faith. It is not going to go away. This book has suggested various options, at home and abroad, of dealing with the Jihadist threat to the Western way of life. A part of coping with, or conquering, this evil virus is to recognise where it comes from and how it incubates. For too long, for all sorts of reasons, and not just political correctness, the militant extremist version of Islam had not been seen to be the danger it really is. A 'virtual caliphate' exists in too many hearts, homes and computers in Britain and the rest of Europe. Understanding and recognising the danger are the first steps to countering it. I don't usually agree with Prime Minister David Cameron, but he is spot on in saying that the Islamic State is a threat to the very existence of Britain and that the fight back requires a 'full-spectrum' response. IS can be defeated militarily in a few years, but the ideology will resurface in another form, just as al-Qaeda morphed into al-Baghdadi's caliphate. So the West needs the patience to continue fighting, on many fronts, a generational or even a multi-generational conflict. When the caliphate was proclaimed in June 2014, it was in effect also a declaration of war on *all* people who are not observant Sunni Muslims. This long fight back will require determination and unity from all faiths, Christians, Jews, and Shia Muslims. Above all, this is also a war within the soul of the Sunni faith. The West may have to do some hard fighting, though Sunni Muslims must all do some hard soul searching as well. It is a very big ask, but Muslims may have to de-radicalise Muhammad before they can de-radicalise and modernise Islam. In secular Britain the vast majority of people don't understand and don't want to understand religion, *any* religion. That ignorance applies in spades to Western politicians. If they had understood the connection between religion and international relations they might have realised that invading Iraq would blow the lid off the long-simmering schism between Sunni and Shia. One of the themes of this book is the probably permanent deleterious effect of Western invasions in the Middle East. I was never a Blairite, though I must confess that I was once gung-ho about humanitarian intervention; now I am a 'recovering interventionist'. The West should avoid military intervention in the Middle East at all costs, unless it is for UN-sanctioned relief efforts such as helping with natural, not man-made, disasters. *In extremis*, such as the irrefutable IS threat to Europe and the Middle East, then careful co-operation with an Arab lead, a genuine not titular coalition, can perhaps succeed in the current fight to the death with the Islamic State.

Therefore, much of the 'solution' to the Jihadist threat must come primarily from Muslims themselves both in the US, Europe and in the Middle East. The West can help and co-operate, but the lead must be Islamic. The crisis is primarily an Islamic one, after all. Muslims must reform themselves, especially their attitudes. They have for too long blamed others for their own weaknesses – especially foreign conspiracies generated by the usual suspects, Zionists/CIA etc.; they are very convenient though generally incorrect scapegoats. Muslims must get over their sense of victimhood by asserting their own positions in the modernity of the twenty-first century. They must overcome the fatal combination of an innate sense of moral superiority vis-à-vis the decadent West and above all the toxic mix of incompetence, arrogance and eternal prevarication. Moderate Muslims say the extremists are not part of Islam. Well, they are, and violent extremists are destroying not only the religion's reputation in the West, but also creating mayhem in the Islamic world, especially Arab countries. The challenges of modernisation and the Sunni-Shia civil war can be fixed only by Muslims taking the lead themselves. It is no good complaining about Western meddling if Muslims make such a hash of organising themselves. The European Union cannot even organise its own currency, so Western smugness is inappropriate. If Muslims lead, then the West can co-operate to physically destroy IS or at least contain the caliphate. Or if the Muslim world can unify sufficiently to decide that a caliphate is what they really want, so be it. Co-operating to end the violent aspects of a caliphate should be primary goals of West *and* East. Destroying or negotiating with a reformed, maybe even tamed, caliphate are the logical alternatives for the West. It may, however, take a latter-day Charles Martel to lead the battles against the Islamic State and its sly companion, the virtual caliphate, lurking in every phone, iPad and computer in the world.

I am writing the final words of this book on 9 August 2015, exactly seventy years after the second atomic bomb was dropped on Japan at Nagasaki. This marked the end of the Second World War. Another nuclear device could start the Third World War. On seeing the effects of the bomb he had done so much to create, Robert Oppenheimer quoted from the Hindu *Bhagavad Gita* 'I am become Death, the destroyer of worlds'. Al-Qaeda has long displayed a similar fascination with weapons of mass destruction (and effect); the Islamic State has experimented with tactical chemical weapons. Moreover, the caliphate is consumed with an overarching belief in the end of days. A nuclear-induced Armageddon would fit snugly into both Sunni and Shia extremist eschatology; and it would be the ultimate blowback for Western intervention. IS could smuggle a lorryload of nuclear material into London or Paris, or use chemical or germ-warfare materials pilfered from al-Assad's stock and deploy a stolen aircraft. Rogue delivery of some kind of WMD is not only possible but likely. The Islamic State wants to re-conquer the lost lands, so it may well be reluctant to nuke the Alhambra in Moorish Spain. IS could spread fear and destruction, however, in northern Europe as part of its drive on southern and central Europe. Just as beheadings and crucifixions are intended to spread panic among local Arab foes so, too, the caliphate of fear could terrify with the use of, or threat of, WMD. Saddam was bluffing. When IS gets hold of WMD it will use them in the name of faith. If the West wants to survive, it needs to resist the caliphate with every device it can, and the most important is the power of the Islamic faith, from Muslim allies, inshallah. In a rapidly proliferating world, we will need all the help we can get, from God or elsewhere.

# Endnotes

[1] Tom Holland, *In the Shadow of the Sword* (Abacus, London, 2013) p.42.

[2] Hugh Kennedy, *The Great Arab Conquests: How the Spread of Islam Changed the World We Live in* (Phoenix, London, 2007) p.57.

[3] Ibid., p.376.

[4] Cited in Eugene Rogan, *The Fall of the Ottomans: The Great War in the Middle East, 1914-1920* (Allen Lane, London, 2015). p.402

[5] Ibid., p. 386.

[6] Cited in James Morris, *Farewell The Trumpets: An Imperial Retreat* (Penguin, London, 1987) p.258.

[7] Norman Stone, 'Too Keen on Saving Private Ryan', *Sunday Times* (London) News Review, 2 August 1998.

[8] Paul Moorcraft, *Omar al-Bashir and Africa's Longest War* (Pen and Sword, Barnsley, 2015) pp.22-36.

[9] Morris, op. cit., p.453.

[10] Paul Moorcraft, *Inside the Danger Zones: Travels to Arresting Places* (Biteback, London, 2010) pp.65-140.

[11] Edward W. Said, *Covering Islam: How the Media and the Experts determine how we see the Rest of the World* (Vintage, London, 1977).

[12] David Loyn, *Frontline: The True Story of the British Mavericks who changed the Face of War Reporting* (Penguin, London, 2005) p.267.

[13] Moorcraft, *Omar al-Bashir and Africa's Longest War,* op. cit., pp.109-16.

[14] Paul Moorcraft, Gwyn Winfield and John Chisholm, *Axis of Evil: The War on Terror* (Pen and Sword, Barnsley, 2005).

[15] Paul Moorcraft, *Total Destruction of the Tamil Tigers: The Rare Victory in Sri Lanka's Long War* (Pen and Sword, Barnsley, 2012).

[16] Of course another British imperial cartographer, Sir Mortimer Durand, had also drawn up the lines of the tribal buffer zone.

[17] For a general discussion of this issue, see Christopher L. Elliott, *High Command: British Military Leadership in the Iraq and Afghanistan Wars* (Hurst, London, 2014).

[18] See Frank Ledwidge, *Losing Small Wars: British Military Failure in Iraq and Afghanistan* (Yale University Press, London, 2012).

[19]  Graham Bound, *At the Going Down of the Sun: Love, Loss and Sacrifice in Afghanistan* (Monday Books, London, 2014).

[20] Lindsey Hilsum, *Sandstorm: Libya in the Time of Revolution* (Faber and Faber, London, 2012). See also Paul Moorcraft's essay review of the same title in the *RUSI Journal,* June/July 2013.

[21] bellingcat.com/news/mena/2014/07/15/identifying-government-positions-during-the-august-21st-sarin-attacks/

[22] Patrick Cockburn, *The Rise of the Islamic State: ISIS and the New Sunni Revolution* (Verso, London, 2015). In this excellent and up-to-date summary, Cockburn makes a similar comparison with the religious wars in Europe.

[23] The PKK is the Turkish abbreviation of the Kurdistan Workers' Party which is synonymous with its armed wing, the People's Defence Forces. It fought a civil war with the central government in Ankara to set up an autonomous/independent state in Turkey. The war from 1984-2013 cost 40,000 lives. The 2013 ceasefire was threatened by the July 2015 Turkish air raids on PKK bases in Iraqi Kurdistan.

[24] The YPG, People's Protection Units, is the armed wing of PYD, the Democratic Union Party, which represents many Kurds in northern Syria.

[25] Trevor Phillips, 'Ten things about race that are true, but we can't say', *Sunday Times* News Review, 15 March 2015.

[26] Douglas Murray, 'The dangerous lie', the *Spectator*, 17 January 2015.

[27] Damian Thompson, 'Waiting for the backlash', the *Spectator*, 6 September 2014.

[28]  I have deliberately concentrated on the Middle Eastern issues and avoided the complex Islamic politics in Malaysia, China and India, as well the largest Muslim country, Indonesia. Its population is 235 million, of which 88 per cent are Muslims.

# Select Bibliography

Ali, Ayaan Hirsi, *Heretic: Why Islam Needs a Reformation Now* (Harper Collins, New York, 2015).

Allen, Charles, *God's Terrorists: The Wahhabi Cult and the Hidden Roots of Modern Jihad* (Little Brown, London, 2006).

Anderson, Jon Lee, *The Fall of Baghdad* (Penguin, London, 2005).

Anonymous, 'The Mystery of Isis', *New York Review of Books*, 13 August 2015.

Bergen, Peter L., *The Longest War: The Enduring Conflict between America and Al-Qaeda* (Free Press, New York, 2011).

Birke, Sarah, 'How Isis Rules', *New York Review of Books*, 5 Feb 2015.

Cockburn, Patrick, *The Rise of the Islamic State: ISIS and the New Sunni Revolution* (Verso, London, 2015).

Fisk, Robert, *The Great War for Civilisation: The Conquest of the Middle East* (Harper Perennial, London, 2006).

Gall, Carlotta, *The Wrong Enemy: America in Afghanistan, 2001-2014* (Howard Mifflin Harcourt, New York, 2014).

Hilsum, Lindsey, *Sandstorm: Libya in the Time of Revolution* (Faber and Faber, London, 2012).

Holland, Tom, *In the Shadow of the Sword: The Battle for Global Empire and the End of the Ancient World* (Abacus, London, London, 2013).

Huntington, Samuel P., *The Clash of Civilizations and the Remaking of World Order* (Touchstone, London, 1998).

Ignatieff, Michael, *Virtual War: Kosovo and Beyond* (Chatto and Windus, London, 2000).

Kennedy, Hugh, *The Great Arab Conquests: How the Spread of Islam Changed the World We Live in* (Phoenix, London, 2007).

Ledwidge, Frank, *Losing Small Wars: British Military Failure in Iraq and Afghanistan* (Yale University Press, London, 2012).

Miles, Hugh, *Al-Jazeera: How Arab TV News Changed the World* (Abacus, London, 2006).

Moeller, Susan, *How the Media Sell Disease, Famine, War and Death* (Routledge, London, 1999).

Moorcraft, Paul, (with Gwyn Winfield and John Chisholm) *Axis of Evil: The War on Terror* (Pen and Sword, Barnsley, Yorkshire, 2005).
———, *Inside the Danger Zones: Travels to Arresting Places* (Biteback, London, 2010).
———, (with Philip M Taylor) *Shooting the Messenger: The Politics of War Reporting* (Biteback, London, 2011).
———, *Total Destruction of the Tamil Tigers: The Rare Victory in Sri Lanka's Long War* (Pen and Sword, Barnsley, Yorkshire, 2012).
———, *Omar al-Bashir and Africa's Longest War* (Pen and Sword, Barnsley, Yorkshire, 2015).
Morell, Michael, *The Great War Of Our Time: The CIA's fight against terrorism from Al-Qaeda to ISIS* (12, New York, 2015).
Pantucci, Raffaello, *'We Love Death as You Love Life': Britain's Suburban Terrorists* (Hurst, London, 2015).
Ricks, Thomas E., *Fiasco: The American Military Adventure in Iraq* (Allen Lane, London 2006).
Rogan, Eugene, *The Fall of the Ottomans: The Great War in the Middle East, 1914-1920* (Allen Lane, London, 2015).
Said, Edward W, *Covering Islam: How the Media and the Experts determine how we see the Rest of the World* (Vintage, London, 1977).
Seib, Philip, *The Al-Jazeera Effect: How the New Global Media Are Reshaping World Politics* (Potomac, Dulles, Virginia, 2008).
Weiss, Michael and Hassan Hassan, *ISIS: Inside the Army of Terror* (Regan Arts, New York, 2015).
Wood, Graeme, 'What Isis Really Wants', *Atlantic Magazine*, March 2015.

# Index